Reach
for the
Stars

by The Nameless Narrator

CJK

Michael Terence
Publishing

First published in paperback by
Michael Terence Publishing in 2021
www.mtp.agency

Copyright © 2021 CJK

CJK has asserted the right to be identified as
the author of this work in accordance with the
Copyright, Designs and Patents Act 1988

ISBN 9781800943056

Cover image
Olesiapaprika
www.123rf.com

Cover design
Copyright © 2020 Michael Terence Publishing

PART ONE

1986

Chapter One

For the past, what, six months or so? Dan had avoided looking her in the eyes.

Four in the morning. His key fit cleanly in the lock, no fumbling. He was sober at least. She tiptoed out of the bedroom where their two-year-old twins slept in their new big boys' beds, either side of their bed.

Head down low, taking care not to step upon the creaky stair, he followed the neck of his guitar into the night light of the landing.

'You're late.'

He started as she spoke.

She'd not planned to say that. She'd planned to say, 'Good gig?' albeit it with sarcastic overtones which he could choose to ignore, or not. She'd not planned to whine and accuse, but she was exhausted; she'd been worried…

'I said… you're late.'

… and Fred and Will had been more demanding than ever today.

Head still down he said,

'I realise I am late. I am totally knackered, and I've got to be up for work at seven, so please can we leave off arguing until the morning.'

'It *is* morning,' she snapped, 'They'll probably be awake in an hour, and I've barely slept.'

He moved to stand his guitar case up against the cupboard at the top of the stairs, and she smelled upon him not sweat; nor cigarettes; nor even alcohol; not hard work; definitely not 'gig'. She smelled upon him an after-shave that she was becoming familiar with, but that she didn't know the name of; she smelled upon him a perfume that had never ever sat in their bathroom or bedroom. She sensed that he'd showered recently, brushed his teeth.

He removed his bow-tie and jacket; hung them over the stair rails.

She then smelled an undertone of something intimate; musky. She felt a rare sexual urge; reached out a hand. He flinched when she touched the thick, dark hair at the back of his head. He'd recently had it cut shorter than she preferred; his curls were no more. She withdrew her fingers as though she'd burned them.

'It's wet.'

She told him.

He turned angrily; nodded, finally looking her in the eyes. And, although angry, she could see that this morning's stress lines were muted; his eyes dreamy, far away; his entire face, softer.

'Yes…'

He spoke slowly, patronizing her.

'Yes… My. Hair. Is. Wet… My. Hair. Is. Wet. With …' he exaggerated the shape of his mouth as if he were talking to the twins, '…*Sweat*. My. Hair. Is. Wet. With. *Sss-sweat?*

But the dress-shirt with its panels down the back and its frills down the front, which she had labouriously ironed for him whilst the twins fought in their playpen, still looked pristine; even the creases in the sleeves remained sharp.

'You can't have been *that* hot and sweaty if you've not even rolled up your shirt sleeves.'

He went into the bathroom.

'It was that posh a wedding, we weren't allowed to take off our jackets; that's why I couldn't roll my sleeves up; we even had to keep our bow ties on.'

His back was to her now, and his lies flowed more easily as he urinated, getting into his story.

'That's why my hair's wet with sweat. Silly, really…'

He shrugged, zipped up his pin-striped trousers.

'Anyway,' she said, 'I've got something for you.'

She handed him a small, round, brown-papered package.

He said nothing, but pulled off the sticky tape. A loose length of steel wire sprang out; jumped down onto the carpet.

'What…?' he said, but didn't look at her.

He pulled off the paper, revealing five more strings, each wound and taped into a circle.

'Guitar strings?' he asked, but again didn't look at her.

'Yes. Guitar strings.'

It was her turn to talk slowly, sarcastically.

'*Strings*… Those. Things. That. Make. A. Guitar… *Sing.*'

He gave a tiny huff of acknowledgment that he thought that quite clever and, hating herself, she felt a tiny lift in her tummy, another little hint of sexual desire.

'They're not *new* strings,' he said, his right-hand sliding one of the spools up and down his naked fourth finger.

She watched him, angry again because he'd always refused to wear a wedding ring. He'd said it would irritate him, especially when he was playing his guitar.

'No, they're not new strings,' she agreed.

'So…?' he looked at her, baffled.

God, he was good.

He continued,

'…I don't get your point.'

'Well, why don't you open up your guitar case, then?'

He turned, calmly and slowly unfastening its buckles.

'No strings!'

He said, astonished.

Without its strings, the acoustic guitar looked strangely blank; empty, lying at rest in its burgundy-lined coffin.

'Yes… No. Fuck-ing. Strings.'

Just like he'd always wanted. No strings. No wedding rings. No baby. Let alone two babies.

'But… why…' he began, '…Why did you take out all the strings?'

'Never mind about that,' she hissed, 'What I want to know is how exactly you managed to play your guitar all night at this hot and sweaty, posh wedding 'do' with no strings to your guitar?'

'Oh right. I *get* you now.'

He even had the gall to smile that smile.

'I get what you mean now.'

God, he was very good.

'I didn't play *this* guitar. As it happened, I probably didn't even need to have taken it. My mate from work, well my mate's brother, was thinking of buying one, and he asked me to try it out for him. I suppose if that guitar had been really crap, I'd have had to have changed it for mine, and then I'd have noticed there were no strings…'

He shrugged, undressing.

How come he found it so easy to tell untruths? How could he sound so convincing when he was obviously lying through his teeth?

He was removing his trousers. And then came one of those instances that made her seriously wonder if she was totally mad to be so suspicious of him. He was wearing an old faded pair of underpants that he'd had for years. *Surely, if he was …* she began to think, then found herself too exhausted to follow her thought process through.

'But…' he continued as he climbed into bed, 'I still don't get why you took all the strings out in the first place.'

And her exhaustion was overtaken by frustration. Why didn't he 'get' her anymore? Why did he constantly have to ask her what she meant by what she'd said? She'd all-on caring for the twins. And yet if she asked for any explanation as to what he was doing, where he was going or where he had been, or what he had meant, he became angry and defensive.

She'd removed the strings whilst Fred and Will fought in the playpen because she felt the need to 'test' her husband; although quite what she would have done had he admitted he'd been with another woman and not playing in the jazz band at a posh wedding-do, had he been found guilty as charged, she really had no idea. But at least, she supposed, it would prove she was not going mad, as he often accused her of being.

'You need locking up,' he'd tell her, calmly.

'Actually, I *am* locked up! I'm locked up in this tiny cottage with these horrendous kids!' she'd cry in miserable frustration, 'And you're never here!'

'I rest my case,' he'd say, going out of the door to work as a care assistant in an old people's home each week-day; going out of the door, guitar in hand two, sometimes three evenings a week to play in a jazz band, occasionally solo classical.

'But, we need the money…' he'd say, with a shrug, when she complained about his gigs. '…You know we do.'

What could she say to that?

He had changed so much recently, but if she ever said as much, he would retort, 'Ditto!' She knew she'd changed. Before the twins she'd been pretty, slim, funny, energetic; she had always taken care of herself, liked to dress nicely. She was the total opposite now. But through no fault of her own; surely, through no fault of her own?

The twins were grinding her down. Her suspicions were grinding her down. She had no one to talk to because she rarely got to finish a sentence and was too tired to speak by the time the twins were finally asleep in their beds.

She climbed into bed beside him.

He yawned, already on the cusp of sleep.

'Anyway, I was ready for a set of new strings.'

After, what, two seconds? He turned over to face her,

'How have they been today, by the way?'

She slammed on the bedside light.

'By the way?! How have they been, by the fucking way?'

He looked shocked, as though he'd never seen her before.

'That says it all, doesn't it? We're out of sight, out of mind. You don't give us a thought all day when I'm looking after them, and all night when you're "gigging".

She drew the inverted commas in the air with her fingers.

'We do have *names* you know. I am not *nameless*. And your twin boys are called Frederick after your dad and William after my dad. We chose their names together. Do you remember? But it's like none of us *even exist!*'

He took her firmly by the shoulders.

'Calm down. Get a grip.'

He sounded a little scared; stared into her eyes, and she thought she saw a glimmer of something different. Was it fear? Or was it understanding? And this time he didn't say she needed locking up.

'…And sometimes I truly don't want to exist.'

A tear trickled down her face. She turned her head to one side and tried to raise her hand to swipe the tear away, but he grabbed her wrist, held it down firmly, gently licked away the salt water. She dissolved inside, and then as he kissed her full on the mouth, long and slow, she melted even more.

He maneuvered her so that she was lying on his side of the bed.

'Let's do it this way,' he said, 'You'll like it, I promise.'

And he raised her legs up high, and entered her.

Her tummy was squashed under the weight of her own legs, and her fluffy-socked feet peered like neglected glove puppets over his humping shoulders. She could not hold back a shocked, ugly snort of a laugh, then squirmed with embarrassment as a tiny fart also escaped her.

'God you're like a child yourself!' he hissed into her ear, then he continued to hump, as she began to cry; uncomfortable, squashed, quashed, humiliated and fearing the twins might wake and see them; she began to cry silent hot tears until he came with a muted groan.

But instead of, as she had expected he would have, instead of snapping,

'*Now* what are you bawling about? What's up, for fuck's sake? You really are mental, aren't you?' then, without waiting for a reply, falling rapidly into a deep sleep through which he'd never hear the twins wake and demand their first of a thousand demands that day.

Instead, he gently asked her,

'What's the matter, babe?'

'You promised I'd like it…' she snuffled, '… but I didn't.'

And he took her in his arms and stroked her hair.

'Shush, babe, shush.'

He'd never called her 'babe' before, and she liked it. He gently kissed her forehead free of its furrows, and tentatively, expertly, sensing her wetness inside her knickers, began to stroke her.

He rubbed her bud. And, starved of adult affection, it rapidly blossomed.

They slept then with their arms around each other for the first time in months, not waking until Dan's alarm went off at half past six and then they smiled at one another. Fred and Will were wide awake but, instead of bawling, were babbling happily across to each other in their beds.

Chapter Two

Following the 'no strings' incident, she presumed from Dan's very slight sheepishness that he was now more aware, and therefore more sympathetic, of how she was feeling; that the twins were exhausting her, and that, on top of the exhaustion, she had suspicions about his fidelity.

Although she believed that he now 'got' the reason why she'd removed his guitar strings, neither the incident, nor the intimacy which had followed it, was mentioned for a long time.

The next time she saw the guitar, it had a set of new strings, and there were a couple of spares in the plush-lined little closet at the base of its neck. No photograph of her though. He'd always used to carry a photograph of her pre-pregnant, lying on an English beach, wearing a black bikini. She didn't question him. But its absence pulled at her heart strings.

Dan's slight sheepishness manifested itself in his sometimes taking the boys for long walks or bike rides upon the High Peak trail, to 'give mummy chance to get on top of things'. They would often finish off at the local pub which had swings and a climbing frame, and all three would return, with their clothes smelling of cigarettes instead of washing powder, Dan's breath stinking of beer, polo mints and the cigarettes which he told her he'd quit, as she had done when she found out she was pregnant.

In fact, aside from the twins beginning to occasionally sleep through the nights, I'm afraid things did not change a great deal for our nameless narrator. Her husband still came home smelling of perfume and mouth wash; looking dreamy and distracted.

One night, shortly after the no-strings incident, slightly pissed and therefore braver, she had suggested and he had agreed, although not particularly enthusiastically, that once a month she would get the twins to bed early and make them both a nice meal so that they could some quality time just to talk; to have time to finish a sentence, to listen to one another; to have a full-blown conversation. This evening was going to be the fifth of those occasions. And yet, despite that to look forward to, she still felt miserable.

As always when she had fed the twins their breakfast that morning, a teaspoon in each hand, hot tears had collected, briefly diverted in the dam of her cheap spectacle rims, then they'd run hot, wet down her cheeks. Her nose had run too, and she'd swiped impatiently at her face with the sleeve of her stained dressing gown.

'Mummy. Thad.'

Fred and Will told her gleefully, as they did each and every morning. She was always worse in the mornings. But this particular morning, she felt more emotional than usual. She was dreading this evening.

'Yes,' she croaked on her morning sobs; forced to agree,

'Yes, boys. Mummy. Is. Sad. Mummy is fucking sad…'

He was right when he told her she needed to get a grip.

'Try to pull yourself together a bit. Get a grip. Be firmer with them. And I'll see you later with a bottle of wine.'

She looked around the kitchen.

The two high chairs that she'd been so proud to buy, had so loved buying that day in Mothercare in Derby; everyone smiling at her and her huge bump, her luxuriant hair and her pretty tie-back maternity dress; bovine and totally and utterly clueless, the two highchairs *were splattered with food, their straps ingrained with dried-on cereal from days, if not, weeks ago.*

The lino on the kitchen floor was slippery with yogurt, the sink filled with half-emptied feeding bottles floating on top of yesterday's dirty plates and dishes, although, apart from the fourth Friday in each month, she could not recall when she'd last eaten a meal served upon a plate or in a bowl. She preferred to exist on the twins' left-overs, alongside salt and vinegar crisps, and cheap vermouth.

The draining board had long since become both crockery cupboard and cutlery drawer; a mountain of pots and utensils, never dried or put away, a downturned cereal bowl at its summit.

The basket in front of the ever-churning washing machine, was overflowing with urine-soaked sheets, baby-grows which were rapidly becoming too small, and stinking sour-milk sicked-upon bibs, turning crusty.

The steriliser unit needed changing. She'd no made-up bottles ready.

She was running out of formula milk again. The *kitchen bin was filled with squashy nappies and used wipes, a smelly carrier bag by its side acting as an overflow; the poor cat's dishes waiting beside it to be washed and replenished.*

Whilst the twins, in their highchairs, messed about with a rusk and juice, and what was left of their breakfast, she tried to quickly get the tiny living room tidy, flinging toys into corners so that they'd have room to play without constantly treading barefoot on bits of hard, pointy plastic. She planned to keep them awake all day so that they would go to bed early whilst she got on with the dozens of tasks she had to do today before half past six, including finding time to cook a meal, and to make herself look, and smell, half decent.

After a couple of minutes in their highchairs, the boys became cross and frustrated; started shouting and straining against their filthy straps, arching their backs and growling. Frightened they might tip up the highchairs onto the slippery yoghurty floor, she cut short her flinging of toys into corners, and hauled them out.

Finding the *two square Duplo bases they were always fighting over, she used them as shovels, scooping up the mess, tipping everything that was on the stained carpet; the bright bits of plastic, the torn and written-upon books and comics, the empty crisp bags, the scraps of scribbled-on paper, the felt tip pens with no lids and no ink, two ice lolly sticks and lots of jigsaw puzzle pieces, and putting it into the toy box.*

Everything swam in the tears which filled her eyes. And she didn't care. At least the rubbish would be out of sight. She would cover it all with a crocheted blanket and the giant jigsaw box with its broken corners and missing pieces. How she'd loved buying them that floor puzzle, Postman Pat and Jess his black and white cat all sitting in the red van. How she'd flushed with pride when the lady behind the counter at The Early Learning Centre had asked her old her little one was and she'd said she had baby twins, both boys.

'How wonderful!' the lady had said, clasping her hands to her chest.

She remembered so clearly one of the very few shopping trips the four of them had undertaken together, she'd seen a lady in her late thirties look at the babies, then turn to her companion and say,

'How come, she's got two, and I can't even have one?'

Her heart had broken hearing the bitterness in the woman's voice, the sadness in her friend's eyes for the unfairness of it all.

'Take them.' She'd wanted to say,

'Take them, please,' she'd wanted to say, 'I'll wheel their pushchair up to Woolworths; leave them there, then you can take over. In their bag, there's everything they should need for the rest of the day. I promise, I'll never say a word. No one need ever know. You'd make them a far better mum than me, I just know you would.'

Now it was impossible to remember just how excited and proud and happy she'd been when they'd gone to Derby City Hospital for a scan, and were told she was expecting twins.

'Are there any twins in your family?' the sonographer had asked them.

'No,' they'd replied.

Well, there are now!' she'd said.

'Congratulations!'

She remembers the cupboard she'd so lovingly filled in preparation for the twins' birth; everything doubled. Her heart bursting with pride, and her huge bump bursting with her two unborn babies, she'd arranged everything so neatly; the baby talc and wipes, the tiny folded-up baby-gros, the fluffy pale yellow pretend-duck towels with hoods; how exciting, how pretty it had all looked.

These days she felt overwhelmed. One day a few weeks back her mum had enquired whether the migraine she'd had the previous day had gone,

'How are you feeling?' she'd asked her.

'Desperate,' she'd replied,

'I feel desperate.'

Had she smiled up at her mum after she'd said that? Or had her eyes filled with tears? She couldn't remember. She was always so tired. Just looking downwards used to make her eyes feel heavy, inclined to droop.

But then one of the twins had yelled or something, and her mum had turned to him to hug him better.

Then she'd waggled her index finger at her grandchildren.

'Boys, you must start behaving better. Your poor mummy just said she's "*desperate!*"

But her mum had been smiling as she'd said the 'D' word, and, with a sinking feeling, she knew then, for sure, that nobody understood how she was feeling.

'What does poor mummy feel?' her mum and then her mother-in-law would ask the twins.

'Deth-prutt'' Fred and Will repeated.

It became a party trick for visitors to giggle at,

'What's your poor mummy feel?'

'Deth-prutt'' Fred and Will would reply to the amusement of all except our nameless narrator, but, hating any form of confrontation, she would smile gently, play along.

Did her mum and her mum in law not understand that, although she loved Fred and Will, she did not want to spend any more time with them? She had too much time with the twins. She wanted time to do other things. Time. To. Do. Other. Things. Not time to play on the floor with the Fred and Will, trying to sound grateful when her mum or her mum in law, or, God forbid, both, bought her mugs of tea, always sugared by her mum in law when she even didn't take sugar.

She was sick to death of her children. And they were sick to death of her.

But she'd sit playing with Duplo or bricks trying to sound enthusiastic as the rain hammered on the windows, trying to sound enthusiastic to please everybody but herself. And the two elder women, they'd be the same age more or less as she was now; that was hard to get her head around, they'd be doing things she'd rather be doing. Why didn't *they* offer to play with the twins and let her do the washing-up, the hoovering, why didn't they let her peg the washing out, Fred and Will's little tops and trousers, their little sweet smelling cardigans, get a breath of cool, fresh air in between the showers; even do the ironing?

They'd sometimes say, 'You look tired. Why don't you go upstairs and have a little lie down?' but that was the last thing she wanted to do. Nor did she want to go out on the **razz**, or shopping, or for a beauty treatment. She hadn't got the energy, she hadn't got the money, she hadn't got the inclination.

She yearned to enjoy her children but, she couldn't.

***

The twins were in bed, and seemed settled. Despite the bad start, they'd not been too difficult today. She'd managed to have a quick dip and wash her hair in their remaining tepid bathwater, and had even made a fisherman's pie earlier, whilst they'd watched most of 'Playschool', and not just the part they called 'the naughty bird bit' at the end.

She sips at a glass of cheap vermouth, puts the stained cushions back on the settee, picks up discarded clothes, smells Fred and Will's soft little-boy vests, removing the soggy nappies from their little jeans, realising that Will has been in damp trousers all afternoon, and realising that, yes, she does love them, she does still love them, of course, she loves them dearly. And she picks up the stained bibs, drops them on the floor in front of the washer. She knows she should go back upstairs, bring down all the other washing, put a good big load on, set the timer for when the electric is on at cheap rate, but the task is too big for her. She will do it in the morning.

And then she wonders how she will feel in the morning?

***

It was getting dark when he arrived, unusually bang on time, walking through the gate into the tiny back yard, with its single peony, its dandelions, its puddles and the rusting, broken Tonka trucks.

She drew the curtains across the kitchen door behind him, poured them a glass of the wine he'd remembered to bring. It was time for their favourite TV programme to begin.

'It'll take about half an hour from now,' she said. 'Do you want a drink and watch Brookside?' She felt nervous, tried not to gulp down her wine.

'I'll record it for you,' he said, and bent to set up the tape. Why hadn't warning bells rung then, when he said he'd record it for *her*. Brookside was one of the few a programmes they both enjoyed, always watched together. His back to her, squatting in front of the television he said,

15

'I could do with having a chat with you actually.'

He sat down, poured himself a small glass of wine.

'Oh, that's good…' she said, laughing slightly, awkwardly, as she sat on the settee beside him, '…because' she touched his knee, 'I'd like to talk to you, too.'

He lit a cigarette. He'd obviously given up pretending that he'd given up smoking. He sipped his wine and she immediately wished she'd sat in the armchair opposite him, as she was unable to see his eyes or his facial expression as he smoked and sipped his wine, flicking the ash into the ash tray, as he always had done, with his long guitarist's thumb nail. The smell of the smoke on her long-empty stomach made her queasy.

She began to say,

'You go first…'

just as he sighed out an extra-long cloud of smoke; an empty speech bubble. It hung in front of them above the coffee table, and then he began to fill it with words she didn't want to understand.

'I know you've had your suspicions. And your suspicions were right; spot on, in fact. I suppose that's the poet in you, always observant…'

'Why? What?'

'I *have* been seeing somebody else. And I'm so sorry, we've tried to end it several times, but, we've both really got feelings for each other.'

'How long?' she whispered, voice cracking.

'Pardon?' he asked.

'How fucking long?' she snapped.

'On and off for two years.'

And the person she now realized she yearned to be, stood up, stared at him icily and said,

'Well, that is fine by me. I'll go and pack the twins' stuff now. And I really hope that the four of you will be very happy.'

Instead she said,

'But, I'm pregnant…'

The VCR machine whirred as it recorded Brookside, unaware that it was witnessing a real-life soap-opera scene.

'…That's what I want to talk to you about.'

The clock on the mantlepiece, a wedding present from her parents, ticked.

'You can't be.'

There was a sleepy moan; Fred, upstairs.

'*Why* can't I be?'

She made as if to stand.

'Leave him.'

She stayed put, on the edge of her seat.

She said nothing.

'Anyway, you'll have to get rid, it's obvious. You can barely cope with two kids, let alone three…'

What a total bastard he really was.

'You arrange to have the abortion, and I can have the twins for a couple of days whilst you get it done.'

She gulped down her wine, devoid of words for a few moments.

'So, whose is it?' he asked her, then shook his head, 'You don't have to answer that; it's not really any of my business under the circumstances.'

'Sorry,' he added, a few seconds later, clearly thinking himself oh so gracious.

'Who's the fuck do you *think* it is?'

And who the fuck did *he* think he was?

'Well, it's obviously not *mine*.'

He ground out his cigarette.

'Why is it "obviously not *yours*"?'

'Well, I'm not here half the time, so *I* don't know what you're doing.'

'Where would I find the time, let alone the energy to shag somebody else? I'm trapped with those two inside this house.'

'Get real, you know we've not done anything in months, nothing for absolutely ages.'

'Five months, yes.'

She noticed that he'd clocked the ever-so slight rounding of her belly where her loose dress had clung to her middle a little as she'd leant forward.

'Five months. Do you remember that gig with 'no strings' attached; that so-called 'gig' which you spent with your puppet on a string, whilst I struggled at home, your twins tied to my apron strings, whilst you broke my heart strings?…'

'How come you've not told me before?'

'You know how I've been since having the twins. All over the place. Coming on twice in a month, then nothing. I thought I was just settling back into a normal routine. Plus, you know my stress and exhaustion levels have been through the roof!'

'Five months?'

'Yes. Five fucking months.'

She could see the realization dawning upon his face. Too late for a termination.

The oven timer began to beep.

And then she could see him thinking,

'How the fuck am I going to tell her?'

Chapter Three

'Ouch!' They were getting worse; coming faster.

A petite nurse swooshed back the curtains, lifted the clipboard from the end of the bed, smiled at him with and said, 'Hiya,' looked at her notes instead of at her.

'Right,' he said hands on his knees, set to rise, 'I'll leave you to it; go and grab a coffee from the machine,' he said.

'If you can *call* it coffee!' petite nurse scoffed.

Her curvy colleague, half covered by a stack of towels added,

'If I were you, I'd opt for the hot chocolate.'

Petite nurse busied herself around her, taking her blood pressure, continuing to talk to her colleague over her shoulder.

'Have you tried that new low-fat stuff yet?' she asked, taking her pulse on the inside of her wrist, looking at the clock on her uniform.

'No,' came the faint reply, her colleague obviously now placing towels onto beds further up the ward.

Petite nurse took her temperature, shook the thermometer;

'You make it just with boiling water…'

'…I still add a drop of milk though.' She said, over her shoulder again.

She then covered over her lower half with a sheet, as though she wasn't really there at all. Perhaps she wasn't? As though she was a dead body rather than a woman in labour, whose entire body was contracting in agony every three minutes.

Petite nurse decided next to speak to her neat stretched bump.

'Right then…'

Did she even exist? This woman who was about to give birth?

'Let's have a look, shall we, see how far you're gone.' She snapped on plastic gloves, rummaged below the sheet and beneath her paper gown.

'Floppy legs,' she said sharply, then inserted something, moved it around inside; an unpleasant stinging sensation but nothing; nothing compared with the pains she was having.

Petite nurse stood, replaced the sheet with a sigh, then snapped off her purple latex.

'You're actually…' she said on a weary sigh, 'you're actually barely two centimeters dilated.'

She disposed of the gloves with a single clap of the lid on the clinical waste bin.

She couldn't have been more shocked had the nurse punched her in the face.

How could she only be that dilated?

Why, her insides were being wrung out like a wet dishcloth, being screwed and turned and twisted as tight as was absolutely possible around and around themselves until no more water could possibly drip.

She felt another contraction coming now. Her muscles squeezing, tightening, squashing: her abdomen a huge stone.

But she said nothing, silenced by the nurse's scorn.

'You're going to be hours yet.'

She was told.

'You've perhaps got a low pain threshold have you?'

'I had twins without a caesarian three years ago,' she tried not to gasp with the pain.

'Oh well,' she laughed, glancing at her curvy colleague who was back at her side, 'you're definitely the child birth expert then!'

She struggled to wipe away a tear without it being seen. The invisible tear. The invisible mother to be.

'Why don't you…' she began, more kindly now; perhaps she'd seen the tear.

'…Why don't you both go home, get a good night's sleep and ask hubby to bring you back in the morning?'

She imagined going all the way back home, in the dark, in agony, and him complaining. He'd had to miss a gig, and she did believe it was a genuine gig, to bring her here.

'Is it all right if we stay over, please…'

She hated the tears that were flowing freely now, as though they had a mind of their own; had been encouraged by that tiny glimpse of kindness.

'…only I really am in a lot of pain.'

She wiped the tears away with her hands, blotted her nose with the cuff of her cardigan sleeve.

The nurse looked again at her notes,

'Well, I suppose you do live a fair distance away. And we're not too busy tonight. We'll sort out a bed on a general ward for you. Get you some paracetamol to help with the discomfort, maybe a little something to calm you a bit.'

At that moment, Dan came back in smelling of cigarettes.

'I took your advice…' he said to petite nurse as he sat down.

'…and I have to say, the hot chocolate was quite nice.'

'Well, it will help keep your blood sugar levels up…' she briefly touched his knee, lowered her voice slightly, '…it looks as though you're in for the long haul.'

Petite nurse swooshed the curtains back closed around her bed.

'What did she mean by that?' he asked, and looked at her for the first time since he'd come back.

'Apparently I'm barely dilated.'

He processed the news, frowned, began to speak; she interrupted him.

'But I honestly, really feel like it's well and truly on its way…' she gasped as another contraction took hold, resisted the urge to reach for his hand.

'…And I am practically full term now.'

'But the nurses know what they're doing. They know best. If they've examined you and measured you, they must be right.'

He'd take advice from them to avoid the coffee, he'd apparently also take advice from them to disbelieve the natural instinct of the mother-to be-of his third child.

'They said we should go back home and come back in the morning.'

'Fuckin' hell…'

he muttered and reached for his denim jacket.

'Best get going again, then.'

'No, please…'

She was trying her best not to cry.

'… I asked if we could stay. Honestly, I'm in that much pain. You will stay with me, won't you?'

Then as the contraction faded, she re-considered,

'…Although I suppose my mum might be relieved if you picked the twins up from hers, if they're not in bed yet. Her back was really painful this morning.'

Like hers was now. No matter how she fidgeted she could not anywhere near comfortable, even as she waited for the next pain.

'Like I'm going to do that! You must be joking!…' he snapped, putting on his jacket,

'…I'm going to get to my gig. You know, to earn some of that stuff that we keep needing more of. You know, that stuff called 'Money'.'

She knew he'd stop at a telephone box, ring her, tell her there'd been a change of plan, that the silly cow wasn't really in labour after all, tell her delightedly that the gig was back on, if she wanted to come along.

'If I make good time, I'll only have missed half the first set.'

And she imagined *her* sitting at the venue, all proud and calm and pretty, nonchalantly drinking her French lager straight from the bottle, a cigarette between her fingers; poised and elegant; in total contrast with her, a blubbering, blubbery ugly mess.

'I'll be back in the morning,' he said, then warned nastily, 'it won't be early though.'

Another pain started to attack, stealing her voice so that she had no strength to speak, not even to say,

'Good bye,' as he drew the curtains closed back around her.

And she was left alone on the trolley, the sides raised like a cot. Drapes shut like those around a coffin at a crematorium.

Aware of a couple talking quietly in the adjoining cubicle, she tried her best to stifle her animal noises; embarrassed by them; ashamed by them. Perhaps she *did* have a low pain threshold?

And she lay there, looking over at her carrier bag of stuff on the floor. Nothing like what she'd taken in with her to have the twins. She remembered at exactly seven months to the day pregnant, '*Twins often arrive up to eight weeks early.*' Neatly and joyously; yes, joyously!; ticking off from the list in the book she'd spent months devouring; reading and re-reading.

She'd arranged everything listed in a proper suitcase borrowed from her mum and dad. Twin One's things. Twin Two's things. All in fragrant whites and yellows. Towels and baby-grows and cardigans and vests, all joyously ticked off and double-checked.

Then Johnson's Baby talc and soap and baby shampoo that she used to love to smell. Sudacrem in case of nappy rash. Tiny disposable nappies, which were only just becoming popular; wipes as they used to be, in a pull-out pot.

Then she'd packed a pile of Proud new mum things. Even a nice new le Jardin body spray and lotion. A magazine to read. Her address book. Some pretty writing paper and matching envelopes! Stamps. Some new stretchy undies. Makeup and a looking glass! Shampoo, conditioner, le Jardin shower gel… A novel from the library to read! … A smart dress to come home in which she still could not zip up.

She really hadn't had a fucking clue, had she?

Three years on, she'd shoved everything into an ugly old bag. After all, she was now an ugly old bag, she was an ugly old bag, a supermarket carrier bag. She threw in an oversized T shirt, an elasticated skirt, big cotton knickers, nappies, some faded baby grows and vests that Fred and Will had long since grown out of. Two small cans of Guiness. Well, why not?

In between contractions she could hear bleepings and buzzings, the nurses' shoes squeaking on the polished floor. The couple in the next cubicle talking softly; it sounded as if they were getting ready to go; not back home, oh no, only *she* was that stupid, they'd be off to the delivery suite, all proud.

She was out of sight.

She was out of mind.

She was out of sight of the baby's father and the hospital staff.

She was out of mind of the baby's father and the hospital staff.

Was she out of her mind?

And then it *was* happening. She knew it was. She felt as though the baby's head was pushing against a cheese grater, or some wire mesh or netting, trying to burst through just one tiny hole. And her entire body was desperately aching, desperately pained dying to stop this pain, but unable to stop the motion causing the pain.

She wanted to run; to run away but was trapped, like the baby, inside her own body. Yet, totally and utterly out of control. Just trying, dying to stop this pain.

And then she felt a sort of change; a sort of lifting; an ever so slight relief in the agony. And she knew she shouldn't push, but she just wanted the pain to end so very much. She was exhausted and sick of fighting. For a second she really didn't care any more. And …

The baby slithered out; a long blue eel, still and silent between her legs.

She tried to sit up to see it and in doing so noticed a black buzzer thing on the arm of the chair at her side. No one had pointed that out to her. He hadn't. They hadn't. But she should have seen it. She should have known there'd be a buzzer.

She pressed it as she sat up-right and saw the mess of blue, of white, of red.

She saw his tiny blue penis.

Not little-boy-blue. Blue. Dark Blue.

The nurse ran in, snipped the cord, scooped up the dark blue baby, took him away.

Tears and sweat, the placenta and blood escaped her. And understanding escaped her too. What had just happened? Whatever had she done? Frightened and alone, she sobbed unbearably hot painful tears wanting to die. Hating herself so much.

***

The nurse came back through the curtains holding something in a white blanket. She handed it over.

'His AGPAR score was very low.'

Her tone was accusatory.

'You're both very lucky.'

And yet she never said a word. Why didn't she? Why didn't she complain that nobody had told her there was a buzzer? Why didn't she complain that she'd been misdiagnosed? Why didn't she complain that she'd been left alone? Why had Dan believed them over her? Why had he left her alone, frightened and in agony?

She said nothing because she was unable to stand up for herself, because she was too shy? Too timid? Too frightened of confrontation? Or because she was lazy? Because she simply couldn't be bothered? Whatever, the answer, she had failed to stand up for her new born son. He'd been born too suddenly. Starved of oxygen. She'd been willing to put his life at risk and had almost lost him.

Dan came through the curtains half an hour later, after she'd been silently checked over and cleaned up. He smelt of cigarettes but worse than that, of that perfume again, and she didn't like the new born baby Ben, for that's what she'd decided to call him, she didn't like Baby Ben smelling *her* perfume in his first couple of hours of life.

'Ay up!' he greeted her, 'You were right then?' he chuckled, presumably surprised that she could actually be right about something.

He reached for his third son's little hand.

'He's ok now then is he? He's going to be all right?' he sounded genuinely concerned; perhaps he was. Nothing would surprise her now. Nothing made sense.

'I take it you're breast feeding,' snapped a nurse she'd not yet seen.

There was no question mark.

'No,' she heard herself respond.

Snappy nurse remained pointedly silent, waiting for excuses. Suddenly angry and exhausted, she thought, Stuff her. She couldn't be bothered to provide excuses.

'But,' she continued, 'I have brought a couple of ready-made bottles and a tin of formula milk with me.'

The nurse's eyes followed hers to the scruffy carrier bag on the floor.

Snappy nurse then said unkindly,

'*Breast is Best*' as the slogan goes. And I'm sure you already know that we do offer support to help mum breast feed.'

Dan suddenly spoke, spoke up for her, and her eyes prickled and tears started as she found herself feeling the most the most ridiculous gratitude.

'My wife tried really hard to breast-feed the twins but we decided in the end it just wasn't worth it.'

She felt like he'd not stood up for her for years.

He continued,

'With bottles you can see exactly how much the babies are taking, and other people can help.'

'Mum could express the milk and then dad could still help.'

'No,' Dan persisted, and she was proud of him, 'we'll stick with formula milk, thanks,' he said.

And she flushed as she stroked Baby's Ben's soft fwispy hair, a slight smile forming on her face.

Perhaps Baby Ben would help get them back together again? Perhaps things were going to be easier from now on?

Chapter Four

Her neighbour Sharon and she had become friendly because Sharon also had two boys from a previous marriage, one a little younger than Will and Fred and one in their class at school. She and Sharon had recently started going to the local pub to sit in the beer garden for an hour or so taking it in turns to play with Baby Ben on Friday teatimes whilst Sharon's partner, Anthony, bravely took all four lads for a kickabout on the nearby playing field.

She and Dan had used to go to the Nelson regularly when she was expecting the twins. In those days there was very little emphasis on not drinking alcohol whilst pregnant, and so she drank; mainly Guinness which is what her midwife told her would make her vegetarian blood thicker.

They had visited The Nelson once since their birth, she, Dan and the twins. A total disaster. Dan had looked so awkward, so uncomfortable, especially when his mates came over to say, or rather to yell, 'Ay-up!' over the twins' constant row.

She'd been so looking forward to the pub visit; she'd so wanted to show off the twins which had made her fairly petite body so huge that towards the end of her pregnancy she'd had fairly wriggle in and out of the pub's tiny toilet cubicles.

She'd wanted so much to show off her babies, now almost a year old, and had expected to be able to show them off with pride. She had been preparing practically all day, trying to disguise her baby fat and her tired eyes, waiting until the last minute to dress them, even allowing them a little sleep midday, as she got thoroughly organised in the hope that the trip would go smoothly; but Fred and Will had done nothing but fight and howl.

She knew she looked fat and frumpy; she'd worn the wrong clothes and had been red and hot and flustered. And no matter what she did to try and distract the twins, and she had brought along a bag full of toys, books and treats, they had continued to fight and to howl.

Her own friends, or women she'd considered friends, had looked embarrassed or pitying, or worse still, smug as they cuddled their own neat little bumps, or their own perfect offspring. She just couldn't stand it. And so, feeling totally ashamed and embarrassed and useless, she'd knocked back her second drink; a large glass of red which had dribbled like blood down her chin.

He'd tutted, then chucked over the tub of baby wipes, snapping, 'God you're even worse than them two!' She was reminded of Baby Ben's conception and she'd left, tearful, pushing the screaming double buggy back home on her own. Dan had stayed until closing time, no doubt laughing with his mates and flirting with the landlady. Maybe even *she* had joined him later.

She now knew that at least part of Dan's discomfort, the discomfort which rubbed off onto his sons and which she took, even accepted, the blame for, was that he knew that others knew he was cheating on his wife, the mother of his twin boys.

This particular Friday teatime was no different. Anthony came back with the happy, red-faced footballers who immediately made their way to Baby Ben, who they cooed at and touched, and he loved all the big boys' attention.

Anthony went to the bar to buy them fruit shoots and crisps, just as a stranger holding a pint came over to their table.

'Ay up Jack.' Sharon greeted him as he sat down beside her. 'Are you all set for tomorrow's match?'

Sharon introduced her as, 'My good friend and neighbour, the terrible twins' Fred and Will's mum,' then continued, 'this is Jack, Anthony's cousin and best friend all rolled into one.'

'Nice to meet you,' Jack nodded at her, then looked back over at Sharon,

'Yes, I was all set for tomorrow's match, but there's some problem with my ticket apparently.'

He sipped his Guiness, staring at the cardboard slip.

'Oh no, does that mean you can't you go, then? '

She noticed that Sharon was slurring slightly. She was halfway down her third pint on an empty stomach.

'It doesn't look like it, unfortunately. Our Anthony says I'm still welcome to stay overnight though, now that I'm here, have a few bevvies and a takeout later, if that's ok with you and the lads?'

'Course it is,' Sharon said, downing her pint,' you are family, after all.'

That sounded nice, our nameless narrator mused, a shared takeaway in front of the tv; get the kids to bed, so tired out from playing football that a rare lie-in might even be on the cards; stay up late, enjoying some stimulating adult conversation instead of just falling out or talking about the kids; a night cap or two…

She did miss times like that.

Anthony and Jack and Sharon and chatted, studying the forged ticket, holding it up to the light, comparing it with the legit one. The boys were offering baby Ben salt and vinegar crisps, and, alongside his Baby Ribena, he loved them.

'Another?' the boys, laughing, kept asking him, and he'd give a big smile and a big nod, take the proffered crisp. 'Ta,' and put it into his own mouth.

And all around her, she could hear people making plans for the weekend.

'Do you fancy going out for a meal tomorrow night?' a young lad asked his girlfriend.

Going out for a meal; that sounded wonderful, unbelievable. Actually getting dressed up and made up; hair done nicely, to sit down at a table with somebody bringing a proper plate of nice food to you, and not having to make do with the twins' left overs or bolt something down whilst they were quiet for two minutes; not having a wriggling child upon your knee whilst you stuffed down rapidly-cooling food. No wonder she never bothered cooking herself a hot meal these days.

'Our Jason could do with some shorts now the weather's picking up…' a woman was speaking whilst her children played nicely on the climbing frame. Mind you, Fred and Will were also playing nicely at the moment, she had to admit; probably trying to keep in her good books in case she might cancel their date with Alton Towers, their date with *Her*.

Knowing a Friday afternoon pint had mellowed her husband, the woman continued, 'So, what do you think about nipping to Derby tomorrow?'

That sounded nice too. A walk round Primark, lunch in one of those new child friendly pubs with a ball pit and ropes to climb.

Just to 'nip' somewhere. Why had she never learned to drive? She felt so isolated, especially now that her parents, particularly her mother, were barely speaking to her, and things were obviously awkward with Dan's side of the family. She was getting so little help.

She kissed Baby Ben on the top of his head, thinking, half-sad, half-happy,

'Just me and you tomorrow, Ben, just me and you all day, and all night...'

Sharon reached over; touched her hand,

'You're a bit quiet, duck. Are you ok?'

She jumped a little.

Then, 'Yeah,' she said, 'Fine. Just, you know, a fed up.'

'Well, *I* would be too, in your shoes. But,' she continued, 'think of it this way; if tomorrow *does* goes ok, at least you'll know you'll be able to get a regular break from the terrible twosome.'

'Yeah, you're right...' She looked around the beer garden, most people in couples; children all playing happily. '... I know...'

She sighed.

There was a couple of moments silence, then Sharon said,

'I'll tell you what, why don't I drive you and Baby Ben and my lads somewhere nice tomorrow?...'

Then she laughed loudly. '...And, don't worry,' she spluttered on her last mouthful of lager, 'I'm not thinking Alton Towers!'

Jack looked up from yet more studying of the ticket,

'Alton Towers?' he smiled, shook his head, 'not my cup of tea.'

'Nor mine.' She managed a shy smile, avoiding his eyes, though empathizing, 'but my lads...' she waved in Fred and Will's direction, '...are looking forward to going tomorrow. Their Dad's taking them there...'

'... along with his new girlfriend!' Sharon slurred, loudly.

For a split second, Jack's eyes met our nameless narrator's. She noticed that his eyes were brown; kind, and she was grateful for his tact when he left the conversation at that, leaning forward to talk more football with Anthony.

As she finished her drink and said no to another one, she briefly considered Sharon's suggestion, but decided against it. After all, she did want to spend some rare quality time with Baby Ben.

And so she said,

'Right lads we'd better get off. You've got a busy day tomorrow'

Her heart fairly sank as they obediently ran to her side, with none of their usual moaning to stay a bit longer; all too eager for tomorrow morning to come round as soon as possible.

'If you change your mind about tomorrow...' was Sharon's passing shot, and,

'Good to meet you,' said Jack with a nod, lifting his almost empty glass in a sort of salute.

***

Although she couldn't see driver or passenger, she recognised the back of Dan's car as it pulled up beneath the sycamore tree at the end of the garden path. Not sure if he planned to come to the front door, maybe even, God forbid, bring *Her* with him, she'd showered, washed her hair, put on mascara and lip gloss, sprayed on some nice fragrance and dressed in an old summer dress that she knew he had once liked.

She gave him a couple of minutes, but when the engine continued to run and she'd heard no doors open or close, she decided, with relief, or perhaps not, that he wasn't going to get out of the car, and so she shouted upstairs to the boys,

'Your dad's here.'

With Her, With Her. She was doubtless here too. The boys fairly galloped down the stairs.

On the front doorstep she gave them both a hug; smelt fabric conditioner, banana shampoo, Lynx Africa...

'Have a nice time...'

31

Above the fleeces tied around their waists, their backpacks bounced excitedly, filled with pac-a-macs, gameboys, a bottle of water, wipes, spare clothes, everything they might possibly need, packed by a well-organised, considerate mum.

Fred and Will hurried down the path towards the waiting car. From here, the woman seated beside her husband was a dark shadow, a cardboard cutout; unreal. Not a threat; she could be ignored.

'…And …' she continued,

'… be good boys…'

But, although she had tried to raise her voice to reach them, it came out hoarse and croaky.

The twins might not have even heard her, especially over Radio One which she had playing in the kitchen, just in case Dan and maybe even *She* came to the door, to show him that Yes, thank you, she was doing just fine, thank you very much; hoping beyond hope, that Gloria Gaynor *'I will Survive'* might just happen to be playing in the background. He had used to constantly mock her middle-of-the-road taste in music, preferring classical or modern jazz. She wondered what Dan's new girlfriend thought of his taste in music; wondered if he mocked her if she hummed along to The Carpenters?

Anyway, she thought, it really didn't matter whether or not Fred and Will had managed to hear her croaky instruction to be good, because she wasn't even sure that she'd even meant it.

In fact, she thought, closing the front door, she'd quite like them to be naughty…

Yes. Be naughty for her. Don't like her. Play up for her. Fight all the time. Demand things. Be rude and nasty …Why not? Let it rain. Let the queues be horrendous. What else? …

But … she lifted a corner of the living room net curtain, if things didn't work out, then he and she *'he and she' like a proper couple; like they had used to be,* he and she would not want to take the twins out again, and then, as Sharon had implied last night, she would never get a proper break from the constant sheer exhaustion, the break she'd been so looking forward to today; just her and Baby Ben…

Through the white lace, she saw that Fred, still the more confident of the twins, was struggling to open the car's back door; and that she and

Dan had both turned their heads, presumably to offer him advice.

…On the other hand, she thought, if things didn't work out, then *She* might get fed up and then they'd split up… and then she and Dan might get back together and …

She saw that Fred was still struggling to open the door … and then…

…*Oh No! She* was getting out of the car.

Oh no; oh no; oh no… She was walking out from the shade of the tree into the early morning sunshine. *Oh no!* She could see that *she* was laughing; shaking her head good-naturedly at Fred.

No!!! Pretty; very pretty…

Oh *No!!!*

A couple of years younger than herself, *Why couldn't she stay sitting down?* … actually, may be a full five years younger than herself…

Please. Stay in the tree's shadow. Please. remain imaginary. I don't want to see you… I don't want to see the real you …

I don't want to see! Slim…

Stop looking! About her own height…

I don't want to see! Long dark hair; wavy…

Stop looking! Nicer hair, thicker than hers, much nicer…

Sunglasses perched on the top of her head … *which he had always said he thought made women look pretentious…!*

Dressed just right for a trip to Alton Towers… *For Goodness sake, put the curtain down!* Dressed absolutely perfectly for a first day out with her new boyfriend and his five-year-old sons.

Flat gladiator-style sandals, an open shirt over a pretty lemon vest top and *Oh God…* faded, soft, good fitting jeans held in place with a narrow leather belt. *God, how she hated women who looked good in belted jeans; a soft, pale leather belt that looked as though she'd worn it often, not bought it especially for the occasion.*

She just knew she'd have got it disastrously wrong. She'd have worn a long, baggy floral top over leggings, not jeans, and would have struggled all day, feet blistering and swelling in high-ish wedge heels, worn to counteract the frumpiness of her shuttledore-top, and immediately regretted.

She opened the car door, and she saw *her* remind the boys to take off their back-packs before they clambered into their exciting new world; into the next chapter of their young lives. Then *she* waited to check they were both safely strapped in.

That was good; responsible… She was probably really nice. In another world they might have been friends, like he'd said that night when he'd dropped the bombshell. But, she couldn't bear to re-visit that one, left it to one side. Because … What?! For Goodness sake, what on earth was she thinking? No, of course they wouldn't, couldn't possibly have been friends. Not even in another world. No way on this earth! Because she hated *her.*

She hated *her,* hated *her, hated her…*

Oh God, what was that noise…?

She hated her and her fucking belted jeans.

What on earth was that noise? It definitely wasn't Ben waking happily in his cot upstairs. It wasn't the radio.

Oh my goodness. The noise was coming from her; coming deep down from her very core; from her breaking heart. She'd finally fully sighed out the breath which she hadn't realized she'd been holding in.

And there had followed the release; a paroxysm of racking sobs.

And through her tears she saw *her, Mollie,* crane her neck and seem to look directly at her. Had *Mollie* heard her bellowing out her ugly noises? Is that why she'd turned? Had Mollie seen the tears on her face as the new foursome had set off to enjoy their fun family trip?

She dropped the lacy net curtain, as though giving up her bridal wear, as though giving up her children, her husband, as though passing her lacy veil onto *her like a baton;* resigned to giving up on their marriage, for a moment wishing that she'd taken up Sharon's offer of last night.

The car disappeared along with her two excited little boys; its noise becoming distant, then gone; off to Alton Towers, and then to stay overnight at Mollie's, Daddy's girlfriend's, house.

'Unless, of course…' and a couple of days ago, she had heard in Dan's telephone-voice relief that she'd agreed to the boys staying the night, and she'd imagined him thumbs-upping to *her; she'd* doubtless have been standing close by as he spoke, '…unless, of course, it doesn't work out,' he'd said in that years-gone-by kindly manner, and she could tell that he thought this unlikely, '…if it doesn't work out, of course, I'll bring them straight back.' He'd said breezily, no doubt all smiles and thumbs-ups to *Her*.

Dan. Presumptuous as always. She should have said firmly down the telephone, 'But, I won't be here.'

She should have said defiantly,

'I have a date.'

But of course she hadn't got a date, and so of course, she said nothing.

Apart from the melancholy sloshing of the washing machine, the house was suddenly so quiet that she could almost hear the silence; and then the first bars of *'Winner Takes it All'* played on the radio, and *Abba* was singing.

> *'… tell me does she kiss*
> *Like I used to kiss you?*
> *Does it feel the same*
> *When she calls your name?'*

and that was it.

She cried and she cried, unashamedly dabbing at her eyes and her nose on the lacy net curtain.

Then she heard Baby Ben stirring upstairs.

God, get a grip. She was being pathetic, playing into their hands. She would have time to try and process all this, to be able to think more about all this tonight when she lay awake as she always did at 3am. Until then forget it! You have a toddler who needs you to take care of him, she told herself.

> *'Somewhere deep inside*
> *You must know I miss you*
> *But what can I say*
> *Rules must be obeyed.'*
>
> *Rules must be obeyed?*

She slammed off the radio and hurried upstairs, filled with a fierce rush of Adrenalin and determination.

It was not curtains yet…

***

Baby Ben was standing up in his cot, looking for all the world as excited and pleased to see her as if he, too, was about to go on an adventure. Smiling widely, yet still managing to keep his dummy in his mouth, he lifted his arms.

And along came one of those strange premonitions that she was becoming used to, that were becoming more frequent, and she was thinking ahead to a time when Ben was stretching, reaching, perhaps for her to put on a jumper, or to take one off, but no, he seemed too old for that, and there was some music, and water, and he was dancing; people were clapping; singing. And there were stars in the sky …

And then she knew for certain that she'd made the right decision in not accepting Sharon's offer.

She lifted him, smiled back at him, and at the soggy nappy sagging between his legs.

'Oh dear, Ben, your nappy's very wet this morning. Let's give you a nice bath before breakfast!'

How much easier everything was with just the one child!

She recalled bathtimes with the twins, even on the rare occasions when Dan or her mum or mother in law had helped her, bathtimes were always to be dreaded; were always a nightmare… Fred and Will used to constantly fight over their toys, especially that one blue boat with a lid, and then they used to keep trying to climb back into the bath, even when it was empty.

One-handed, with Ben expertly balanced on her hip, she put in the plug, turned on the taps, squeezed in Matey bubble bath, lay him on a towel on his changing mat while she got ready clean clothes and nappy.

While Ben was in the bath, she knelt beside him, singing a song the twins had used to sing in infant school, as she gently blobbed Matey bubbles all over his face,

> *There was an old man called Michael Fin-egan*
> *He grew whiskers on his chin-egan,'*
> *Then the wind came round and blew them in again.'*

She blew off the foam, and he laughed, and squealed and shook his little head.

'Poor old Michael Fin-egan,
Begin again!'

Then, her eyes wide open, fixed upon his, she slowly, exaggeratedly raised her shoulders, taking a long, long, deep intake of breath, which he copied, *'Ffff-uhhh!…'*

'…The-errrre …' and her voice rose, and slowed, teasing him, and he clapped his hands, in gleeful anticipation as she began again…

'… was a little boy called Ben-Ben-Benagan.'

And he laughed, eyes screwed up tightly as she patted the bubbles onto his face and his hair in time with her singing.

'He grew whiskers on his chinn-egen
The wind came round and blew them in again
Poor little Ben-Ben-Ben …
Begin again!'

But this time she didn't begin again. Her voice tailed off, and, as Ben realised he wasn't going to get another verse today, he looked a little disappointed, playing instead with the bubbles in the bath.

Then she said,

'Just me and you … all day today, Ben!' she said, and hated that her voice broke.

She tried again, pointing this time,

'Just me … and you.'

That was a bit better.

She gently rubbed baby shampoo into his hair, then carefully rinsed it off, pouring water from a plastic jug, feeling his fontanel, now almost closed.

'All day and … all night… too. That'll be nice, won't it?' she forced a smile,

'Just Baby Ben and Mummy?'

He thoughtfully examined the froth of bubbles sitting on his knee,

'Mama?' he said, as he touched it with his little fingers.

Had she heard him properly? She held her breath, the only sound her tummy rumbling, then,

'Mama.'

He spoke again to his knee,

'Yes,' she said loudly; delighted, 'Mama!'

Not wanting to distract him by touching him, she willed him to look at her, pointing to herself,

'Mama'

Then she pointed to her little boy,

'Ben'

Still looking at the bathwater, he said,

'Ben'

And then he lifted his face, gazed straight into her tear-filled eyes, and said to her,

'Mama'

and then,

'Ben.'

'Good boy!' she shouted, lifting him from the water, hugging his wet body tight to her cotton nightee.

'Clever boy!' she said.

Exhilarated, she turned to see who else had heard her baby's first words, as any parent would. But of course there was no one. Nobody to share her proud moment. Of course, what had she been thinking?

His big brothers had gone out with his daddy and his daddy's girlfriend; his daddy's slim, pretty, belted-jeaned, nice-haired girlfriend.

And whilst Ben fiddled with one of the tiny pink ribbons on her nightee, she croaked, a little deflated.

'Today we will be just Mummy and Clever Baby Ben'

She put him back into the bath, weeping a few hot tears which added to water's depth, and she would always remember saying,

'I love you so much Baby Ben. We've already been through such a lot together. And I promise you that no matter what happens, I will always love you.'

***

And after bathing him, she continued to get a grip like she'd told herself to, like she always did and like she was going to have to do so many times in the future.

She gave Ben his cereal, eating the little he left for her own breakfast, put a wash on, including the twins' bedding, pegged a load out, tidied all the twins' and Baby Ben's stuff, trying so hard not to think about *her*, about him and *her*, because she knew, as she'd already thought and would think many more times that day, that the time for that would come later; later when she was lying on her own in bed having had a couple of drinks, Baby Ben asleep in his cot at the foot of the bed. The house quiet; the twins' beds empty because they were going to stay at *hers, at their daddy's girlfriend's house.*

Ben had gone to sleep in his baby-bouncer chair, and she was thinking about to start making them both a nice little picnic to eat in the garden when there was a gentle knock at the door.

Her first thought was, was it them come back? She had feelings like this all the time; that Dan would surely sooner or later choose to return to her, full of regrets, because even now, even now, she could not believe what had happened between them. Why, they'd always loved each other so much. They'd met at school, had been girlfriend and boyfriend since they were fifteen, right the way through to marriage at twenty-four, twins at twenty-six. And she would have him back; oh, goodness, she would thank her lucky stars if he came back; she would take him back like a shot.

But it wasn't him. It was…

Oh!

A big bunch of flowers, so pretty; greenery topped with blues and peach and purple and white, and when they were moved to one side, a man's face smiled at her.

It was Jack from last night.

'What?…' she said, and she couldn't help smiling at his happy, open face,

'I knew they were off to Alton Towers…'

and he thrust the bouquet towards her.

'… so to cheer you up I've brought you flowers!'

'Thank you!'

She took them from him,

'Oh thank you, that's really kind. Come on in.'

And they were soon talking easily as she searched for something a to put the flowers in. Shit, did she even possess a vase? *He'd* very rarely brought her flowers, and if he had, he'd looked so uncomfortable holding them.

She said, realising that last night she'd not commented on the fake ticket,

'I'm sorry for you not being able to go to the match. Sharon often tells me how much Anthony enjoys watching Liverpool play. I bet you're well fed-up.'

She said as she poured water into a Pyrex measuring jug; again that strange premonition feeling; *in years to come she knew she would be pouring water into a jug, but she would be shouting; frightened.*

'Well, yes,' he replied, 'I can't deny that, but it's my own fault. Our Anthony did warn me there were some dodgy touters doing the rounds.'

She removed the clear plastic from the flowers with scissors, fussing, not sure what the was doing, but happily arranging them in the jug.

Jack laughed,

'Isn't it funny in how in films, women immediately start searching for a vase when a man brings her a bouquet. Like the flowers will die in thirty seconds flat if they don't get put in water.'

She laughed, 'I think it's probably partly to cover up their embarrassment,' she said.

'Are *you* embarrassed?'

She turned to him, 'Honestly, and to my own surprise, no, not in the least bit.'

'That's good then,' he smiled.

'I'm just grateful for the…' she laughed, stuck for words, '…for the thoughtful thought'

'Well I guessed you might be on a bit of a downer today, although …'

and she saw his eyes taking in the pretty dress she'd put on for Dan's benefit in case he came to the door; she'd been wearing leggings last night.

'… for all I know I'm holding you up from a luncheon date?'

And she remembered how presumptuous Dan had been over the telephone, when he'd never for one second considered the possibility that she might not be at home if he chose to bring their children back to her early.

'Oh God, no,' she managed a laugh, 'just me and Baby Ben today. I think 'luncheon' will consist of a little picnic in the garden, surrounded by the twins' quilt covers, sheets and pillow-cases drying on the washing line!'

'Well, leave them to their white-knuckle rides, I say. A little picnic in the garden with baby Ben sounds much nicer to me.'

As though responding to the sound of his name, Ben stirred in his chair the corner of the room.

Jack immediately crouched down beside him.

'Ay up matey,'

Jack said, and Ben smiled at him, slowly, sleepily uncurling and yawning, stretching up his arms; *again that feeling…*

'My sister's little girl's about this age,' he said, picking up one of the toys beside Ben's chair to show him.

She replied with pride,

'Ben actually said his first word, well his first *two* words this morning'

'Oh brilliant,' he said, 'What were they?'

And they continued to chat away as she prepared sandwiches, put salt and vinegar crisps into bowls.

'Would you like a drink of tea or coffee?' she asked him.

'That would be lovely,' Jack said.

'Or a beer? A hair of the dog?'

'Even better,' he laughed.

PART TWO

2000

Chapter Five

She ran up the stairs,

'Honestly, Ben, you can be so clumsy at times!'

And as it so often did nowadays, especially since she and Jack had had a little boy called Kenny, another frazzled voice talked to her in the back of her mind.

It's no use crying over spilt milk… It's no use crying over spilt milk …

She sometimes thought she was going mad.

She was pretty sure there was an old sweatshirt of the twins in the charity-bag drawer; frayed at the cuffs, a pen-stain near the school logo, but it would do for today; no-one bothered on a Friday.

Everything in the drawer was tangled, like it had just come out of the washer; but dry, smelling slightly, ever so slightly of detergent; smelling more strongly of young boy and of the outdoors, of some sort of herb, thyme perhaps?

She pulled a length of soft cotton fabric, began to separate it from its nest of cast-offs.

Ouch! A sudden shock of static electricity.

Oh! What was that pushed up the sleeve? Hidden up the navy-blue sleeve?

What trick was hidden up his sleeve?

What trick was hidden up his sleeve?

An empty plastic own brand cola bottle? The top half of an empty plastic pop bottle, greasy, scorched paper masking-taped to form a dirty tight drumskin base. Alien amongst the cuddly pyjamas, the now too-short grey school trousers.

Was it some sort of percussion instrument? What on earth was it? She balanced it on her palm, bewildered. She smelled it and it smelt like her uncle's pipe used to smell.

'Don't sniff at that, Mum.'

She jumped,

'You might get high!' Ben laughed.

She turned, to him,

'Why? What … who's is it?'

He lowered his head, much taller than her already, looked her straight in the eyes.

'It's called a bong. It's one of my mate's big brother's.'

A Bong. Bong. Stupid word. Stupid word.

'He was at the skate-park last night, and his girlfriend turned up, so he asked me to look after it for him.'

Ding Dong Bong.

He held out his hand for it.

'Don't worry I'll drop it him off on my way to school.'

He'd been good, even way back then; the morning after his thirteenth birthday.

'Make sure you do…' she said, handing the homemade bong back to him; *handing the homemade bong back to him on a plate.*

He took the old sweatshirt, as she continued,

'…and, whatever you do…' *whatever you do, whatever you do — surely 'whatever you do' gives you carte-blanche to do whatever else you want to do, except precisely the thing which you specifically specify?*

'…Whatever you do, please don't bring anything like that in here again!'

Was she giving him scope; plenty of scope to do even worse?

'I won't,' he said, holding the bong. Did that hold look practised? Did the way he held the contraption look relaxed? He somehow balanced it beneath his chin whilst tying the spare sweatshirt sleeves tight around his waist. Were such objects familiar to him?

Did it really belong to the big brother of one of his mates?

She decided there and then not to mention what she'd found to Jack, or Fred and Will, who were now nineteen, and had moved into a flat with a couple of mates. She didn't think they'd believe Ben. And then it would all kick off.

But *she* believed Ben…

Didn't she?

***

After a tea that same Friday, Ben said,

'That was lovely, that was,' always polite; always helpful, rinsing his plate, glass and fork, then,

'What're you playing on, lil bro'?' he asked seven-year-old Kenny who was on the sofa, knees raised, head leaning against his dad's arm.

'Mario,' he yawned, staring down at his rapid thumbs.

Ben watched his half-brother's screen, transfixed for a moment, then,

'I'm off to the skate park,' he said, pulling down his beanie hat over the long hair he'd straightened with her imitation GHD's, and as she opened the fridge to reach for a bottle of wine, she shouted,

'We've got to be all packed and ready to go to Praia da Rocha by dinner time tomorrow! So I want you in by half-nine at the very latest!'

'OK,' Ben said and the porch door shut.

Ben was a fantastic skater, the sort that even a couple of grumpy old men might stop and admire. The skateboard seemed to be tied to his feet; an integral part of him. Up on down the slopes, even up and down steps; even along handrails!

Her heart jumping as high as her son jumped, she'd watch him through her fingers; proud and appalled.

> *All smiled*
> *who saw my son*
> *jump thro' the air*
> *Wearing beanie hat*
> *Long hair …*

Ben and his mates loved the new ramps which the Town Council had recently provided upon the old playing field. There were now picnic benches too, where groups of girls sat and giggled, tossing their long hair, listening to their radio and pretending not to watch the skater boys, whilst carers played with children on the brand new swings, slide and see-saw.

Always extra-tired on a Friday night for she now worked full time as an Admin Assistant, and always slightly pissed most nights because she still liked her wine, by the end of the second episode of Coronation Street our nameless narrator was ready to go to bed, and read, or possibly write some poetry, until beckoned by an inadequate sleep.

'I'm off upstairs then; busy day tomorrow!' she said to Jack, who had just carried a sleeping Kenny to bed, and was looking forward to watching one of 'his' drama series on TV with a large gin and tonic.

'Don't forget Ben's got his own key now.'

It had been one of his *Now You're a Teenager* birthday presents.

She drew the curtains.

'The nights are suddenly drawing in, aren't they?…'

Jack didn't reply. The older Jack had mellowed into a kind man of few words.

'…I'd better go put the outside light on for him.'

She opened the back door, stepped down into the porch full of dried-muddy football boots and coats and wellies, reached across to turn on the outside light. Whoops! She slid forward, her right leg outstretched.

Ouch!

Ben's skateboard, spitefully struck the inside of her ankle. She rubbed it, then lifted the board to lean it against the hoover out of harm's way, never ceasing to marvel how he could possibly balance and manoeuvre such a huge, heavy, clumsy thing.

… and yet she'd called him clumsy only that morning… And yet she'd called him clumsy only that morning …

He was far from clumsy. She must bite her tongue a bit more.

Strange that he'd not taken his skateboard with him tonight… he must have taken his rollerblades with, for a change. She had a quick rummage around. No sign of them; that must be it.

… Then one day
he wasn't there

didn't go to the park
Til after dark
and left his skateboard at home
Sad to say
He was to learn a new
more dangerous way to play
and fly thro' the sky
On a chemical high.

***

Final Night in Prai da Rocha

Ben and Kenny had always been happy to attend the Clube Praia da Rocha hotel's Kids' Club, even though because of the six year age gap, they were normally put into separate groups within that same club.

'Can't *I* go to the kids club disco, too?…'

Kenny had called from the boys' bedroom as they were changing out of their beachwear.

'I've never been to a disco. Felicity and Jade are going and Felicity's even twelve days *younger* than me.'

'Ooh, I don't think so,' our nameless narrator had called back to him, 'Perhaps next time we come.'

For of course, back then it was harder to keep in touch; there were few mobile phones.

But Jack had said quietly,

'I don't see why not. We could have a couple of drinks at Pepe's Bar. Just the two of us…'

She was tempted. Much as she loved their holidays with the children, how she had wished she'd never given into them and bought them those blessed fishing nets that morning!

It had been a stressful last day of the holiday.

They'd all paddled in the sea amongst a myriad of tiny silver fish which Ben was determined to catch.

'Oh, please, just let me get one, please!'

The fish which Kenny could feel around his legs, but could not see in the glimmering water,

'But, I can't see any fish, I can't see any fishes!' he wailed.

'Got one!'

Ben was delighted with the silver fish he'd netted,

'When I leave school I think I'll be professional skateboarder and then when I retire, I'll be a fisherman and live here in Praia da Rocha.'

And she had one of those sinking strange feelings that were occurring more and more.

I don't know why but something tells me you're not going to be either of those things.

✳✳✳

'Why can't I even *see* any fish?'

Kenny had continued to wail until Jack managed to catch him one whilst Kenny 'controlled' the net.

After they'd returned the fish to their water, they had walked along the crowded Praia da Rocha streets seeking somewhere for lunch. Whichever way Ben and Kenny had held the ridiculously long sticks, nets-up or nets-down, they'd been in constantly in danger of either tripping somebody over or of poking somebody in the eye.

Her stress levels had been through the roof...

Jack reached for her hand,

'What do you think, duck? It would be nice to totally relax for a couple of hours, wouldn't it?'

'Well, I suppose it is our last night.'

She was persuaded.

And so she said,

'You wouldn't mind taking Kenny to the Disco with you, would you, Ben? Looking after him whilst Jack and I pop to Pepe's Bar?'

Kenny looked at the floor, an anxious smile on his seven-year-old face. The slightest of pauses followed, and he risked a pleading glance at Ben, maybe preparing himself for a 'No', and as yet unsure of how he might react to that.

Ben shrugged,

'Yeah, ok…'

Another pause, then,

'…just so long as he doesn't start crying or anything.'

She felt the back of Kenny's neck tense beneath her hand.

'Like I'm going to start crying!' he protested, ready to charge at his big brother as little brothers do.

But then, with a flick of his long hair, Ben had flung a winning smile at Kenny and instead of running, fists flying, Kenny ran, arms open wide, into his big brother's hug.

God how she'd loved them; how she still loved them so much.

'Thanks Ben,' she said.

'Good lad,' said Jack gruffly, ruffling Ben's hair.

'You've got to let me pick your clothes and everything though,' he said.

Kenny happily agreed, 'OK.'

'First thing, have you had your shower?'

'Yes.'

She noticed, with a smile, that Kenny was talking more quietly than usual, trying his hardest not to be annoying, trying his best not to give his big brother an excuse not to take him.

'And have you had your hair washed?… Mum, have you washed his hair?'

He was touching examining Kenny's long hair; fair and fluffy, so different from his own.

'Yes,' she'd said, from beneath the folds of the nicest dress she'd packed.

'Show us what clothes you've got, then?'

'There's these…'

Kenny shyly opened the bottom drawer of the unit they were sharing,

'…and then there's my Pokemon things in that cupboard.'

'They're a bit baby…' he caught his mum's eye in the bathroom mirror, as she did her makeup '…er they're a bit young for a disco,' Ben said, 'have you brought your footy shirt?'

'Yeah!' Kenny had forgotten about that.

'Right, wear that with these.'

He handed him a pair of what she called long shorts, white ones,

'…And I'll wear the same.'

Kenny was thrilled,

'Then we'll be dressed identical, like Fred and Will in that photo in the living room.'

She continued to watch them through the bathroom mirror, making a special effort with her makeup.

'Right,' said Ben, 'now let's sort your weird hair out.' He began to gel the tips, standing back every now and again to view his handiwork.

At first Kenny had pulled silly faces at himself in the mirror, then astounded at his own rapid transformation, he became shy of his own face; the face in front of him, the face that he knew so well was morphing into that of a much bigger boy. And so he looked away; looked down; played with his fingers.

'Wow, you do look smart,' she and Jack had said, smiling, 'very trendy'

'You can have a spray of my Lynx if you like…'

Ben gave Kenny the can. '… even though it's about all gone.'

'Cool!' said Kenny, screwing up his entire face; spraying himself inexpertly all over.

'I expect Jack's got something you can borrow if you need it, Ben, although I don't know what you *do* with all your body sprays and deodorants,' she said.

Of course, she had a pretty good idea now.

'Eurgh! Kenny, your trainers are all sandy. Give them here.'

Ben had banged the shoes together on the balcony.

Then he pulled a couple of baby wipes from the bathroom.

'You ought to do this every morning, lil bro' he advised, 'I do. It keeps them looking nice and new.'

She had taken a photograph of the two boys, dressed identically, tanned and gorgeous, ready for Kenny's first-ever disco.

She'd still got that picture. She still looked at it from time to time. It lay beneath the stash in her bedside drawer, protected by a polypocket taken from work.

She'd loved how Ben had introduced Kenny to the other youngsters, whilst she and Jack had hovered, suddenly unsure if and when to make their move to Pepe's Bar.

'This is my little bro,' he'd said, arm around him.

'What's his name?' Jade had asked Ben, whilst Kenny and Felicity silently stared at one another, marvelling at how grown-up their kids' club friend suddenly looked.

'Kenny,' Ben had said, 'Kenny after Kenny Dalglish. Aren't you, mate?'

Kenny had stared shyly down at his good-as-new white trainers.

'Ah-hah!' said one of the kids' club assistants, a lad about Fred and Will's age, 'Hence the cool shirts!'

She saw both of them swell with pride. Ben was already at an age when he could hide this with total conviction from all but herself. Tears stung her eyes, when she saw that Kenny was trying to act as cool as his big brother; trying his very best not to look too pleased, pushing his tongue into the inside of his cheek to prevent his smile spreading.

Jack and the Kids Club assistant had a quick word about their beloved football team, and then they'd told him they were only going to Pepe's bar, four doors down, blew the boys a kiss and waved goodbye.

About two hours or so later, they came back slightly drunken, with about ten minutes of the disco left to go.

'…And now the prize for best boy dancer goes to …'

'Ben!'

God how glad she was that they'd come back with little time to spare.

Everyone was cheering and clapping as the music started.

She'd felt so proud…

'When the world, leaves you feeling blue
You can count on me, I will be there for you
When it seems, all you hopes and dreams
Are a million miles away, I will re-assure you

We've got to all stick together
Good friends, there for each other
Never ever forget that …

I've got you and you've got me, so

Reach

and he'd stretched and he'd reached

for the stars

so that even his gel-spiked hair seemed to stretch and to reach,

Climb every mountain higher

and he'd stood on the tiptoes of the trainers he loved to keep so white
and so clean,

Reach for the stars

and he'd punched the air with his fist,

Follow your heart's desire

and he'd sung along;

Reach for the stars

With such a smile upon his face.

And when that rainbow's shining over you
That's when your dreams will all come true

There's a place waiting just for you (just for you)
Is a special place where your dreams all come true
Fly away (fly away) swim the ocean blue (swim the ocean blue)
Drive that open road, leave the past behind you
Don't stop gotta keep moving
Your hopes,…'

She had believed then that, despite his rocky start in life, Ben surely did
have everything to live for. Why, he might even become a professional

skateboarder and, in later life, retire a fisherman in Praia da Rocha. Why ever not?!

Why had she been getting so many negative voices inside her head?

Ben had absolutely everything. Opportunities there for the taking.

Wonderful things within reach.

And then, just as our nameless narrator truly thought she might burst with pride, Ben clapped and stamped his feet to the audience, who immediately joined in, then beckoned to Kenny who, no longer trying to hide his enormous smile, ran to dance beside his big brother.

***

The following morning, the last morning of their holiday, she'd woken up feeling lovely, thanking her lucky stars …

'Reach for the Stars!' still playing in her mind.

… that she'd not booked the early flight even though it had been £30 cheaper. Now they wouldn't need to rush about; they had all morning to pack. She lay there admiring her tanned legs against the white sheets. They'd all had such a lovely time!

Jack was still sleeping beside her; and she could hear none of the normal chatter from the boys' room.

Then she heard Kenny,

'Erreugh! It *stinks* in here!'

Ben had probably farted; typical boyish humour. Then she heard Kenny get out of his bed,

'Erreugh, Mum! There's all sick on my bed!'

She leapt out of her bed, and went into their room where Kenny was pointing at his sheet; multi-coloured with sick-spatters, lumps of chips; stinking doner meat; alcohol, and … something else?

Her own stomach lurched.

'Were you poorly in the night?' she asked Kenny, knowing full-well the answer.

An unfamiliar person crouched on the floor in the corner; an unfamiliar voice, slurred, a crushed silver can lay beside him and one of the blessed fishing nets. The fishing net had trapped lumps of sick; served as a sieve. Mucussy liquid pooled all round it.

'No, I was. Soz, Mum.'

'What do you mean?'

'I wen' out, one of lad helps kids' club.'

Ben could barely speak; smart clothes covered in vomit; shorts clinging to him, wet through.

'So?' asked Kenny, 'Why did you have to be sick on *my* bed?'

'Can't find bog, dark, can I?'

Then Ben burst out laughing,

'Why do you have to be sick on my bed? Why do you have to be sick on my bed?' You're like Goldilocks, 'Whose been sleeping in my bed!'

He put his head down onto his arms laughing hysterically, madly.

'Is Ben actually pissed up?' asked Kenny.

'It looks like it. He's been a very stupid boy,' she said looking at Ben,

'Haven't you?' and her heart jumped and raced because his eyes weren't Ben's eyes. They were someone else's. They were no longer Ben's eyes. They certainly weren't a boy's eyes.

And she knew, she just knew that this would not be the first time she would see him like this …

'Haven't you?' and her voice had become tight and scratchy; like it had been when she'd found the bong; a new voice, a voice that was to be hers from now on.

Jack grabbed him roughly.

'Here, let's get you in the shower!'

Oh My God! What a horrible, stinking mess!

She gathered together the sicked-on bedding, put it outside the bathroom, ready to try and rinse off when they'd finished in the shower.

'He's not just been drinking!' yelled J, 'He's got fags and a lighter in his pocket!'

Jack yelled, slinging his stepson's filthy shorts out of the shower door, followed by a packet of Rizlas, a disposable lighter, half a packet of Portuguese cigarettes, *a square corner from the flap torn off...*

What a horrible end to the holiday!

She went to Ben's drawer, found him a clean set of clothes, put them out ready on the bare mattress, placed the rest of his clothes in his suitcase. She'd better leave his thick, grey hoodie out with his back pack, it was bound to be cold back in England.

His hoodie felt different. Her heart sank. What was that lurking in its front pouch? She knew without looking. Hidden from view, like a baby kangaroo sleeping in his mother's pouch.

Ben was standing beside her, towel around him.

'What did I tell you the other morning?' she hissed.

'You said never to bring anything like that 'in here' again. Well, it's not 'in here' as in 'our house' is it?' *It was so unlike Ben to be 'smart', to answer her back. Something talking for him.* 'We're not at home, we're in Portgual on holiday...'

Something was talking for him; and it frightened her.

Yes, we are on holiday and we were having a lovely, lovely time...

'Anyway,' he continued, 'Did you know you can get served alcohol at sixteen in Portugal? And legally smoke cigarettes? So I don't know what Jack's going off on one for.'

Chapter Six

She knew she needed help; she knew Ben needed help; but she didn't know who to turn to.

She knew nothing about drugs, and she didn't know anyone who did; Jack certainly didn't. He didn't even want to talk about it. He said she should ring Dan; let him sort it out. But she didn't want to. Something was stopping her, although she didn't know what.

All she she did know was she felt ashamed; not so much of Ben, but of herself. Ashamed of herself, and so incredibly guilty.

During her lunchtime, she'd recently been to the group surgery for her yearly blood pressure check,

'It is a little raised again, I'm afraid…'

The nurse had said with a sympathetic sigh, staring at her computer screen.

'…But we'll leave your medication as it is for the time being. If you find yourself getting stressed, do something that you know will calm you; a walk perhaps, or some deep breathing exercises…'

'Yes, I will do,' she lied.

'Also, try your best to cut down on the salt and, just remind me again, how much alcohol do you drink?'

'Not much,' she lied, 'Perhaps a couple at the weekend; only socially, really.'

On her way out, she took a copy of the leaflet which had caught her attention whilst she had been sitting in the waiting room. She whisked it into her bag, as if she were shop-lifting, her face burning in case anybody had seen her.

She read it when she got back home…

SPODA

Support for Parents of Drug Addicts.

"A little support can have wide positive consequences.

One of the pioneers in developing services to address the wide range of issues facing families and carers affected by another person's substance use.

SPODA's services include telephone helpline, support groups, one to one work, education sessions, respite and alternative therapies.

Service offered:

Support for anyone whose life is affected by someone else's substance use.

Specialist support for grandparents/kinship carers who are caring for a child due to parental substance use, for families that have been bereaved due to a loved one's substance use, and for prisoners' families. Specialist support for families affected by someone else's dual diagnosis.

Target group: Families and carers of substance users.

Area served: Derbyshire, excluding Derby City.

How to contact: Phone or write.

Then she poured a glass of wine, and sat on the bottom stair, receiver squashed between her ear and shoulder, the landline telephone upon her lap purring, like a cat; the grey spiralling wire, its tail. She paused, her damp, shaky fingers twisting and turning the cable. What sort of mother finds a bong hidden in a child's school uniform, and then in his holiday hoody? She took a gulp of wine, inhaled deeply and dialled the number on the flyer.

She'd have to be quick. Ben and Kenny were upstairs putting on their Trick or Treating gear. Jack would be back from work soon.

'SPODA. Good evening. Derek speaking. 'Ow may I help you?'

Young. Male. Approachable. Yes, nice. He sounded nice. Bit posh perhaps, although he had distinctly dropped the aitch in 'how', which was a bit odd; perhaps, she thought, he was pretending to be common, although she considered herself fairly common, and she didn't drop her aitches…

'Er…' she began, 'I found a bong thing in my son's, well in our spare-clothes drawer. And when we were on holiday I found another one in his hoodie's pouch thing…'

She sensed Derek was making notes. She thought she could hear the sound of his pen scratching above the melancholy sloshing of her washing machine.

She'd just put in the first load of the weekend, Ben and Kenny's school uniforms. She'd held them briefly to her face, as she had the twins' clothes that afternoon before Dan had dropped his bombshell; before she'd dropped hers. She smelled innocence, fabric conditioner, school dinners and mown grass, a little sweat, tainted with something else; something alien.

Derek hadn't spoken so she carried on.

'…Well, I know it's do with drugs. Like a funny bong thing. He has been a bit sort of dreary, his eyes look funny sometimes, there's a bit of a smell…'

She was rambling.

'…I don't know anything about drugs. I know he had a few cans of beer on holiday, on the last night, he was very sick, and I think he probably smokes normal cigarettes, maybe even everyday. But …'

She was repeating herself.

'…His eyes look funny…'

Derek's pen formed a full stop.

'Right.'

'…And when I think back he has smelt of cigarettes for a while, but the last couple of weeks or so it's been a different sort of smoky smell, and he's seemed a bit different somehow…'

A. Full. Stop.

Shut. Up.

'First things first…'

She breathed out a shuddery breath, swallowed a dry lump, hoped he couldn't hear the slight tearing sound in her throat as it wrenched. She tried to tame her voice, that new scratchy, tight voice that had, just recently adopted her.

More writing…

'…if that's all right…'

A rustling of paper.

'…with you?'

'Yes, that's fine.' she squeaked.

'Right.'

Another. Full. Stop.

We'll start again,' a tiny mirthless chuckle.

She imagined him sighing, putting down his pen, perhaps indicating to a colleague that he could do with a brew, please, a good strong coffee.

Or maybe, he was silently making those rabbit ear gestures people do.

'ow old is your son?'

'Thirteen.'

She sensed a split second's hesitation on his part, then, because she wanted to make it quite clear, she added,

'Only-just-thirteen; a couple of weeks ago.'

'Yes, well…'

My God, he was almost *laughing*.

'…that *is* a little younger than most lads start on The Weed…'

He was almost fucking laughing.

'…Yes, admittedly a tad younger than most, but I really wouldn't stress unduly…'

Derek would be leaning back in his twizel chair, smart shoes crossed at his ankles, perhaps clicking his smart pen top, up and down, up and down.

'…I mean, at the end of the day,' *up and down, up and down,* 'what can you expect?'

She had cleared her throat. Perhaps in readiness to challenge him, to tell him how extremely worried she was; how horribly guilty she felt, because she knew, she absolutely knew she must have done something wrong; but she was cut off before she could begin as Derek raised and slowed down his voice and spoke through a long, weary sort of sigh.

'When all said and done. Weed is One 'ell of a Lot Cheaper than Alcohol... Amongst that age group, it's more Readily Available than Alcohol... and Believe you me...It is One 'ell of a Lot Better for You than Alcohol.'

SPODA's mission statement was:

"A little support can have wide positive consequences: Support for anyone whose life is affected by someone else's substance use."

A spokesperson for SPODA had told her unequivocally that:

'When all said and done. Weed is One 'ell of a Lot Cheaper than Alcohol... Amongst that age group, it's more Readily Available than Alcohol... and Believe you me...It is One 'ell of a Lot Better for You than Alcohol.'

That last, was SPODA's message to a deeply concerned parent.

There had followed a confused, palpable pause.

'Oh right. OK.'

'But, I'll make a note that you called...'

She sensed him writing again, could almost hear his careless scrawling. Another full stop. A rustling of paper. A slurpy sip from the mug of coffee he'd been handed.

'...I 'ope that's 'elped...'

Another. Full. Stop.

And, again, she heard that scratchy, tight, or was it just a little less scratchy and tight now? The voice that had said,

'Thank you.'

(Thank you?!)

In a rush to hang up and, she imagined, to dunk his chocolate biscuit, Derek finished by hurriedly saying,

'Don't 'esitate to ring us again,' which with his dropped aitches sounded like, 'Don't ever ring us again.'

And she didn't.

Our nameless narrator never rung SPODA again, and she would most definitely never recommend their services.

Yet, at the time; at the time, she had felt so *relieved!*

Frumpy; Old-fashioned; Stupid; Old; Behind the Times; Over-protective; Naïve; Foolish; Silly.

But, relieved?

Yes, very relieved.

Ultimately, very relieved.

Now she knew not to worry. She knew that Ben was just behaving like many lads of his age. Just, what did they call it, 'experimenting'? And, just because none of the other mums spoke about their worries, who was to say that every student in his year group was not 'using' ('using': was that the right term?) weed, or maybe worse? You heard stuff about Ecstasy, too.

Of course, she'd been over-reacting. Everyone took… everyone took … what did they call them? That was it! …Everyone took 'recreational' drugs these days!

'We're off then, mum.'

Ben was wearing a horrific mask, black trackie bottoms and a black skin tight top with luminous ribs. Kenny wore a Dracula cloak, and Ben had used one of her old lipsticks to make the blood around his mouth.

'He won't put his Dracula teeth in though, mum,' Ben moaned.

'They hurt my mouth,' Kenny explained.

'Let me have them, then.' And Ben shoved in the canine teeth, 'Do they show through my mask's mouth hole, mum?' he said, a little muffled.

She smiled at him, 'Yes.' And her heart lifted.

Of course, at the end of the day, Ben was just a kid! A kid dressed up for trick or treating in the hope of plenty of sweets.

A kid, but growing up, and sometimes experimenting like everybody else was doing. Just like she and her friends had used to drink and smoke. But instead of the Babychams and Cherry 'B's they'd drank, and the Benson's and Hedges they'd smoked, teens today were smoking Weed, swallowing Ectasy, and, of course, still drinking, strong cheap lager and the new Hooch Alcopops, she presumed.

She felt another lurch of relief, was ready for her second glass of wine.

'Stick together round town, then, lads, and be back at half past eight at the very latest.'

She closed the door on them, then immediately felt worried again, remembering something Will had said a while back. He'd said that there were rumours round the small town, where he worked in a mattress factory, that Ben was taking more than weed, and that he was stealing to feed his habit. But, there again, Will had referred to what the people were saying as 'rumours', and surely 'rumours' were more often false rather than the truth?

She sighed, turned on the regional news.

And, of course, she suddenly thought, feeling a little better, out of her four sons, Will had always clashed with Ben more than the others did; maybe his 'tale-telling' was some form of complicated brotherly rivalry? God, she hoped so…

Somebody on the television was being interviewed about Halloween; apparently it originated from Pagan times. She knew her sister-in law-hadn't liked the idea of Kenny dressing up as Dracula, then going out and 'celebrating' this non-Christian date.

She got on well with Alice, and had talked to her about Ben's problems, as she was the closest she had to a sister. Alice had found religion later in life and had suggested going to church might help him. She attended a church which had helped many people who had previously been addicts. In fact, Alice said, she would ask her friend if she had any advice. Susan had apparently been in a total mess, but with God's help had turned things round overnight! Susan was now a preacher.

'Leave it with me,' Alice had said, but because they both had busy lives she heard nothing further from her for quite some time.

***

Towards the end of November, she returned home from work to find, Shit! yet another of those badly photocopied, standard letters from the school, the relevant parts deleted and/or hurriedly filled in, in red pen. They always read:

For the attention of the parents/carers of BEN ...... Year 9

'We know you realise the importance of a good overall education for all our students, however we regret to inform you that BEN has today been removed from ... (subject)/was late for assembly/did not show up for period .../did not show up for detention. (Delete as appropriate) Please take the time to speak with BEN about this.

She knew Valerie Jones's handwriting off by heart; that stuck-up school secretary. And she knew, she just knew, that Valerie Jones would now know Ben's address off by heart, yes, even his postcode.

She did speak to Ben each and every time she received one of these letters, but they still kept on coming.

The post today had arrived early, before they'd even set off for work. Oh no! another standard letter from the school *and* a bank statement. What a great start to Monday morning!

She angrily tore up the letter from the school without opening the brown envelope. She knew what it was going to say. She was cross because it would refer to Friday, and it served to now dampen what had been a nice weekend, during which she'd truly thought Ben maybe turning the corner, getting fed up with experimenting with recreational drugs; he'd only been to the skate-park once, and then had not stayed long. His eyes had looked normal, and his speech hadn't been slurred. Why, he had played some carols on the piano and had even joined in with decorating the Christmas tree!

She sighed, *There was always something!* ... and opened her bank statement.

She could see straight away that her bank had changed its format; they were always changing things, just like they did at work; always such a waste of money and paper! However, the date was still in the same place; still as difficult to locate. It was the body of the statement itself that looked totally different from usual. What were all those little acronyms, ATM, ATM, ATM, ATM ... What were all those capital letters listed way down the left-hand side of the page? She turned over the sheet ...ATM, ATM, ATM, ATM ... and halfway down the second side?

ATM, ATM, ATM, ATM ...

What did that mean? At the moment? Her eyes had been drawn down the list, now they travelled across to the right-hand side…

'What is it?' Jack asked, his car engine running.

'Oh nothing,' she said, 'just rubbish.'

She shoved everything into her work bag, and got into the car.

She arrived at work and went straight into the Ladies loo.

'Have you had a nice weekend?' a colleague asked, drying her hands.

Shit, she'd have to pretend to need the loo now.

'Yes, lovely thanks…'

She locked the cubicle door behind her.

'…Did you?'

She sat on the toilet, pulled out the bank statement.

ATM Co-op £10

ATM Co-op £10.

Again, and again and again… Most days in November, apart from the line which showed her salary had been paid in.

Fucking Hell Fire.

She needed to ring Ben before he got to school, if of course he was headed for school and if he wasn't, she needed to make sure he was headed for school and not to the Co-op.

With shaking fingers, she opened her purse. Flicked through the cards. Why could she never be bothered to put them neatly, properly in the little transparent slots? Why were they all always in a slippery clump together? Why did she have so many loyalty cards, most of them pretty much useless?

Divided loyalties? Divided loyalties?

Her brain began to work overtime, as it was prone to these days, whenever she felt panicked.

Divided loyalties.

She tried to fan the cards open like a pack of playing-cards.

Pick a card. Pick a card.

She thought she already knew which card Ben had picked.

One fell onto the floor; Fred's business card. Always a bit of a loner, he'd moved to Skye with his dog to repair dry stone walls and do incredible paintings of the Aurora Borealis there; also Dan sometimes joked to get away from Will, who had used to begin most of the twins' arguments.

Oh no! Another card fell into the loo.

The NatWest one, that was the missing one. Unless, please God, please God, that was the card that had fallen upside down to the bottom of the loo. She pulled it out, wet, turned it over. It wasn't her debit card. It was one of Jack's Painting & Decorating business cards.

She was going to have ring him. She had to. No doubt her colleague would be telling her boss she'd just seen her in the loo. She'd have to say she'd had a phone call from her parents, something like that. *Because they were becoming more and more of a worry, too; they were becoming more of a worry…*

She walked down the back stairs to the quiet area at the back of the building. She was getting used to that wall, the twiddly little bit of dried up ivy sticking out of a crevice, which she fiddled with whilst she talked; to the brightly-coloured pebble trapped in between two flagstones, which she always tried to lift up with the toe of her work shoe. She'd started ringing him most lunchtimes. Just to check, just to check he was OK; that he was in school, and so on.

'Hello.'

'I've had another letter from the school,' she hissed. 'You weren't there for at least one lesson on Friday, were you?'

'I didn't feel well mum… I don't feel well now…'

She began to speak, but he continued,

'…I am going though. I am on my way to school now. I'm walking down now with Kenny. Speak to him, if you don't believe me.'

'Good,' she said, conscious of the time passing on; it must be ten to nine by now, 'but I need to talk to you about something else, too.'

'What?'

'You know.'

'What?'

'Where's my fucking debit card?'

'How the fuck would *I* know? I swear down mum, I don't know what you're on about it. I swear down.'

God, he was good …

'Anyway, how would I know your pin number?'

She switched her phone off.

She'd have to ring NatWest, but she hadn't got her card with her account details on had she? Ben had got it.

Or had he? Had he? … Was she jumping to conclusions? Always thinking the worst of him… What was wrong with her?…

She'd have to log on to her on-line banking on her work pc, even though they were no longer supposed to use the Internet. But, then she remembered her password was at home.

Why was everything so fucking complicated?

At twelve o'clock, the papers on her work desk moved, and her heart sank. She just knew it would be Ben.

She read his text,

'Mum where are you?'

What did he mean,

'Mum where are you?'

Where did he *think* she was?

Shit. He must be totally out of it; lost all track of dates and times. She went down those back steps, again, too distressed to lean against the wall, rang his number.

'What do you mean 'where am I?' '

'You're supposed to be here,'Ben replied.

'Where? What do you mean?'

'At school, you and Jack. Mr Best, and everyone else is here.'

Shit, oh shit shit shit.

What was wrong with her?

Of course, she'd stopped opening those letters from the school; had been tearing them up and throwing them away. So blasé, thinking she was so clever, so rebellious; she'd enjoying tearing them up because she thought she already knew what they said.

She'd obviously missed reading the one which had invited her and Jack to a meeting at the school; a meeting they'd arranged especially to talk about Ben.

A meeting for Ben's benefit… A meeting for Ben's benefit…

God, she was so useless.

She'd have to ring for a taxi.

'What time was it meant to start?'

'11.45'

They were going to think she was such a rubbish mum.

I am a rubbish mum. I am a shit shit shit mum.

'I'm coming now. Why didn't you mention it this morning?' she flung at him, rushing back up the steps to the office, making hurried apologies.

It would take fifteen minutes to get to the school by taxi. She was dying to go to the loo, she was sweating and dishevelled and …

Why hadn't she'd said she'd got a migraine? Why hadn't she said she'd never received the letter?

She nipped in the staff toilet, horrified by her appearance in the mirror, then knocked on the Headteacher's door.

Valerie Jones was poised with her pen and notebook.

The air in Mr Best's office was pissed off and stale.

'Hi Mum,' said Ben, with his best smile; then tutted, slowly shook his head, mock-telling her off,

'I don't know, mum, fancy forgetting.'

'I know. I'm sorry Ben. We've been that busy at work recently,' she said, 'It totally slipped my mind. I'm so sorry to have kept you all waiting.'

She looked round at the several fed-up faces. Tummies were rumbling. she sat in one of the two vacant plastic chairs.

'Is Ben's stepdad Jack not coming?' asked Mr Best.

'No. I'm sorry, he can't. He's that busy with work at the moment. Everybody asks for him in the weeks up to Christmas.'

That had all sounded bad. It sounded like they both put their work ahead of Ben.

'Right,' said Mr Best, 'Let's just set the scene here for the benefit of the minutes, shall we?

Minutes? God, this was serious stuff.

She could see Valerie Jones listing Jack under *'apologies were received from'.*

Let's go round and introduce ourselves, if you want to start Miss Blakemoor.

'Hi, I'm Ben's year tutor.'

'Hello, I'm Helen Knifeton, Governor with a special interest in truancy'

'Hi, Phil Gratton, PT department.'

'Valerie James, just admin.'

Mr Best laughed, 'Don't say 'just' Mrs James. Certainly not 'just admin'.'

Shit it was her next.

'I'm Ben's mum.'

'Thank you, and I take it you all know who I am.'

There was some polite laughter, then, 'I also take it you all know who Ben is, as without Ben this meeting wouldn't be taking place.'

There was some awkward noises and rustlings, fidgetings.

'Thank you all for coming. Right well, whilst you were on your way, we've been able to have a little chat to Ben about why he's been missing so much school recently, and getting his side of events and the situation at home, that sort of thing. We understand he's very good on his skateboard and skates, rollerblades? Rollerblades?'

'Oh yes he is, he's always at the new skate park.'

She sensed they'd been waiting for her to say more. But, she wasn't sure what else to say; she was finding it hard to concentrate…

She had to try for Ben's benefit.

She must try for Ben's benefit.

Shit, she'd still got her debit card to cancel. And what if it wasn't Ben who'd got hold of it? Someone else could take out all of her money, her overdraft facility, the lot. Not just £10 here and there…

'Yes. Precisely and although that's extremely admirable especially in this day and age when so many students seem to prefer to be playing these new-fanged video games rather than taking physical exercise, obviously Ben's school work is of vital importance to his later life. As you know he will start studying for his GCSE's in the New Year.'

The meeting continued for another ten minutes or so, during which it was agreed that Ben should give a roller blade and/or skateboarding demonstration at the Christmas Fayre, on the new skate-park where carols and refreshments were planned; weather permitting, of course. They'd all chuckled.

She was pleased. They would get to the bottom of the debit card thing when they got home. In the meantime, things were looking up.

They walked home together.

'I think that's a brilliant idea for you to give demonstrations on your roller blades or skateboard at the Christmas Fayre isn't it? You'll love doing that won't you? I bet grandma and granddad and Fred and Will and everyone will love to come and watch.'

'I know but I've not got my blades any more.'

'What do you mean you've not got them any more?'

'Someone must have nicked them…'

They carried on walking up the steep hill, in silence.

He turned to the side to look at her, '…and my skateboard.'

Chapter Seven

The flood-lit, frosty, skateboard demonstration had been a success, although she could tell that Ben was not at his best; was not so confident on the board he'd borrowed for the occasion. She was put in mind of Dan on the night of Ben's conception when he'd alleged he'd borrowed a mate's guitar to play at that supposed 'posh wedding-do'.

Unfortunately, despite help and support from the caring staff at his school, Ben was eventually excluded; he simply would not stay in school, and he'd stolen a teacher's purse. Of course, exclusion was exactly what he wanted. She tried to talk to him; to spend more time with him. But she had to work.

Dan occasionally had him at weekends but he and Mollie now lived in Sheffield and were concerned that he'd get tempted into even more trouble in a big city.

She took him to the doctors but they spouted the same sort of stuff as Derek from SPODA had. Yes, they had a GP who specialised in Drug Addiction but she only dealt with heroin addicts and that type of thing. And Ben was not a heroin addict, was he? She didn't know. She had her suspicions that he might be. Or at least might be well on the way to becoming a heroin addict.

And so, our nameless narrator was grateful to Jack's sister, Alice, when she finally managed to arrange a mutually convenient date for a meeting for herself and Ben to meet with Susan.

Anything was worth a try…

She'd already caught two buses to get into Chesterfield and now she and Ben were trying to find the train station. She forced a laugh; what a nuisance that he'd inherited her appalling sense of direction! After twenty minutes of wandering round in the heat she pointed up at the rail sign 'At last!' she said, avoiding to mention how the poet in her had immediately noticed that the arrow was pointing upwards as if towards Heaven.

'Oh yeah, right.'

He sounded disappointed, and when she saw his face, she realised he'd been deliberately not helping her with her directions; hoping she'd give up on the idea; frustrated, overheated.

'You know,' Ben refused to meet her eyes, 'I really could do without this, mum.'

He reached for a cigarette, fumbling deep in his pocket for his lighter, '…*Fuck's sake…*' until he found it.

'…I could really do without this.'

There was a split-second pause during which she resisted pointing out that he'd brought all this upon himself, because he hadn't; it was her, it was all her fault, wasn't it?

Then, truly exhausted, she said,

'And so could I, Ben… So could I. Believe. You. Me.'

And, because she was feeling anxious and panicked, her brain began working overtime as it always did, and she pictured herself saying,

'*Come on…*'

And in a sweaty, shared hullucinary state, unaware of the people all around them, she'd dump all their luggage, all their baggage on the floor where they stood.

Then she'd take his hand. And they'd walk through the rotating door onto the platform.

Ben would gracefully jump down onto the train track, then lift his arm as though reaching for the stars; help her down to his level.

Then she'd say,

'Let's just lie ourselves down to rest here upon the train tracks.'

And they would do just that.

Instead she says, '*Come on* … It's worth a try.'

She forces out a little laugh,

'It's not like we've got anything much to lose.'

He coughs his short, little phlegmy smoker's cough, sighs again, a puff of smoke.

She buys their tickets, quietly proud that she manages the machine whilst less confident others, queue impatiently at windows to be served. They push the tickets into the turn stile slots; where greedy metal mouths snatch them from their fingers, spit them out at the other end.

A train stands there ready; hissing, hot and impatient.

'Is this the right train?' they ask a porter who looks at them blankly, 'er, sorry, to Nottingham?' Yes, despite her success with the ticket machine; still a pair of country bumpkins; one a drug addict.

Although she'd expressed concern that Ben would be travelling backwards, which would surely make him feel sick and dizzy, he insists he'll be fine. The journey would take less than ten minutes, after all.

She noticed him glance, but for less than half a second at the girl seated adjacent to them. 'She's pretty' she could see him thinking; tanned, bare legged wearing a mini skirt and chunky heels, dark shiny hair, her pretty face breaking into a slightly shy smile every so often as she sees something that pleases her on the screen with which she scrolls with long beautiful nails; stroking and loving it like a pet on its lead of pink earbuds. Then, she knew he'd be thinking, 'Yes. She's pretty all right, but she's '*nice* pretty'. Way out of my league.'

But why? She needn't be. She needn't be out of your league; not if you sorted yourself out.

And as his heavy, sleepy eyes fall closed, her own eyes fill with tears, especially when she glimpses the pretty girl sneaking a look at Ben.

She woke him five minutes later, and he immediately, instinctively fumbled for his Rizla papers and filters, his rolling tobacco which sits inside some folded colourful card; it had reminded her of one of those fortune teller things they used to make at primary school, before the term 'origami' had been heard of.

'Pick a colour, then pick a number then pick another number.'

Then you'd lift up the corner for the answer which would have been something like, 'You love Stephen Crowder' or 'You love Mr Crane': she had loved Mr Crane, if truth be told, or 'You are going to marry Mr Harvey' or 'You will have four children' or 'You will have a son who is an addict.'

Who'd have thought it? She'd have thought marrying Mr Crane more likely than having an addict son. Daintily he picks three, maybe four, tiny bits from the orange shreds like dried up marmalade, and adds these to the initial pinch of tobacco which sits upon its filter paper.

'It is just normal stuff,' she says, feeling she must comment, but deliberately avoiding the question mark, not wanting to jeopardise anything when they'd come this far.

He licks the edge of the paper carefully with the very tip of his tongue, and says, 'Yes,' without looking at her, his next skinny cigarette lodged behind his ear.

He starts to light it as they disembark.

'Excuse me!' a lady porter shouts. 'No smoking anywhere on the station.'

'Sorry, duck,' he says. She loves that he gives the grumpy cow a grin, that he calls her 'duck', that he apologises.

She loves that, in return, she awards him the tiniest of shrugs and a miniscule smile, as if to say, 'I know it's a bit "jobs-worth", love, but Rules is rules. And I don't make them.'

'Right,' she says, 'which way, now?'

An arrow points straight up again, and again the irony is not lost on her, and her heart beat increases.

Perhaps, just perhaps this visit might be a turning point.

They obediently, doggedly, follow the crowd up the steps, out of the station.

'Susan should be waiting for us. Can't see anyone though.'

Ben was drawing on his cigarette,

'Pick up point?... pick up point? ...' she said, gazing helplessly, nervously all around, 'Look for a sign for 'pick up point.' '

She knew Ben did not care how late Susan was, or even if she didn't come at all. And, if truth be told, she now truly wishes they'd stayed upon the train. It had been going all the way up to Edinburgh. They would have had hours to talk together, to plan their fresh start; undistracted; uninterrupted. They'd have been there by evening. Anonymity in their favour.

'Oh...!' There was Susan, tall and blonde, waving, black sunglasses on top of her big hair;

'...there she is.'

She was driving a massive white vehicle with tinted windows; a hearse in negative.

'I could really do without this, Mum,' Ben had said again, shaking his head; and yet, resigned. He firmly crushed out his cigarette.

The journey only took a few minutes.

'Oh dear, it looks like you might have a visitor already,' she'd said, noticing a small man wearing a skull-cap, hovering beside Susan's back door. Susan said nothing as she parked up, but our nameless narrator's heart sank; perhaps they'd come all this way for nothing. Susan was quite probably about to hear of someone in far more urgent need of her help than Ben.

Then she felt relieved, if that was so, at least the pressure would be off. She and Ben could still have a nice day, get the train back into Nottingham, have a good long chat over a nice lunch, do some shopping…

The heat hit them all as they climbed out of the car.

'Hiya Hon,'

Susan gave the guy in the skull cap a quick hug and a kiss,

'Good to see you. '

She then stretched up on her tiptoes, fumbling for the spare back door key high up in a gap in the wall. She guessed that Susan deliberately allowed Ben to see where she kept her key, wanted him to appreciate that she trusted him and that he should therefore reciprocate that trust.

'This is Alice's sister-in-law and her son, Ben.'

Susan said, then dived into her downstairs loo, calling through the slightly open door,

'Make them a tea or coffee will you Asher… or a cold drink.'

The four of them sat around the coffee table in Susan's living room, where it felt so cool and spacious, airy, minimalist. Ben's living room was minimalist, of course, but for very different reasons. This room had two rugs you'd want to run your fingers through, to pull and to fondle; a polished tinted glass coffee table, a couple of framed photos on the stone hearth, a wood burner in the far corner, a large black plasma TV; all natural colours, a vase of fresh, fleshy lilies. Yes. Of course, Susan's living room was a living room. Ben's was a living *dying* room.

'Right,' Susan said and smiled, sheepishly, 'I think you may have already realised, this is all a bit of a 'set-up'; a well-meaning 'set up'. I invited Asher to come along too. I hope you don't mind, but we thought knowing that you were going to be meeting the two of us might have felt a bit too much, especially for Ben.'

She was right, of course Susan was right, she had had all on getting Ben here as it was.

And so they sat. She remained silent, whilst Asher and Susan asked Ben questions which he willingly answered, looking directly at them, with the whites of his eyes, with his pin-prick pupils, wearing his heart on his sleeve, and, she suddenly noticed, since he'd removed his jacket, with marks on his arms; pastel, lilac smudges like chalk.

And he told them that that he had been involved with drugs since he was thirteen, and she remembered that morning she'd found the bong when she was looking for a spare school sweatshirt; that the reason he had turned to drugs was because he was 'young and stupid'.

Beneath the little Jewish cap, Asher had dark, cropped hair, a soft, unlined, kind face. And his clear, bright as bright eyes never, ever, not once, moved away from Ben. He wore cream-coloured linen trousers, beige loafers, no visible socks, a striped granddad shirt with a dark waist coat on top.

Then there was a brief lull in the conversation as Susan offered biscuits and they sipped their drinks.

She noticed that Ben's eyes were taking note of, flickering around, the beautiful room.

'*Ben.*'

Asher sounded surprisingly sharp.

'*Look at me.*'

And Ben's eyes came to rest upon Asher's.

'Look at me, Ben.'

Ben cleared his throat.

'Keep on looking at me.'

And Ben did look at Asher.

And Asher said,

"Ben' means 'Son' in Hebrew.'

'Son.'

And Ben leaned further forward on the chair, as though there was a magnetic attraction between the two of them. He placed his hands flat upon his thighs, like a much older man, a might do prior to standing.

'Look at me hard. Son.'

And perhaps for a split second Ben had intended to rise, to stand, to run out of the door.

'Son.'

But instead of running, Ben sat, stiff, as though turned to stone. His face and lips even turning a little grey. A statue.

Utter silence fell.

She'd never heard a silence like it.

Until that moment, she'd been unaware of the traffic whooshing past on the road outside the open window; unaware of a washing machine sloshing, melancholy, in the background, unaware of the birds that had been chirruping; and had a child been crying somewhere; had a dog had been barking?

The washer must have finished its cycle; there must have been a gap in the steady stream of traffic; the child had been placated; the dog, too; and the birds, maybe taking a break? Were these coincidences? Surely not.

Silence.

The silence before the storm?

'Look at me, Ben.'

Utter silence.

'Look at me, Son.'

And Ben continued to gaze, unblinking at Asher.

'I used to be worse than you.'

Utter silence and stillness.

'I. Used. To. Be. Worse. Than. You.'

Complete and utter silence, apart from a gulp.

A further silence. Ben's eyes opened wide, and those pin-prick pupils expanded.

'Did you?' Ben was incredulous.

'Definitely. I was in the fucking gutter, mate. People were literally kicking me, spitting on me, Son. And deservedly so, Son. I was in a very bad place, mate, far worse than you are.'

Our nameless narrator and Susan had sat silent throughout, but she now became aware that she had been constantly, nervously fiddling with the little tag at the end of the string attached to her teabag. She'd been rubbing and rolling it between her left thumb and finger, up and down into an ever tightening, tiny tube, as if making her own miniscule cigarette. Some of the yellow lettering had come off onto her trembling, sweaty fingers, like a nicotine stain; or gold leaf.

She was sweating beneath her cotton maxi skirt, the salt water, like tears, coursing down the insides of her legs. She placed her mug, empty apart from the soggy herbal teabag, onto the tinted glass coffee table as quietly as she could, aware of her hand shaking.

She resisted a sudden urge to smash her mug down; to shatter the glass, into shards, into glass daggers, like the beautiful visual disturbances that accompanied her ever-increasing migraines.

She rearranged her feet more comfortably, raised her knees slightly, rested her wrists upon her thighs, and slowly pressed each finger in turn end to end against its opposite to stop her hands shaking. She pushed her fingers together as hard as she could, forming a steeple, then pressed her palms against each other. That's how she'd been taught to pray, she realised; that's how she'd been taught to pray when she was a child at All Saints Junior School.

And then Susan began to speak, and she said,

'You will see signs,' she said. 'You will see signs and when you do, when you do, Ben, you will… break.'

Susan's voice rang out loud as loud,

'You will Break. Believe you me, Ben, You. Will. Break.'

And her voice broke a little as she emphasised the word.

'You will … bbrrreak.'

There was a short silence, then, she spoke more quickly.

'Well, you've tried everything else, haven't you, Ben? You've tried weed, you've tried amphetamine; you've tried smack and crack. You might as well give God a try. What have you got to lose?'

'Nothing,' Ben croaked.

'Exactly. Nothing.'

'I was addicted for years. I was forty when my addictions went. They went over night. And not a sign of a come-down the following morning. Imagine that. Overnight.'

'That sounds wonderful,' Ben breathed.

'It *was* wonderful. It was *the* best thing. The best thing ever.' Susan said, and then,

'So, now let's say a prayer.'

Ben lowered his head low, low down, as he had done on the train when he'd briefly slept. She bowed her head, too; she bowed her head over her steepled, praying hands.

And Susan prayed. Susan prayed that when Ben lay his head to rest that very night he would slumber like a baby, that he would have the best night's sleep he had had for a long, long time.

Susan prayed that Ben would find the strength within himself to open up his mind to God.

And Susan prayed that through God, Ben would find the strength to fight his addictions.

And then Susan began to speak in Tongues, which flickered off her tongue like living flames, like the flames that flickered inside her wood burner during the winter months.

And then Asher began to whisper beneath Susan's Tongues.

Whispering Asher, his very name a whisper.

'… and let us pray for Ben's mum too, for Ben's long-suffering mum.'

Her heart lurched; surprised and enormously touched.

And then Asher's voice rose above Susan's Tongues.

'Help Ben's mum to sleep at night; not lie awake in her own private Hell.'

How did Asher know? How on earth did Asher know she lay awake every single morning at three o'clock; worry and guilt gnawing at her very core. How did he know?

Because she did. Oh God, every single night she lay awake in her own private Hell. She really did.

And Susan continued to pray in Tongues, and Asher's voice rose, and they harmonised perfectly.

And then, the sweat still trickling down her legs, the summer thunder began to rumble, and the rain began to fall.

And Susan's voice rose above the thunder, and Asher's responses grew more impassioned.

And the thunder rumbled; and Ben remained still and silent.

And then she began, she began to weep hot, hot tears. She began to weep as she'd surely known she would. At first she was able to brush the tears away, unseen, unheard, with her fingers, but then they came like the rainstorm, thick and fast. She tried blotting at them with the hem of her long cotton skirt, and a sob escaped her.

Susan was still praying in Tongues, louder now, and Asher's whispers also became louder, echoing her, slightly behind. And she could no longer hold in her sobs and her shoulders shook; as though shaking free their heavy burden.

And the rain splattered, applauding upon the windows behind her. And the thunder clapped too.

And Susan reached over to her, put her arms around her; pulled her close towards her.

Ben slowly raised his head as though he had been gently roused from sleeping, shook his head slightly from side to side.

And Asher asked Ben for his mobile phone number and he gave him his.

'If you need help, or just someone who understands to talk to, or someone to pray for you, I am at the end of the phone. But I will wait for you to contact me, Son. I'll wait for you to contact me.'

And then Ben and Asher shook hands; a long slow two-handed handshake, full of feeling.

And then all of a sudden, everything was 'normal' again.

Asher and Susan were laughing and bickering good-naturedly as to whether the small local train station around the corner served the same line as she and Ben had come on, which would save them having to go back to the main Nottingham train station.

'It doesn't matter about taking us to the station, Susan,' she'd said gathering her belongings together, 'I'll ring for a taxi.'

Ben was putting on his jacket and his rucksack onto his back again.

But Susan wouldn't take no for an answer. Melancholy music played on the CD player and Susan sang softly along. She and Ben said nothing. What was there to say?

Again the journey passed in minutes.

Susan gave them each a big hug,

'Take care. Keep in touch.'

They stood in front of the main entrance to the train station; the grey concrete steaming after the rain storm.

'Wow!' our nameless narrator had said.

And Ben had said nothing. He didn't need too. She knew that he knew exactly what she meant, and he knew that she knew that.

They had just stood there for a few moments, the noise of the traffic and the heat of the day gradually returning them to normality; the sun beating upon her face where tears had so recently fallen.

The air had that earthy smell, as it does after a refreshing rainfall. She'd felt numb.

'What just happened?' she asked, 'What just happened…?'

'I don't know, Mum. '

He began to roll a cigarette, his fingers trembling slightly.

'But whatever happened, it's not cured me of wanting one of these.'

He chuckled, that little throaty laugh, which she'd not, she realised, heard for a long; a very long time.

Wouldn't it be nice if the story of our nameless narrator and her son Ben ended here? Ended here with this message of Hope. But I'm afraid, dear reader, that it doesn't.

She and Ben often talk about their visit to Susan and Asher, and she has encouraged Ben to ring or text Asher. But so far, I'm afraid, he hasn't done.

PART THREE

2005

Chapter Eight

She checked her phone. Where the fuck was Dan? He had said he'd be here for his son. And his case was first on today's list of Courtroom number one's sessions.

Ben's skinny frame behind the glass screen was tiny, hunched, bent forward. A uniformed policewoman stood beside him.

'All rise,' the Clerk to the Court boomed, secreting her mobile phone somewhere between the folds of her billowing black witch's cape.

The Clerk's glossy hair flows over her shoulders contrasting with her white woolly wig. It reminds her of Ben's hair beneath his beanie hat. He wears his hair shorter these days.

And so our nameless narrator rose, a *thorn amongst roses*, her seat flipping up obediently behind her; Dan's which she'd saved for him, remained unoccupied.

The last time she'd sat in one of these sorts of chairs she'd been at the cinema with Ben and Kenny. They used to love going on the bus to the cinemas, as they called them, they'd laughed at her when she'd called them the 'pictures'; laughed even more when their grandma called them 'the flicks'. The 'flicks' was the same era as 'Fin' used to appear at the end of the film.

'Fin' how he used to laugh at that word when it appeared at the end of the Laurel and Hardy videos he used to watch at his Grandma and Grandad's, almost as much as that word, as at the two funny men's antics. Quite why it had tickled him so much, she still wasn't sure. They'd loved the extortionately priced pop and the popcorn during the film; the pizza at PizzaLand afterwards.

'I'm full up mum. I'm totally Fin!' he'd tell her.

He somehow managed to catch her eye, above all the other people seated in the court waiting for their loved ones' cases to be heard; the clerks, the solicitors, the barrister and the judge, incongruous, all looking so young in their gowns and wigs, like children who'd been rummaging in the dressing-up box, wearing mum's frock, shuffling along in mum's clicky-clacky shoes.

They checked their mobile phones for one last time, then switched them off, mirroring the waiting defendants and their family and friends. He awarded her one of those smiles that he'd used to do when he was much younger, the one in most of his school photos, head to one side, not quite shy, but definitely unsure.

Apart from the shudders which intermittently racked his body; he was obviously, what he called 'rattling', he could have been leaning against a wall, waiting for a bus, scrolling and texting with one hand, whilst the other bounced a few coins in his trousers' pocket, perhaps holding a roll-up between a stained thumb and finger.

But his hands were out of sight for some reason; behind his back.

She remembered that game they used to play with a ball as children. Whenever you you dropped the ball, and she did, often, they would call you 'butter fingers', and you had to kneel down, on one knee, then two, then put one hand behind your back, and then two.

He didn't normally stand like that. Why was he standing like that?

Posh people on holiday in Praia da Rocha stood like that, those women in beige trousers and cream blouses, those women with caramel hair neatly bobbed, hard skin removed from their heels, their manicures and pedicures recently topped up; those women who stood, hands behind their backs watching their quiet, well-behaved offspring.

Their leathery, paunched husbands could never quite relax and chose, instead of lolling on the sands or playing ball or even briskly walking, to gaze out to sea for a few minutes, hands behind their backs, sometimes upon their hips, then to silently turn and gaze at their family as though watching over them like the seagulls on the stones watched them; the stones like abandoned naughty giants' boots.

Was Ben bowing down in the face of so much authority? Or had he hurt his back? Was he poorly? Had he tummy ache?

Or perhaps someone had someone just kneed him in the stomach?

Her own stomach lurched at the thought: that beautiful olive-skinned flat belly, the line of dark hair parting its skin; a line of dark hair that she imagined others had licked, had kissed; the white scars like ghosts, that others had perhaps traced, where she knew he'd used her small vegetable peeler to pare away layers from his own core.

The late morning sun, cold and cruel, flashed silver somewhere behind him. Of course, she thought, skin turning cold, pores opening like flowers. How stupid, how naïve she was. He was hunched because he was handcuffed. Handcuff-Hunched. His arms were tied. His hands were tied behind his back, just as hers were. His hands were tied high up on his back.

> *Just eighteen;*
> *Handcuffed-hunched*
> *behind a screen,*
> *My son's investigated*
> *for drugs-related*
> *crimes.*
> *Quietly*
> *I cry.*
> *The fault is*
> *surely mine!*
> *He was such a*
> *joyful boy;*
> *We always had*
> *Such fun...'*

What if he started to cry, wanted to wipe his eyes, his nose?

She could see he was sniffing; always sniffing; a side-effect of coke. She wanted to go to him with one of the useless, shredded tissues which she found in every pocket, every bag she possessed; all rolled into damp pellets of tears and sweat and snot.

She wanted to wipe his eyes, his nose. Like he was a baby again. Like he was a baby with all his life in front of him. His little mouth yet to kiss; yet to taste anything more than milk or water; yet to talk, yet to say 'Moma,' as he had that day in the bath, the day Jack had brought her flowers, all those years ago. The unexpected, beautiful baby who, despite all the odds, had grown inside her and survived his harrowing birth.

What if he wanted to give her a hug? What if she wanted her to give him a hug? And she did. Oh God. She so much wanted to hug him.

But, her hands were tied. Her hands were tied; just as his hands were tied.

And she found herself steepling her fingers, much as she had done when they'd been to Susan's, praying; finger tips pressing as tight together as they possibly could.

Their hands were tied. She wished Ben was still tied to her apron strings; wished she'd insisted he remained tied longer to her apron strings, instead of allowing him to go to the new skate-park.

Her entire mouth and throat were dry; she wanted to sip from the plastic bottle of lukewarm water, but that had been confiscated from her in the entrance when they'd searched her bag.

'There's a vending machine on the next floor.' She'd been informed.

But she'd had no one-pound coins. Her tongue practically scraped her lips; the inside of her mouth, she was so dry.

She noticed Ben lower his head slightly; press his forehead against his left shoulder, as if to rub at an itch, or maybe to pray as they had done on their visit to Susan's that day, or perhaps to blot away the sweat that so often wet his face, especially when he was rattling, making him look shiny, plastic; a waxwork parody of his true self.

Or maybe, *and her heart broke*, maybe he was lowering his head to wipe away his tears. Her own eyes filled with hot tears and her mouth became still dryer. She was frightened lest the tears fall. She'd got to stay strong for him. She bit the inside of her cheek, willing her teeth to leave a painful ulcer; she fought to breathe slowly, normally; to avoid gulping or hiccupping. She pressed her fingernails into the inside of her wrists; willing her neglected nails to draw blood.

His pale grey trackie bottoms were stained with something rust-coloured, he'd tucked them into his black sports socks, revealing grubby trainers, one with a length of knotted string for a lace.

He wore a Raw Star T-shirt, its turquoise suited him. She'd bought it for him last Christmas from TK Maxx. He'd liked it, but a few days later said the colour showed-up the almost-constant sweat beneath his arms. She must have looked a little hurt. 'I'll still wear it though, mum,' he'd said, 'I normally wear something on top anyway, so it doesn't matter,' which was true she had realised, until that day at Susan's, when he'd revealed his bare arms. Prior to that, if ever he was obviously feeling the heat, he'd shrug off his hoodie or sweatshirt, but would always leave the sleeves over his forearms, like ladies' long evening gloves. She'd wondered why he did that.

'Take it off completely, why don't you?' she'd asked him a few times.

'Can't be arsed,' he'd say, and then, 'Anyway, I'm back off out in a minute.'

And off he'd go, shrugging his top back up to the tattoo of a star which a mate had penned for him on the nape of his neck. Since going to Susan's she now knew why he kept his forearms covered, because they were covered with marks like love-bites.

But they were far from love bites. And 'hate' bites nowhere near described how she felt about the heroin to which Ben was addicted.

'Disgusting!'

'Despicable!'

'Obscene!'

were the words the Judge was using to describe how he felt about Ben, and how he'd had been caught thieving off elderly neighbours to feed his drug habit.

She could sense people trying their best to resist looking at her as she sat alone,

Alone!

beginning to sob, at the back of the room, yes, on one of those push up-pull down seats like she was eating popcorn with Ben and Kenny, back at the fucking cinema or something. God, how she wished she was.

Then,

'Take him down'

He turned and screamed.

'Mum. You promised!'

And she had promised him everything would be ok. She had promised.

***

'Take *him*
Down'
I hate the fear
upon his face;
How I wish
that I could
take his place.'

She froze and afterwards wondered each and every day for many years to come whether if she had have stepped towards him, the court would have allowed her to give him a hug, to whisper him some words of small comfort.

And his gaunt face, his eyes anxious, dry and panicked, had caught hers and it was as though there were only the two of them in the room. His mouth remained open like a little bird anxious for succour, and that image would remain imprinted on her retina, in her mind's eye for ever. How she wished she could handcuff herself to him; re-attach their shared umbilical cord.

She left the Courtroom. It's true, she thought, as she sat on one of the toilets; shock can make you numb. The mirror opposite her was glass-free, and she stared at her distorted reflection; a frowning white face, tense and taut.

Then she grabbed some paper towels, and sat on one of the benches in the waiting area outside Courtroom number one's huge door. She sat amongst the youngsters all on their phones, all hunched over, not because of handcuffs but because they were all looking at their ever-open prayer-book phones; bowed, as though seated on church pews.

And she sat there, alone,

A*lone!*

and she cried.

Now that Ben was not there to see her, she didn't care how much she cried; now that Ben was being transported in a black maria to Nottingham prison, where he was to to serve a sentence of five months. She cried all the tears she'd breathed through and bitten back and fought away, ignoring a well-meaning pat on the hand by a passing lady in a pink mac.

Half an hour later, she walked down the main Court steps into the foyer, everything glimmering and unreal, floating on the liquid of her tears. She ignored the man who'd searched her shoulder bag, and had taken her bottle of tap water. 'Just open your makeup bag, too, will you?' he'd requested, and she'd been embarrassed at the state of its contents, so familiar that it had become invisible to her; scraps of tissue and toilet paper; everything coated with cheap bronzing powder. His wife was probably one of the beige brigade.

She ignored him as he shouted after her,

'Are you all right, madam?'

She pointedly shoved at the rotating door much harder than was necessary, so hard that it rotated more than she'd expected and thus she felt a sensation akin to going back from whence she'd started.

'There was a little boy called
Ben-Ben Ben-agen …

…
Poor little Ben-Ben
Ben…
Begin -Agen.'

God, how she wished he could. How she wished they both could.

Begin Again.

She knew there was a Wetherspoon's close to the Chesterfield Magistrates court, and so that is where she headed, through another rotating door, pushed more cautiously this time.

She realised that the sky outside must have been bright as she entered the pub's darkness. The condiments and sticky menus were the brightest things in there. The weekday pre-lunchtime punters looked dull and drab; just like her. The smell of their doorway cigarettes lingered upon her hair and clothes.

Would they let him have a cigarette? Just a normal one? She didn't know. She hoped so.

The comforting stench of beer and spirits was all around her; beer and spirits drunk for relief rather than for pleasure. She should, she thought briefly, have bought herself a pint; that would have quenched her thirst, lubricated her mouth and throat. She tried to sip the large Pinot, partly because it tasted disgustingly acidic on her emptied stomach; emptied when she was violently sick with anxiety first thing this morning; and partly because she knew that if she wasn't careful, she would be tempted to gulp it down.

Who cares? Who cares if I gulp it down? Who cares if I drink myself to death? I deserve to drink myself to death. It would be better for everybody if I was dead.

Time stood still as she drank her second glass of wine. She didn't care what the other people thought of her; that middle-aged woman in creased smart clothes, who made a couple of texts, then turned off her phone and drank alone in one of the dark alcoves. That woman who quickly drank two large glasses of Pinot before twelve noon; who didn't even study her phone or the menu in an attempt to disguise her misery. Despite her tears, dabbed at with a red serviette, her legs remained crossed, as they had been in court; her face chiselled and defiant.

She went to the bar. She waited her turn impatiently, and one of the men awaiting his next pint, said to the barman,

'Serve this lady first.'

She nearly didn't reply, so miserable and defeated she felt, but that wasn't in her nature, so instead she said,

'Thank you.'

'That's all right, love,' the guy said, 'You look like you need it more than me... At a guess, I'd say you've been in that there big building over the way?...'

She nodded.

'...Not a nice place to spend your morning,' he said as he took his pint.

How nice it was to receive some sympathy; but how awful too; the tears fairly welled up again.

She gulped and squeaked,

'Thank you,' then went back to her table.

He'd been so nice. Why couldn't Dan have been nicer to her, then none of this would have happened.

And why the fuck hadn't he come with her, come to support her and Ben?

Anger rose inside her. She turned to her phone.

'Sorry.

Car problems this morning.

Let me know what transpired.'

Bastard.

Had he never head of buses? Those vehicles she travelled on all the time, carrying heavy bags of stuff for *their* son.

Their son who was now imprisoned.

Chapter Nine

Although she'd determinedly looked up bus timetables and had concluded that the journey, if long, was perfectly do-able, Jack had insisted on driving her; on coming with her, and as they got out of the car, and he took her trembly hand, rubbing his thumb against her palm, she was pleased he had.

A tall, old building, Her Majesty's Prison, Nottingham was a surrounded by grubby annexes. They followed the signs for the visitors' centre and she felt her jaw tensing, her face hardening, becoming chiselled, as it had that day in Court, deliberately defiant, preparing for something, perhaps for people pointing and whispering; challenging the two of them, she wasn't sure what, but it was not going to be pleasant, that she was sure of.

But, of course, and the thought lifted her spirits a little, but of course she mustn't forget that she was being allowed to see Ben for the first time in five weeks! They had been writing to one another; proper letters, which she would keep forever. Proper old-fashioned letters, written in his handwriting; she loved the feel of the underside of each page where as always, he'd pressed down so hard with his pen! They'd even had a brief chat over the telephone on his first night inside, and he'd sounded ok. he'd never used a payphone before.

'Mum,' he'd said, 'I can't believe some people didn't have a phone at all, not even a landline. That they had to go and queue outside and put money in to call people.'

'Oh yes,' she'd said, feeling suddenly very old, 'I can remember using telephone boxes. In fact, in your dad's village people knew the number of the telephone on the village green and someone would always answer it if it rang and go and fetch somebody from one of the neighbour's houses to come and talk to whoever it was on the phone!'

Ben had been incredulous!

Considering how large the prison was, its visitors centre, like its car park, was small. Two or three people stood outside smoking, looking lost without their mobile phones. Perhaps visitors were rare. She didn't know. Neither she nor Jack them had ever been to a prison before. All she knew was that Ben had rung her and told her that he was now being allowed visitors. She had gone on-line and requested to see him, then she'd received a standard email back a day later saying that he had accepted the visit, that it would take place on such a day at such a time, and had listed what they should and should not bring.

Inside the visitors' centre it was stuffy and smelled, she thought, of vomit. It was full of mainly young women and lots of little children. She looked around for a sign or some instructions as to what to do; but couldn't see any. Everyone else looked as if they knew exactly what they were doing.

A blonde woman, with a coloured tattoo of roses and thorns growing up her left leg, caught her eye,

'Is this your first time?'

She held a wriggling toddler against her hip; he was clutching a beaker, temporarily housed in a sealed bag marked 'Property of Her Majesty's Prison Service'.

Far from looking defiant, our nameless narrator obviously looked as lost as she felt.

'Yes…' she croaked,

She was grateful the woman had spoken quietly, discreetly.

'…We're not sure what to do,' she and Jack said at the same time; as one, at one.

'No, I know what it's like …' replied the woman, '… It's like everything else…'

she shot a look at the navy-uniformed receptionist '…No one never tells you *nottin'*!'

She went on to explain through somehow comforting cigarette- breath, 'Queue up at the desk, see that clipboard? Write your names by the next free number, then get a visitors' slip from that box, fill it all in, then give it back to her. She'll read out a few numbers, so listen out cos some of them only read them the once, then you're stuffed. Then you'll get to go into the next room, and then the next, and then the actual visiting room. What else?…'

She adjusted the little boy up higher to her waist, '…Oh yeah, get a locker, there should still be some free at this time. They're a pound.

I've always got some pound coins if you've no change. Put your phone and everything in there, except your passports or your utility bills and your money bag so you can get him, and you's, a drink or whatever.'

'Thanks ever so much.'

'I don't recommend the coffee though.'

She was taken back to that day Ben was born in the hospital. Now she was going to visit him locked up in prison. Who'd have believed it?

She smiled at her, sadly, but the woman didn't return her smile, just said,

'Hot chocolate's your best bet.'

Of course, the prison visitors' centre, was for all intents and purposes, a waiting room, just as each and every one of its cells was a waiting room. The visitors waiting for permission to see their loved ones; the prisoners waiting for the go-ahead to see their visitors. But, of course, like Ben, the prisoners were also waiting for something far, far bigger. The prisoners were awaiting their release; their return to freedom.

When she and Jack had sorted everything out, they sat on two of the low stained chairs, amongst children clambering all over the kiddies' bright coloured plastic furniture.

She smiled at the little ones dressed up smart, ready to see their dads; the little lads in new trainers, which flashed behind them like police cars as they toddled, little checked shirts with proper collars, close-cropped hair; the little girls in pretty dresses, and pale pink socks; the young mums with their long hair up, trying to placate their children with books and dummies, delicate tattoos on their wrists and their feet, on the nape of their necks, smiling shyly at one another; at one another's children.

One was heavily pregnant. It must be so hard for them, she thought, the father of the baby, inside. His baby inside his missus. His missus continuing with life on the outside. On the outside looking in. Waiting for her man and for her baby's release. Wanting and waiting and ready to love and to tend to both of them…

She went to the loo. The ladies was unpleasant; its toilet hard to flush, its mirror not of glass, but of a shiny, scratched metal like the mirrors in the Court. She presumed this was to prevent people from smashing the glass; an urge she sometimes had, from brandishing, threatening, stabbing with the mirror's shards, catching the sun, twinkling rainbow migraine colours. It also hid people from their true self; distorted their reflection; made everything seem unreal.

At least, she thought, at least one of these mirrors could not break and cause the person who'd broken it to endure seven years of bad luck. Some of the offenders here would be in for seven years, or even more; maybe for life. It didn't bear thinking about.

She stared again at her reflection as she washed her hands, and again felt a strange premonition-type of feeling.

She was cleaning a steamy mirror and something bad was happening behind her but she didn't know what…

Mirror mirror on the wall who is the fairest of them all? Certainly not her. She felt so old nowadays. The visitors all seemed to be young, mainly female, obviously wives or girlfriends.

Somebody else came in and switched on the light,

'It's always so pissing dark in here,' the teenager said as she went into the cubicle.

As she dried her hands she glanced at posters which told her not to wear revealing clothes during her visit. She wasn't sure then if her skirt might be a bit on the short side; pulled it down. Other posters asked if she or somebody she knew was suffering domestic abuse, or was having problems with alcohol or substance misuse; that was ironic. Another warned her against smuggling drugs or mobile phones into the visiting room.

And so they sat, she clutching their passports, gas and electricity bills, a clear bank-bag of coins, along with their visitors' slip, number 6913. They sat and they waited for their number to come up; like waiting for the lottery results on a Saturday night.

If only, she thought, although she no longer had the energy to play the Lottery; still, *if only…*

When the next ten numbers, were read out, 6913 was included.

'That's us.'

They were taken with the others whose numbers had also been read out, into another room. Here their passports were checked and they were searched.

So like going on holiday; so unlike going on holiday…

She was asked to open her mouth, lift her tongue, take off her shoes, stand legs apart and arms outstretched. The officer searching her noticed a tissue tucked up her sleeve ready for any tears and immediately took that from her.

She remembered that day all those years ago finding that Bong thing hidden up the sleeve of an old school sweatshirt. *What trick had he got up his sleeve?* Felt tears prickle her eyes. She would just have to use her sleeve to wipe them away now that the tissue had been confiscated.

The woman next to her was ordered to take down her hair, and hidden inside her bun was a tiny white mobile phone.

Keep it under your hat, keep it under your hat…

The woman's phone was silently placed in a sealed bag, but she was allowed into the third room with the rest of them. This was more like a corridor with lines across the floor on which you each stood. A beautiful Alsatian sniffer dog came up to each one of them. She longed to bend down, to bury her fingers in his mane, to fuss him.

They were led back outside into the fresh air, to queue with their fellow visitors, to hand over their passports to an officer behind a grille, and then the door was opened for each of them in turn with a huge key attached to a chain in the officer's pocket.

However had things come to this?

She gazed up at the huge arched gates topped with tangles of sparkling, barbed wire scratching at the pale blue sky, her anxious mind beginning to work overtime.

Amongst the fast-moving clouds, the birds flew free; *like tea-leaves, thieves - cockney rhyming slang, or an ever-moving, ever-changing dot to dot puzzle, swooping and diving above the prisoners; flying high; high-flying; high-flyers above the jail birds.*

And then there a plane, unzipping the sky, or a needle; yes, a needle, joining together the gossamer cloud veils, stitching them up; stitching them up; she wondered how many prisoners had been stitched up; perhaps Ben had been.

She wishes she was in that plane going on holiday – or, no, running away; never to return.

Then they went into the main hall up to an officer sitting at a lectern with a large squared plan of the room in front of him.

He smiled at her,

'Hello.'

'We're here to see my son, Ben. Sorry we've not been before.'

'I'll put you up in the corner, love, next to the door which he'll be coming in through. Table number 63.'

He was nice, in fact most of the officers, despite their uniform, the keys, the pager, the chain of their handcuffs trailing from their back pockets, most of the officers had kind, if weary, wary eyes.

They sat beneath the clock.

And then the door at the side of them opened and in came the prisoners. All dressed in reflective tabards over grey joggers and sweatshirts.

She could tell straight away that Ben had been using his charm when she heard him speak to one of the lady officers ushering them in,

She turned to watch him.

'Are you all right, Miss?' he asked the officer with a smile.

'I'm fine, thank you Benjamin.'

She liked how she used his full name, as she ticked him off on her list.

'You've got visitors today, have you, Benjamin?'

'Yes, Miss,' he said, 'My mum and my step-dad… Oh, there they are! I can see them just there!' and he smiled, excited, and caught our nameless narrator's eye, hurried over to them.

'Errr!' said the officer; that noise that teachers make, 'Errr!' Benjamin, no rushing or sudden movements, please!'

He turned round, 'Sorry Miss.'

God, he looked so much happier than when she'd last seen him in the Court room.

'Ahh! It's so good to see you!' he said reaching out for her.

She began to stand, and then, stopped, unsure,

'Are we allowed…?'

'Course we are!' he reassured her, and she looked around and everywhere people were hugging, and holding up smiling children and babies.

Tears filled her eyes and she hugged him; smelt cigarettes.

'Can I have something to eat, only I'm starving?' he asked, 'I'll pay you back when I get out.'

'Don't be silly,' she said.

Jack went to the hatch at the other side of the room to queue for three hot chocolates, a cheese and ham sandwich, a Mars bar, '…oh and a bag of salt and vinegar crisps, please,' he'd added.

'So how are you?' she asked.

And he talked, as he ate. And she listened and felt happier.

'They're reducing my methadone. It's horrible, I'm right rattling when I wake up. But at least I'm doing it.'

Oh brilliant. If they can get him off the drugs, prison is definitely the best place for him. And he seems quite content, even, happy…

'My pad mate knows one of Shelley's brothers.'

Oh good

'I'm reading a book, there's a library thing.'

Oh good

'There's a couple of pool tables. I beat this lad the other night.'

Oh good.

'We've got a little tele in our pad.'

Oh good.

'I would like to be able to buy some decent toiletries though mum and some crisps and stuff, and some 'bacca. Sorry mum.'

Of course.

'I've got a canteen card. You can't bring money or post a cheque. You have to buy something called a postal order, and you have to put Nottingham HMPS. They'll tell you what to do.'

And then the bell rang its three-minute warning.

'Ah that went too quick,' he said.

'I know it did.'

And she stood and they hugged. And she did not want to ever let go of him.

'You're in the best place, kiddo,' Jack said, as he and Ben shook hands.

'I know,' Ben nodded, 'I'll ring you from the payphone in a couple of days mum.

As the Prison Officer allowed each one of them individually back through the tall iron gate, with a turn of the enormous key on his enormous bunch of keys, she saw that it was not just her; most of the women were weeping, letting free the tears that they bravely managed to hold back whilst talking, whilst laughing, even whilst hugging and saying goodbye to their loved one.

'Thank you,' each one of them said to the officer, their voices breaking, the irony not lost on either the visitor or the officer.

Thank you for letting me go free. Thank you for letting me walk away from the one I love. Away from the one I love who cannot walk away.

She knew that they would all, again, be wiping those tears away after their next visit. For it never got any easier. It never got easy; that walking away.

***

She queued at the local post office the next day, calling straight from work.

'Can I have a postal order please?' her face had become that chiselled, defiant one, her voice that stretched and tight one.

The woman behind the counter in the mauve acrylic cardigan, reached into a drawer, pulled out a postal order, date-stamped it. Our nameless narrator saw her clock the county council ID badge which still hung from her neck, and then she asked,

'Who's it for?'

'HMPS Nottingham,' she replied, 'and ten first …'

'Who's it for?'

She interrupted,

'Ben ...'

'I don't need his name,' she snapped, although our nameless narrator just knew she'd have stored his full name in her memory to bandy about later,

'I just need his *prison number.*'

She said deliberately loudly, so that everyone in the queue could here.

And the woman in the mauve acrylic cardigan stared at her, pen poised.

She fished in her pocket, pulled out the post it note, she hadn't yet committed he number to memory.

'A7322DG'

The woman shoved it under the hatch, then said, 'That's twenty pounds plus the processing fee ... that's ...' she worked it out slowly on her calculator.

She hadn't realised there would be an extra charge on top of the postal order's face value, but she wasn't going to let this bitch know that.

'And ten first ...'

The bitch opened the folder with stamps in it, and she could see her thinking 'Ah, so he's going to be in at least ten weeks then'.

'...ten first class stamps,' she ended.

She seemed to take ages tearing the stamps' perforations, then shoved them through.

She fished in her purse as the bitch said, 'The right change would be good.'

Was it her imagination or did the woman hold the twenty pound note up to the light to check its authentic y a little longer than she normally would? Did people always check both sides of a note?

Did people always push coins through like that, rather than neatly putting them into your palm?

She went over to one of the two booths, at the back of the room, got out the long letter which she'd written in her lunch break, and the envelope which she'd already addressed, put the postal order inside it.

Someone had left the polythene wrapping from a greetings card on the shelf next to the tied- down pen.

'Congratulations New Baby!' said its label.

'Can you please put any waste in the bin?' she woman shouted over at her. She wanted to say it wasn't her waste, but her eyes were filling with tears and so she did as she was told.

She sealed the envelope wishing she could kiss him, stuck on the stamp. Went outside to post it.

✳✳✳

A few days later, she was at work when her phone caused the papers on her desk to vibrate, and a text message flashed up,

'Mum its Ben ring this number please.'

Oh no. How had he got hold of a mobile phone? Had he escaped?

She was worried, hesitated. She was at work. Should she ring it? Was it safe to ring it? Would it get him into trouble? Or rather, more trouble than he was already in?

A moment later, and another message,

'Ring it now please'

She locked her screen,

'Sorry, just got to make a quick phone call.'

She walked downstairs to the back yard, fiddled with the branch poking through the wall, rubbed at that pebble and the fag ends trapped between the flag stones.

'Ben it's me. How… Did you get the postal…'

'Mum! he interrupted her, distressed,

'Listen! Have you got a pen?'

'No'

She heard a stranger's voice swear. Who was that?

'I'll get one.'

She raced back up the stairs. Grabbed a pen and what was left of a pad of post it notes from her desk, avoided the concerned, inquisitive, prying eyes of her colleagues.

'Hiya,'

One of the ladies from the office upstairs was just coming out of the loo. They normally had a bit of a chat.

Mouthing, 'Sorry,' she held her phone back up to her ear, raised her hand in greeting,

'Mum?' she heard, 'Hurry up.'

His voice was strained, strange; he sounded short of breath, breathless, but not breathless like he'd been running…

'Fucking hell, go steady mate,' she heard him say.

…Breathless like

'What do you want?' she asked.

Breathless like

'You've got to pay 50 quid into this account mum.'

Breathless like

'What? What?'

Breathless

What? What?

Breathless like he was being *strangled.*

Fingers sweating and shaking, damn stupid, useless pens they had at work nowadays, scratchy and stupid little post -t notes. She held it in her palm. Nowhere flat to rest the pad.

He coughed, cleared his throat, branch name, sort code, then began to read out an account number, hesitated,

'Does that say 6913?' she heard him ask,

'Course it is, what do you think it is? Can't you fucking read?' somebody snapped.

And she wanted to jump down into her mobile phone and to stab the Bastard.

Then the Bastard took over the mobile phone.

'Make sure you do it Mrs Ben's mum cos he owes me and I hate chasing debts.'

Now *she* was breathless, hyper-ventilating, shaking all over. She leaned against the wall, palms down, legs astride, forehead pushed against the rough, cold stone. as though she was being searched.

Would there ever be a time when Ben was not in trouble?

Chapter Ten

Whenever she rings him, she knows from the very first syllable he utters, what state he is in.

Today he immediately knows who she is; he is not slurry-slow, or frantic-fast.

But he *is* croaky-quiet.

'Ay up,' mum."

Straight away she is concerned.

'Ben, you don't sound very well. Have you got a bad throat?'

'No!' he hissed impatient, 'I just don't want *her* to hear me…'

'Who?' she asked, 'What do you mean? Who don't you want to hear you?'

He cleared his throat, swallowed, even trying to do that quietly.

'*Her*. Her Upstairs. I don't know her name.'

He paused, and then, louder,

'Mum, she's driving me mad!'

He sounded tearful. Her heart sank. He'd seemed so content; so settled in the little council flat which Dan; yes, Dan(!), had sorted for him before his release from prison.

'Why? What's she doing?'

She really didn't need this. But there again, nor did he.

'She just never stops banging all day and all night long. *Bang! Bang! Bang!* I can't stand it.'

'Your neighbour?'

'Yeah, her upstairs. I don't know her name, but all day and all night long. *Constant. Great. Big. Bangs!*'

'That sounds weird. So, what's she doing to make that noise all the time?'

'I don't know mum. I bumped into her on the stairs yesterday and I said, "What's with all the banging? It's driving me mad." And she just looked at me gone-out and said, "What banging? I don't know what you're on about."

Anyway, I've rang the council and they said to keep a record, write everything down with dates and times. But then it's just her word against mine, isn't it? So can I borrow that old tape recorder, so I can prove it to them … and to you because even *you* don't sound like you believe me!' he hissed.

'Yes, I'll bring it with me on Saturday; the day after tomorrow.'

'You'll come and see me on Saturday, will you?' he repeated, now using his usual, fairly loud, voice.

It wasn't the first time she'd noticed him echoing what she was saying whilst on the telephone, almost as though there was a third party present whom he wanted to overhear the conversation.

'Yes, but it will just be a flying visit I'm afraid, because I've promised Will and Shelley that I will have Jake in the afternoon.

And so, with a constant nagging ache at the back of her mind, she rewound a couple of old cassettes and checked the microphone was still working, 'Testing, testing. 123.' hating the tight scratchy voice that had become hers.

She caught the bus to his new flat, carrying the tape recorder and cassettes. When she arrived she would planned to nip down with him to his local Co-op and Farmfoods, which were very handy; just round the corner, as was the Pharmacy where he picked up and took his Subutex methadone substitute each morning.; buy him whatever food he fancied. He'd lost a lot of weight in prison. She checked the two folded tenners and her debit card were pushed well out of sight down in the slots in her phone case.

His flat was smack in the middle of the building. The banging neighbour above him and apparently an ex-army guy below. Her mind was starting to work overtime again.

Smack bang, Smack banging. Smack head, Smack head banger.

His living room window, smack bang, in the middle of the other windows.

She pressed number six, *lucky six* and heard the click as he picked up the handset in his hallway. She spoke through wind-swept hair into the grille.

'It's only me… Mum.'

The grille reminded her of the prison; the grille behind which the kind-faced guard had sat, where the smell of the prisoners' lunch cooking had mixed with the cold frosty air and had made her feel nauseous, yet hungry, because neither she nor Jack could face food before a visit. They preferred to get it over with then call at Wetherspoons for a cooked breakfast and a couple of pints on the way home.

She trudged up the concrete steps, as always with that sinking feeling. He stood at his door, lifted the chain, with a rattle, again reminding her of the prison, and she went into his living room.

Despite the cold weather, the window was wide open, part of the slightly too-short, slightly too-narrow curtains billowed, trying to escape their rail in search of fresh air; although, to be fair, it smelled nice and fresh in here; it was just a bit cold. She could hear the material, snapping; like sheets hanging on a clothes line on a blustery day. How she wished she was unpegging washing, smelling the fragrance,

And so she closed the window with a snap, immediately echoed by,

'Mum, what're you doing? What've you shut that for?'

Then his voice dropped back to a hissing whisper, as he re-opened the window.

'It *stinks* in here. Can't you smell it?'

'No. I was just thinking how it nice and fresh it smells in here.'

'Well, I think it stinks… '

Her heart rate increased.

'…Everywhere in this shithole stinks like something dying.'

He was frightening her.

'The smell is so strong, I can even taste it on the tip of my tongue.'

'Well, *I* can't smell anything.'

Exasperation flooded his face; one of the very few times she'd known him lost for words.

She continued,

'If you *can* smell something, is it something dodgy that's still lingering in the air; something that you've been smoking? Do you think it might be that that you can still smell? Or, I don't know…' for she didn't; she didn't know fuck-all about drugs, '…can the smell or taste, or both, of whatever it is you've taken, can the smell or taste get stuck inside your nose or mouth?'

'Mum! Do you think I'm totally stupid? I don't want to end up back Inside, do I? I've hardly touched that shit for months! Although, having said that, at least Jail smelt nicer than place; except for when my pad-mate had a shite;' he considered, unsmiling, 'Actually, no, the smell in here is *worse* than Krys's shites!'

He lit what looked like a normal cigarette.

'Anyway,' he hissed, 'have you brought that thing, mum?'

'Yes,' she said and began to unpack the carrier bag the recorder was sitting in the bottom of. She went into the kitchen, putting tins of food onto the side,

'I got you some nice crusty bread, salt and vinegar crisps, of course! And a couple of tins of beans and sausages, you used to like those…'

you used to like those … when you were a little boy who laughed a lot and loved skateboarding, and loved S- Club Seven and our family holidays in Praia da Rocha.

'… and a newspaper, your magazine, and some other stuff to look at, and some fruit; that will do you good, and of course, the most important thing…'

She placed the tape recorder and two spare cassettes besides the latest copy of 'History' magazine.

'…I've set it all up,' she was carrying it back into the living room, 'so you just need to press *'Play'* when she starts…'

She placed it firmly put it onto the coffee table.

'*Shush mum!*'

Ben pointed up to the ceiling. He used to punch his fist into the air, not point his bitten, nicotine-stained finger; he used to sing along, all smiles, to his favourite song.

'I keep trying to tell you, she's listening.'

His eyes were terrified.

'She's. Always. Listening. She's listening to every single thing we say.'

She tried to keep her tone of voice light.

'Well, at least she's not banging…'

She paused. Listened. Silence.

'I can't hear a thing. Can you?' she asked, quietly.

'She won't bang about whilst *you're* here, will she?'

She shook her head. It wasn't like him to snap at her.

She could tell that he really believed the things he was accusing his neighbour of. Perhaps he *was* telling the truth; she didn't know what to believe. He was utterly convincing.

She left him seated on his squashy corduroy sofa, rolling another fag and she walked into the bathroom; a smell of bleach, into the kitchen, a smell of stale food, into the bedroom, more fresh air. No horrible smells…

She'd have to go shortly, and didn't want to leave him on bad terms, although he would have his proof now, and if she wasn't going to bang whilst ever *she* was still there, she'd have to go in order for the tape recorder to pick up anything.

She'd offered to have Jim whilst Will and S went to Derby shopping to buy outfits and a gift for their friends' wedding. She walked over to the bedroom window; almost tripped over the end of the kitchen broom poking out from beneath his bed.

'Ow!'

She picked it up. She must have shouted out, because he came in the doorway, hissing,

'Mum, are you deliberately making as much noise as you can?!'

'Sorry but I nearly tripped … Why is the broom under your bed?'

'I've started to use it to bang back at her.'

And suddenly he laughed, but it wasn't a proper laugh; it didn't meet his angry eyes.

'Mum, you look just like a witch with your messy wind-swept hair, wearing that black jacket, holding that broom…'

'Thanks very much!' she said, trying to laugh, and to sound far more light hearted than she felt.

She wished she could fly away, carry him with her on the back of the broomstick.

Fly away.

Somewhere over the rainbow …

If happy little bluebirds fly,

then why, oh why, can't I?…

Had she sung that out loud? Had she aggravated him?

She didn't think she had said, or sung anything out loud; she had thought it was her usual panicky anxious mind doing its usual thing.

But he was suddenly more angry than ever.

He snatched the broom from her; his face suddenly transformed, ugly, contorted.

'Yes, you do. You do look like a witch, like her upstairs.'

He banged the ceiling with the broom end.

'She's. A. Fuck….Ing. Witch. Bitch! Witch!'

Each yell punctuated with a thud, so forceful that the bare light bulb swung.

The silence afterwards seemed more silent than ever.

'Stop it!'

She tried to grab the broom off him.

'I've not heard one thing since I've been here.'

'I've told you, she's not going to do anything whilst you're here, will she?'

'I don't know.' Her voice rose. 'Why not?' her voice rose.

'Because she's fucking evil. It's her who makes this place stink!'

But it doesn't stink, and I've not even heard one footstep from upstairs.

'Why what does she do? What does she do to make it stink?'

'She drops lumps of her own shit down inside the walls, in like the cavity bits. Great rotting turds. That's why it stinks.'

He went back into the living room. She followed, whispered,

'Ben I'm really sorry but I'm going to have to go, I'm having Jim this afternoon. I've got to get the next bus. But, like I said, the tape-recorder's all set up. Just press 'Play' when she starts banging.'

They went down the concrete steps together, and he talked rapidly; quietly again.

'She's following me now. I can hear her walking at exactly the same time as me. She spies on me all the time; she knows exactly what I'm thinking and she follows me everywhere I go. And when I'm on my own, she *bangs…*'

'I've filled in one of her spy holes in the bathroom. I stuffed a baby wipe in it, but she can still see through it a little bit. She talks to me, like the other day I'd dropped my fag lighter and it went under the settee and she said,

'You want to be careful, you do.'

***

Of course, our nameless narrrator rang Ben the following morning.

'Has she been any quieter?' she asked.

'Well, I've got a mate staying with me for a few days. She doesn't make any noise when he's here, and the smell's even gone.'

She had never felt so relieved. She'd 'Googled' it and had been prepared to ring 111 if his hallucinations persisted. Hopefully, it was a post-drugs related paranoid episode which had now passed. She hoped so.

She also hoped the 'mate' who he told her was called Paddy, was a nice lad. A 'nice lad'? Who on earth did she think she was to hope her druggie son had a 'nice' mate?

She visited again the following weekend.

The door was wedged open and Ben and another man, presumably

Paddy were talking, or rather, grunting and huffing and puffing.

'Hello. It's only me!'

'Come on, you cunting thing!'

The washing machine had been pulled out of its normal place and had been turned sideways.

'Soz mum,' he said, 'but we've got to get this washer to someone and we can't detach it from its wastepipe.'

Like he had been attached to their shared umbilical cord, safe and sound in her womb. If only was still there.

Ben was rubbing the base of his back where his boxers rose above his trackie bottoms. Paddy was bent down pulling at and turning the pipe.

'This is Paddy, mum.'

'Hello.' Paddy looked up at her, shaking back long floppy hair. Smiled. He looked nice. Friendly.

'Paddy's mate's going to do my washing from now on, so I don't need this anymore. I'll be able to get you all nice Christmas presents this year.'

'I don't think...' Paddy huffed and puffed 'I don't think...' as he pulled, 'I don't think it's going to shift, Ben.'

Then he stood, panting, hands on hips.

'Paddy mate, it's fuckin' got to shift. I promised it to him by two o'clock!'

Why, she wondered, why would anyone fix such an exact deadline on the delivery of a second-hand washing machine?

Briefly rested, and his determination renewed, Ben said, 'Shove over!' and tried his luck again.

She glanced at her mobile phone 14.03.

Ben struggled and swore, then stood rubbing his back, lighting one of his tiny roll-ups.

'Here I'll have another go!' Paddy bent down again.

Ben's mobile phone rang and he picked it up, clocked who was calling and blew smoke, 'Fucking Hell,' out with a mutter, 'it's him!'

She could hear a male voice on other end, speaking quickly; aggressively.

Ben's face paled despite his recent exertions and more sweat began to roll down his cheek like tears. Or were they tears?

Were they tears?

He drew on his cigarette.

'Yeah, No, I swear down, mate!'

There followed more threatening sounds. Then,

'We're just having a bit of trouble detaching the wastepipe…' he explained, 'You haven't got an adjustable spanner have you, mate?'

And she heard the guy respond in an absolute rage. So loud that Ben was forced to held the handset away from his ear, and she heard,

'Are you *totally* taking the piss now?'

Of course, it would be his dealer.

'Are you totally taking the piss?!!'

God, how she hated him. How she hated that stranger at the other end of the phone so much. How dare he threaten her son? How dare he frighten him?

Ben put his mobile phone down. She could still here the man ranting on the other end.

'Here, let *me* have a go!' she said.

'*You'll* never shift it, mum.'

'If *we* can't shift it …'Paddy said.

They both stood, hands on hips, as she grasped one of his two tea towels.

She recognised it as one of a pair she'd bought back from Portugal, years ago. She squatted down.

Bastard. She turned. Bastard. She turned the knob. The Bastard.

She wished she could.

Turn Back Time

The teatowel gave her a good grip; a good grasp.

Bastard. Knob. *If I could turn back time.*

She thought as she turned and pulled.

Anger was making her strong.

Bastard. Knob. *If I could turn back time.*

Anger was fuelling her; making her very strong.

And then …

Off it came, a grubby, white umbilical cord and

'Fucking hell!'

Snake-like, it coiled, turned upon her; spewing cold water.

She gasped, reached for coil, remembering those guitar strings she'd removed the day of Ben's conception; toppled backwards.

She flung the pipe on top of two mugs which lay in the washing up bowl; one had no handle. Paddy held out his hand, helped her up,

'Careful, you don't slip.'

That was nice of him.

She blotted at her jacket with the teatowels.

'Fuckin' hell, mum!'

For a split second, a smile ran across his entire face. Not like the smile and the harsh laughter of last weekend when he'd said she looked like a witch with the broomstick. A genuine smile. And she realised she'd not seen a smile reach his eyes in years. He picked up his mobile phone, spoke into it, grinning.

'Done it mate!'

Mate?? Why call him 'Mate'? Still, what did she know?…

'Bout fuckin' time' she heard him say; more conciliatory now.

'We'll be round with it in two minutes, mate.'

They somehow managed the washing machine as she lifted the pipes and the power cable, holding them up like a wedding train as they walked the washer down the narrow hallway and down the stairs.

'We'll be all right now mum. You go and put the kettle on.

***

Paddy had become a permanent fixture at Ben's place. And for a good few months, our nameless narrator was far less stressed. She knew Ben was still attending the Pharmacy each morning for his methadone substitute and a blocker which would block the effects of heroin should he ever be tempted to take that shit again; and she suspected he and Paddy smoked a bit of Weed, but she found herself thinking back to what the SPODA guy had said. At least Ben was no longer taking that awful stuff, that Spice, or Black Mamba, or whatever they called it now; she believed him when he said he'd done with that.

Things, at last, seemed to be on an even keel. Paddy was a regular church-goer and had even persuaded Ben to go to church with him. Perhaps, she thought on more than one occasion, perhaps God really might provide the answer? The two guys also attended the Poppy Day memorial service outside the Town Hall.

'I'm much happier now Mum' he'd tell her when she rang, 'It's lovely to know there's someone else sleeping in the other room; someone to talk to and watch tele with; and we take it in turns to make tea every night. He made me a right nice meal yesterday.'

And best, yet, Paddy had helped him to fill in a form, and he had been accepted for a Council bridging loan. Over £340! 'I'm going to give you a hundred quid, mum, straight away, I'm going to give you a hundred quid mum, next time I see you, and then I'm going to get you and everyone really nice Christmas presents.'

I'm going to save it, put it away safe. Make a fresh start. And she seems to have stopped her banging. And the smells have gone, except for Paddy's farts!' and he laughed, and she heard Paddy laughing too, and she felt better than she had for a long, long time.

She said she'd visit him in two weeks' time, pick up his washing. She could even do Paddy's if he wanted.

Tuesday morning at work, 10.10am. Two missed calls from an unknown caller. It had to be him. She knew, she knew; she just knew it was him. Heart sinking, heart racing, fingers shaking, she locked her keyboard; unlocked her heart, went down the back stairs, stood in the little back yard, poking at that pebble with her toe.

Before she could say,

'Did you ring?' or 'What's up?' she heard,

'Mum!'

and she knew; she knew and she just knew.

'You'll never guess what's happened!' and she knew; she knew and she just knew.

And she knew; she knew and she just knew it was going to be bad.

'What?'

His voice stretched tight and high; loud.

'Mum' he sobbed. 'He's done a runner. He's fucked off. Nicked my money.'

Very bad…

'Oh B…' she said, her mind already buffering, whirling, her head aching, thinking what to do next, as she stood and listened; her breath condensing in the air, a net, a shroud, an empty useless speech bubble, for what could she say? What could she say?

What could she say over his sobs but,

'Bastard'

Someone walking their dog glanced back at her.

She turned around to face the stonework of the building, fighting an urge to head butt the lintel, to smash her phone against it and run.

'How could he? After all I've done for him. I've fed him. I've shared everything with him.'

Her heart broke for him; for the unfairness of it all.

What could she say? What could she do? except say 'I'm coming…' and run upstairs, ask for the rest of the day off because she had problems; she had problems, again, '…has problems, again' she imagined her boss telling the rest of the office with a sigh, a voice betraying a little impatience, a slight emphasis to the word 'again', and she imagined the others, re-arranging their work loads, rearranging the rotas, pretending to one another that they didn't mind, that they understood, that there for the grace of God, then over a glass or two of wine moaning about her to their partner, who'd agree that it wasn't fair, that the entire office seemed to be at the beck and call of a druggie, a smack head. She'd been going to stay late tonight because … needed to go to her daughters' parent evening; her daughter who was a good girl, who worked hard. She and … had gone to after school club together. She and … had sung songs and listened to stories together.

She rings for a taxi, already planning to tell J that she'd caught a bus. Her entire life was about to continue, after that brief interlude of calm, it was about to continue again with its mass of lies; a mess of stress and sleeplessness; of guilt and heartache.

She is glad that the driver senses she wants to remain quiet. Or, perhaps he has his own problems to mull over. For who knows? The windscreen wipers, his frequent sighs, the drumming of his fingers when they stop, the squeak of his gear stick and the radio playing Keane, 'Somewhere only we know.'

Somewhere only she and Ben knew with their lives of shared stress and sleeplessness, of danger and crime, of guilt and heartache. And she knew as soon as the sad melody unfolded, she knew and she just knew that she was going to cry; not just a few tears but a torrent.

The driver didn't quite move his head to look at her when she let out a sort of squeak, but she felt his body tighten. He spoke to the steering wheel.

'Are you all right, love?'

'Yeah,' she said, and because he sounded embarrassed and because he sounded kind, she tried to smile, to be upbeat on his behalf.

'Just family…'

She wiped hot tears upon her scarf, fished for money and a tip, in her purse.

'Just family stuff.'

They'd pulled up outside the low rise block of flats. Most of the curtains remained clumsily pulled. Union Jack flags and skulls and crossbones covered up some.

The driver took the money. *He took the money. Paddy took Ben's money. Bastard.*

He took the money and then said,

'D'you want me to hang about, love?'

That was nice of him.

'No you're all right. Thanks.' She shut the car door, shut out Keane, although they continued to sing in her head.

Somewhere only we go.

Somewhere only she would go.

The handle to the door of his flat came off in her hand. She heard him fumbling with the chain on the other side. Again, the memory of prison.

A smell of wet towels and roll-ups.

His eyes were pink-rimmed pin pricks.

'Mum,' he put his head upon her chest.

'Oh, mum.'

His living room door rested against the hall wall, its top hinge catching the sun where he'd torn it from the raw plug in his rage, its top hinge catching the sun like, like his handcuffs had that day in court. the front of his top kitchen drawer had been pulled from the rest of the unit In his bitter disappointment; in his sheer frustration and sorrow. Forms and letters lay there, none containing even a tiny hint of hope or good news.

One of the neat little click-top tubs she'd given him sat without its lid on the floor, its lid where it had come to rest when thrown in horrified disappoint; disbelief, against the skirting board. The neat little click-top tub that had been filled with his money. Now it was empty. 'All but 20 quid,' he snuffled, 'at least he was good enough to leave me enough for a decent smoke.' And he sounded grateful for that. And her heart broke for him all over again.

She wanted to find paddy and kill him. Wrap that washing machine waste pipe around his pipe around his neck and strangle him.

And now it was gone. Gone with that bastard. Ben thumped the broken door. Screamed in pain and swore. The guy from below replied from beneath the floor. He screamed back at him. Raised his fist. Then put it up to her own face to study. It was too close to see, she pushed it back. Distorted. Purple and blue. Hi s gnawed knuckles were hidden blurred beneath what looked like a swelling boxing glove. He asked for boxing gloves and a punch bag one Christmas. His big brother

Matthew had shown him what to do. Had she been right to encourage such sport? Was it even 'sport'?

Blurred. The knuckles that would appear even more blurred if she shed the tears that were threatening to fall. The knuckles that she should perhaps have more readily rapped: a rap across the knuckles never did a child any harm, her grandma used to say with a knowing sniff.

And the water on the floor. Water mixed with vomit, she now saw. She grabbed one of the brown bath towels which lived, forever wet and crouching and smelling, on the floor in a little alcove in the hallway.

'Leave it mum,' he was saying, 'I'll do it later when I put that bastard's shit in the bins round the back…

And now his voice had begun to slur, like he couldn't be bothered to open his mouth, and he was swaying a little. Something appeared to be kicking was kicking in. But what could she say?

Except,

'You know I'll give it you back, Ben, if you can keep on track, a bit at a time. I'm sure the police will get it back anyway…'

'They won't though mum. I've rang them. It's my word against his. I've no proof. They said they'll look out for him, but He's vanished.'

There was quiet for a moment and she hoped the woman upstairs would not start banging and dropping her shit down the walls again now that Paddy had gone.

'Mum, I've not even dared to go into my living room yet. So many happy memories, Mum. I really liked him…'

And, remembering that anal discharge in the prison visiting room that time when he was in prison, and having also witnessed the easy affectionate way Ben had with openly gay men, she realised for the first time that there may had been a sexual element to their relationship.

'…And I thought he liked me.'

Paddy's stuff had been piled in a neat pile upon the floor in front of the sofa. Three bulky bin bags topped by a thin faded duvet.

On top of the duvet lay a dark blue book ; a thick paperback book, an elastic band around it.

Face-down

She turned the book over.

The Holy Bible.

A bit of paper

'Sorry mate. Love you loads x'

Ben sobbed, then disappeared into the kitchen. She heard him opening cupboards.

The worst of it wasn't the shock.

The worst of it was that she *wasn't* shocked.

Not in the least little bit.

She wasn't the least little bit shocked when he held the syringe between his lips, the lips which had sucked the bottle she'd proffered, the lips which had kissed her cheek, the lips which she'd refused to give her breast. That guilt again. Should she have heeded petite and curvy nurses' advice all those years ago?

His left arm reached out for help; for help which she couldn't give him; beseeching, but his hand not open; his good fist was clenched tight, ready to punch if restrained. His right arm pulled at the loose end of a trainer lace to tighten the tourniquet around his arm.

He slapped the inside of his left elbow quickly and sharply.

'Come on! Come on!' he urged his vein to rise.

Chapter Eleven

Jake was playing at being shy, hiding behind his mum as she sat at the kitchen table.

'Don't be so silly; give Nana her invite,' Shelley said twisting to face him,

'What on earth's the matter with you?'

But Jake shook his head, refused to hand over the blue envelope.

'You want Nana to come to your party, don't you?'

'Yes'

'Well then?...'

'Oh, for goodness sake,' snapped Will, passing our nameless narrator the envelope,

'Here you are, mum. All written in Jake's own fair hand.'

'Oh, thank you Jake,' she said smiling at him, before 'What beautiful writing.'

Jake bobbed back behind his mum,

'You are a clever boy,'

She began to open the envelope.

'Yes,' said Shelley, 'I just made a list of everybody's names and he wrote every single invite all by himself.'

'Wow, very well done!' she said, unfolding the Spiderman notepaper and beginning to read,

'Come to my birthday party at The Jungle...'

'...*The Jungle!?*' she laughed, '...that's a long way to go for a birthday party!'

Jake peeped from round his mum, caught his dad's eye and giggled with him.

'Oh, I see, "the Jungle Play Area, in Chesterfield." That sounds fun!... "On, oh this Saturday! at 2 o'clock to 4 o'clock. Love from Jake to

Nana and Grandad and Unkel Ben'"'

'Ben!?' Will looked furious, 'Why have you let him put that wanker on?'

'I've not let him do anything, I just wrote the list,' Shelley said, 'and I can assure you Ben wasn't on it!

'Why didn't you check them all?'

'Well he'd licked all the envelopes by then.'

No wonder Jake had been nervous about giving her the invitation! She'd best try to diffuse the situation. She was getting used to trying to diffuse such situations…

'I would absolutely love to come, thank you very much, Jake! But I'm afraid I'm not sure if Ben will be able to come; he might be busy.'

'Busy? Huh, busy! … I know Kenny's always busy and Fred's in Skye, but, but…'

Will scoffed,

'Ben!' he spat, 'He doesn't know the *meaning* of the word 'busy'.'

And Shelley gave a little laugh, 'But you do have to admire Jake's determination, duck. He did keep saying he wanted Uncle Ben to come…'

And then Jake came from behind Shelley, stood up straight and said,

'I *do* want Uncle Ben to come… Please. I've not seen him for *ages.'*

'Yeah!' said Will, 'Well we all know why *that* is!'

'It is *Jake's* birthday, duck,' said S.

'OK. But there's no way I'm paying for him; he'll have to pay to get in as an extra' Will said. 'We've only ordered food for twenty guests. And, remember, I'm really not happy about it. If he puts a foot wrong, he's out!'

'Don't worry,' she found herself saying, 'I'll keep an eye on Ben;' well aware of the irony of minding a grown man at a child's birthday party…

***

The children had just finished their birthday dinner; jungle juice to drink, then chicken nuggets or vegetable nuggets for the veggi and vegan children, with chips covered in red sauce from squeezy bottles, followed by cup- cakes, all iced with animal faces.

And so here they were. Well, all except Jack who had a bit of a cold, although she suspected he wouldn't mind missing it too much because Liverpool were playing Manchester City on the television at 3 pm.

'The Jungle' was one of those places that children like, and, that most parents, although previously complaining about how 'ghastly' such places were, will eventually have to admit to liking. The extra money is usually well worth paying to relieve the stress; reduce the pressure of hosting children's parties, especially once Pass the Parcel and Musical Statutes and supermarket birthday cake don't quite cut it any more.

It seemed Jake was sharing his party with two other birthday animals, twin girls, also five. On arrival all three had had their faces painted as lions. Then Amy and May were dressed as lionesses in furry costumes, complete with tails, big paddy paws and everything. Jake was thrilled to have an actual lion costume. Why, he had a longer, bushier tail than the girls, and he even had an actual mane! So there were about thirty five children all told. All had had their faces painted as different jungle animals; although not as lions, but monkeys, parrots, tigers, and so on.

'I'm the only actual lion, aren't I, Nana?'shouted Jake over the music.

It was noisy, bright and brash; typically described as 'Cheap and Cheerful', but it certainly wasn't particularly cheap and that afternoon it wasn't especially cheerful either. Many of the grown-up guests looked bored and miserable, as did most of the helpers, and a couple of children were crying all over their animal makeup; they were from the Amy and May's party, thankfully not from Jake's. Little white paper serviettes, adorned with smears of tears, face paint, grease and 'red' sauce, fluttered in the breeze from electric fans amongst people's feet.

'Yes, I think you are the only lion!'

But she didn't think he'd heard her.

Gosh, the music was loud; very very loud.

'In the jungle, the mighty jungle, the lion sleeps tonight!...''

blared on raucous repeat. That sleeping lion must be stone deaf, she thought.

There were mums and dads sitting round the plastic tables on plastic chairs, drinking plastic-tasting beer from tiny plastic beakers. But there were ropes and ladders and ball pools and steps and slides. Most grownups were hunched over their phones, stroking them like pets. In fact, unless taking posed pictures of their happy child and friends to post on Facebook later, or unless approached directly, 'Mum, watch me on the slide', 'Mum can I have another drink?', 'Mum when is it time to go back home?' they barely glanced at their over-dressed, sweaty kids.

And long forgotten faded birds and monkeys gazed from their endangered rain forest wallpaper, as yet another jungle birthday party unfolded before them.

'Ping!' A text from Ben 'I'm here at reception.' At least he'd managed to get on the right bus on his own, and wasn't too late.

'Aren't I Nana?' yelled Jake again, 'aren't I the only actual lion here?'

She stood to go and meet Ben, picking up her bag as though nipping to the loo.

'Yes,' she said, 'Well, apart from those two over there,' she shouted and pointed to Amy and May.

'Nana, they're just lion- *nesses*,' he scoffed.

'Oh, Jake!' she said with a short laugh, but decided to say nothing more. She was determined not to interfere with the upbringing of any grandchildren, she was determined to leave the parenting side of things, in the more-than capable hands of their parents.

She headed for the reception checking the eight pound coins were still in her bag's outside pocket. Why was her mind; why was her heart racing so?

He looked a bit of a mess, and smelled of cigarettes and a little sweaty. He wore a dark hoody to cover his arms, and to cover his face if need be, a shirt with its collar raised to conceal another amateur tattoo, but nice cargo-style trousers, clean trainers.

'I'll pay for Jake's Uncle,' she said to the girl who stood texting at the till, and placed the coins on the counter. 'OK,' she barely looked up as she stamped Ben's hand, and said, 'Have a great Jungle party.'

They walked back in. 'It's not my cup of tea,' she said to him, 'but Jake and all his friends are enjoying it!'

She got them both a beaker of beer from another texting girl.

They sat for a few moments with Will, who greeted Ben with a curt, unsmiling nod, followed by a slow, sad shake of his head.

Jake was now with his friends on the rope bridge. All wore their blue sashes over their bodies to distinguish them from Amy and May's party animals who wore pink. They watched each child walk oh so carefully along the wibbly-wobbly rope bridge, arms outstretched to balance. She loved how each of them high-fived the staff-member Tiger who waited at the end. Youngsters these days were so tactile, none of the awkwardness of most of her generation. She tried to take a picture with her phone; knew she would fail to capture the moment.

Jake suddenly noticed Ben, and came running, ducking down to avoid the slimy snakes which hung from the entrance of the tunnel into the soft area.

'He was all smiles. Uncle Ben!' He'd not seen him since before he'd been in prison.

'Ay up Jake.' Ben bent down to give his little nephew a hug, 'Happy Birthday, mate!'

Damn, she'd forgotten to bring the card and little present she'd wrapped up for Ben to give him. But she knew immediately that a birthday present was the last thing on either of their minds. Jake wrapped his little arms around his uncle's legs and squeezed his eyes tight shut with pleasure. Seeing his Unkel Ben was by far Jake's favorite present. She saw the sparkle of tears in Ben's eyes, felt them instantly mirrored in her own.

'Where you going?' Jake's best friend had come running over to him. 'It's the best bit. It's free time now.'

'This is my Uncle Ben.' Jake told Riley, then lowered his voice, 'He's been in real, actual jail.'

'Oh,' said Riley.

'Come on, then, you two,' said Ben, 'I'll be the nasty hunter man and you two can be the big brave lion and big brave tiger!'

'Can you play with all of us?' asked Jake.

Are you sure grown-ups are allowed in the play area?' she asked, gazing around.

'Grown up?' Will scoffed, and briefly she hated him, and hated even

more that Ben had had to muster up the strength to pretend not to hear him.

'Yeah mum, look, they turn a blind eye...' just like he'd just turned a deaf ear, '...they turn a blind eye during the half-hour free time,' and he pointed at a couple of adults helping children on the equipment, 'So long as they're over eighteen and,' he laughed, 'skinny enough to fit through the tunnel.' He whipped off his hoody to reveal a T shirt covering his slim torso, arms clear of marks.

She was so proud of him. For twenty minutes he was run ragged, playing a huge game of Tig with Jake and all of his friends. Ducking and diving; chasing and laughing. The smile never left his face, although she knew his eyes would still hold that anxious look, the look that she knew was permanently reflected in her own eyes; the anxious look they'd both hold until the day they died.

He pretended to be terrified at the top of the Giraffe slide, and then Jake pushed him really hard, and he whizzed down the giraffe slide, lying down, to all the children's delight!

Jake and his friends were in their element, although, she thought, they must be getting very warm; very thirsty.

She stood at the front of the netting, holding cups of orange jungle juice which, and several children ran up to her and drank. Some including Jake still clung to the monkey bars, where Ben was reaching up to help the smaller children as they made their way across.

Oh no. Her heart sank a little when Jake stood in the ball-pit and began to bounce one of the light-blue and green little balls up and down, catching it neatly each time upon his flat palm. He looked suddenly bored; sensing the best bit of his birthday party was now over. Uncle Ben smiled at him, his head to one side, 'Very good catching,' he puffed, then looked away for a second, coughing, still catching his breath.

Just before Jake had managed to grasp the ball seven times, he missed catching it, and as he scooped the ball up, his eyes became suddenly wary, avoiding his Uncle Ben's. What might he be able to get away with?

Jake was by no means, a 'naughty' child but she could see his mind working; could he get away with more than he could with mummy and daddy? After all, he knew they'd nipped out to do something to do with cutting the jungle birthday cake and checking the jungle party bags in the next room. And so he presumed that Nana and the helpers had been left in charge for five minutes or so. He didn't think Uncle Ben would be left in charge, although he wasn't quite sure why.

He suddenly realised that all of his friends were watching him. And so he began to throw the ball much higher, play acting, shouting and whooping and laughing as he dived to catch it; missing every time. Ben had turned his attention back to him again, and was standing, head to the side, a slight smile on his face, saying nothing; after all, his nephew was keeping the ball within the pool, wasn't he? He wasn't throwing the ball at anybody.

She noticed Jake waiver, look up at Ben, catch his eye for a split second, then decide to fling a ball at his chest. Ben caught it neatly, one handed, 'Good catch!' shouted Riley.

But Ben's expression changed to serious, 'No … you mustn't do that,' Ben was looking round, hoping to discreetly catch the attention of one of the helpers who were dealing with a wailing child from the twins' party. Jake glanced at his friends, wondering whether he dare to throw another, and then judging by one or two of their faces, decided that he would.

This time, lower and much harder, the ball bounced upon the flap of one of Ben's many cargo-trouser pockets; he attempted to catch it but missed and it caught beneath the flap, and he scooped it awkwardly up from underneath his pocket and off his thigh back into the ball pit.

Jake glanced across at them. She shook her head, and made her cross face.

'Jake, stop that! It's naughty!' she mouthed, her heart beginning to race again, especially when she saw that Will and Shelley had just come back into the room. She had so wanted Ben to make a good impression today, so that Will would let him see Jake on a regular basis.

'Hmmph!' puffed Jake through his big mane and mask. Perhaps Uncle Ben wasn't going to be such good fun after all. He sat down in the ball pool; head in hands, cross-legged, but she could tell it was a token protest, and he soon began to thoughtfully sift through the green and blue balls as the helpers slowly returned from their break.

'You all right, birthday Lion?' the Parrot helper asked, pushing her phone into the back pocket of her jeans, and Jake nodded.

Ben stood for a moment gazing up at the nets above him, at the other animal children running around, his hands upon his hips, probably ready for a cigarette; if not something stronger.

'Jake. Come and get a drink!' she shouted but he ignored her, because as young children so often do, he'd all of a sudden got his second wind and was now entertaining the ball pit helper Parrot woman, as well as his friends, and Uncle.

He was playing at drowning in the balls, waving,

'I'm drown-ding!' Jake was saying, throwing balls up and around it so that they almost looked looked like waves in the sea. Arms and legs flailing. How she laughed. Other people laughed, too.

'I'm Drown-ding!'

And just as Ben had done throughout his life, he was ducking and diving, as though in the shallow-end of the swimming pool; just like he'd ducked and dived and struggled against temptation and trouble all of his life.

Jake fell backwards into the moving pit. It was weird how the balls looked fluid, all in differing shades of blue and green to resemble a jungle drinking pool; they flowed like water, swallowing him up, burying him. Water. And she felt one of those strange premenition-type feelings; pictured herself struggling; drowning in very deep water, and for a moment she could not get her breath.

She must get another drink. It was very warm in here. She began to fumble in her purse for change; she'd get Ben one, too. And Jake had still not been for his jungle juice. She headed for the little bar area.

And still the music played, and still the children ran and shouted, and still the parents sat hunched over their phones, many with carrier bags of shopping at their feet, stuff they'd bought from the B&M Bargains next door, their free hands helping themselves and their kids with their nuggets and chips and red sauce. And still, babies watched the older children play, goggled eyed and dummy mouthed, and toddlers played Lego on their ipads.

And then a whistle sounded.

And still the music played, and still the children ran and shouted and still the parents stroked their phones, their free hands helping themselves and their kids with their nuggets and chips and red sauces. And still, babies and toddlers watched goggled eyed and dummy mouthed, and toddlers played Lego on ipads.

She turned back to see where the whistle had come from. The Parrot woman helper.

'In the Jungle …'

A nasty skid and then the music stopped.

A child was crying 'Where's the music gone?'

'Ssh,' his mum was saying.

Then everyone was quiet apart from something making old man noises.

The woman who'd stamped their hands was hurrying holding a green box; a green box with a white cross; a first aid box. She bent double to make her way through the scary snake tunnel.

Surely they realised J was just messing about? Pretending to drown in the coloured balls?

But the strange grinding, growling noises were coming from Jake.

'Daddy,' a child asked, 'did that boy turn into a real lion?'

Of course, that's was he was doing, pretending he was a real animal; well I never, the little monkey, or, rather, the big lion!

His body was almost covered by the balls but his arms were raised as though he'd been punching the air along to the music. Or was he doing a high five? Reaching for the stars? Just like B n had done when he'd danced so happily all those years ago.

But no, Jake's arms were stiff: motionless.

Something was wrong: something was terribly wrong.

She ran to the netting, legs weak; couldn't see Jake's face because of his mane and all that dark brown and yellow grease paint.

The netting stopped her in her tracks. She would never fit through the narrow, tunnel, although the little first aider was on her way.

She could hear somebody speaking into their mobile phone, requesting an ambulance, their voice shaky.

Ben was lifting Jake from the ball pit, placing him on the floor then carefully, purposefully turning him over onto his side, raising his leg so that he wouldn't roll back again, gently tilting his head back a little way to keep his airway clear.

And then Will was there, beside her, at the netting.

Screaming,

'Bring him to me!'

'I've put him on his side,' Ben said, 'In the recovery position.'

And then everybody was talking at the same time.

'That mane thing's in the way.'

'He's fitting. Best leave him be. Leave him be.'

'Sounds like asthma to me. Does he want to borrow my inhaler?'

'He's too bloody hot in all that stuff. That's what it'll be. Rip it all off him.'

Will was too big to get through the little kiddies' tunnel way. And he was slamming himself up against the netting like a fly trying to escape a spider's web; star jumping. Screaming and screaming at Ben. Trying to tear at the nylon netting with his fingers, then with his teeth. 'Bring him here!' he was yelling!'

'Bring him fucking here! Pass him over.'

'No. I don't want to move him,' said Ben, 'He's safe, he's breathing; he's in the recovery position. I passed a first aid course in the nick.'

'Well that says fucking everything, doesn't it?!' yelled Will.

'He's done the right thing,' said the tiny first aider, and patted Ben's shoulder.

Then her heart stopped, and she thought back to what had happened earlier…

Everyone was talking again.

'What colour is he?'

'Is he blue?'

Her heart stopped and she felt cold; and she remembered that ball getting caught on Ben's trouser pocket.

'Can't tell with all that face paint on. Did he have a colour on his lips too?'

'Stop him biting his tongue.'

'Take that fucking makeup off. Why haven't you got a defib at the ready?'

'I thought everywhere had to have a defib these days.'

Her heart stopped and she went cold and she felt sick, and she remembered Ben scooping the ball from beneath the flap of his pocket.

'Our village has got one in the old telephone box.'

'I used to be a first aider, and I think…

Why did everyone have to talk at the same time?

'That's a good idea. Ours just has old library books in it.'

Her heart stopped and she went cold and she felt sick, and she wanted to die for all their sakes. She truly did.

'Paramedics are on their way. Ambulance station is only a couple of miles out of town.'

All I know is, Just don't give him owt to eat or drink. Whatever you do, don't give him owt to eat or drink.'

A huge wave if sheer terror flashed through her.

What had happened when Ben missed catching that ball, and it had somehow got caught beneath the flap of his pocket as he'd scooped it away? What if a drug had been in Ben's pocket and it had fallen out and poisoned little Jake?

It might have been secreted there years ago; Ben would have forgotten; he didn't have his clothes washed particularly regularly. What if a drug had fallen out, and then, as Jake was laughing and shouting, flinging the balls all around, and, she gulped, having the time of his short life; what if it had got into his mouth? What if he'd swallowed something poisonous? What if he'd swallowed a drug? A drug. Oh my God. She should tell somebody.

But then the Parrot helper said,

'He's coming round.'

They could all hear incoherent murmurs and moans, confused; but not distressed.

'Oh thank God, thank God,' they all said for a couple of minutes, and then Will turned on Ben,

'It's *you* who's caused this to happen!'

'What the fuck do you mean?'

'Summat came out of your pocket when you was playing catch with him. I reckon I saw it flirt out of that pocket,' he pointed to the one above his knee.

'What you on about?'

'What do you think I'm fucking on about? Drugs of course. And he's picked it up and swallowed it. And,' he turned to Shelley, who was crying pitifully, the shock now kicking in. 'You see… This is why I didn't want him to come.'

'If owt's happened to him, I'll kill you. In fact,' he lunged again at the netting, 'I'm going to kill you anyway!'

'There must be another way in for emergencies.'

He turned, furious with frustration to the helpers who had gathered up the children and advised parents and carers to leave.

'Try these, mate,' the guy who'd been sitting next to them walked up tearing the cardboard back from a new pair of B&M Bargains kitchen scissors, 'Need bloody scissors to get into the packet! Don't know if they'll be strong enough to get through the netting, mind.'

'I'll try anything,' said Will, immediately trying but failing to cut the wire,

'Fucking hell! Just bring our little lad here to us.'

And then the ambulance crew arrived, with wire cutters, quickly cutting through the netting and then carefully through Jake's lion mane and costume They placed Jake onto a child-sized stretcher which immediately made her think of pall bearers bearing a child-sized coffin.

As they lifted him, they all heard his normal voice, surprised but not slurry or groggy,

'Mummy? Daddy?'

Her heart fairly leapt with relief.

'You're going to be fine, matey,' the tattooed paramedic said, and then turned to them.

'He's going to be absolutely fine.'

And her heart fairly leapt with relief again.

'Looks like he's had what we call a febrile convulsion. He'd got overheated; dehydrated. '

He turned to Ben who was rubbing his eyes, 'You did well there, mate.'

Thank God … thank God…

'Just taking you to hospital to check you over, matey,' he said to Jake. And Shelley followed her little boy, holding his hand as he lay on the stretcher.

'Can Uncle Ben come with me?'

'Not now; perhaps later,' said Shelley, smoothing his hair against his hot forehead.

Ben walked through the netting and into our nameless narrator's arms.

'Thanks Ben, you were brilliant,' she hugged him.

'Ouch!' Ben shouted out, felt round to the base of his back, brought his hand back, fingers covered in blood.

'…And don't you go touching anyone with that blood, you dirty druggie!' sobbed Will.

'Let me have a look at that wound, mate,' said a third paramedic who'd seen Will stab at Ben with the kitchen scissors.

'Do you want to press charges?'

'God, no, I don't want to involve the police,' Ben said, a tiny laugh in his voice, and the paramedic, Bless him, Bless people like him, he caught Ben's eye and smiled, 'Understood, mate.'

'It's shallow, but you will need a couple of stitches, though. Let's sit over there, now it's quiet and I can sort you out.'

'They were brand new scissors,' she said 'so it is a clean wound.'

'Yeah, and he can keep 'em. I don't want AIDS,' said the guy who'd lent them to Will, then continued,

'But they did cost eight me quid.'

He was showing her the B&M receipt. She reached in her purse to pay him.

'Keep the change.'

He snatched the ten pound note from her hand, and glared at her; the dirty druggie's mother.

Chapter Twelve

Tim sits beside her, fascinated, but nervous, his ears pricking then flattening each time there's a crackle or a pop. She places another log on top of the bed of hot orange gems. The amber flames look like ghosts But *what do ghosts look like? What do ghosts look like?* with their transparent, pale blue pointed hoods, their bodies ever moving, frantic, fluid.

She loves how the fire spits and pops and crackles and roars; how it smells of all that's natural as she closes the door upon the living heat. And as the fire settles a little behind the glass, she loves how the flames mourn flickering in a ring, a ring wringing their hands around the wooden coffin, grieving and praying for oxygen. It must be horrible not to be able to breathe, to be fighting for breath.

She loves how they seem to be trying beat out their own fire, or how they fight to escape themselves, frantically, desperately fleeing their own flames. She wishes she had the strength to do the same. She puts on the black gauntlet, sweeps ashes off the tiled hearth, partly Cinderella, partly wicked witch.

And she remembered that day in Ben's flat when he'd been banging on his ceiling because he truly believed that the young woman upstairs was out to get him; stalking him, and it suddenly came to her, haunting him. Yes it was as though the woman upstairs had haunted him.

Wicked witch rather than Cinderella was more apt today; another Halloween. How quickly they came along.

Also, she was wearing black. She had intended to change into something more colourful because Will and Shelley were bringing little Jake, but she always covered everything with a scruffy stained apron, so it really didn't matter.

She doesn't see Jake very often these days. She can no longer face catching buses other than just to work and back, and she knows they won't visit without a proper reason because the episode at The Jungle play centre is still raw.

Like everybody else in her life, but with greater reason than most, they believe her too accepting of Ben's situation; too soft on him. But today, as Jake will have been to a friend's Halloween-cum-birthday party not far away, they are going to call in. She quickly moves the matches up high upon the book case; places the fireguard she always uses when he visits, firmly around the stove.

She has not heard from Ben for nearly a week now, and she is worried sick about him. She checks her phone, hoping against hope that he might have texted her whilst she was upstairs, telling herself that this will be the very last time she looks at her phone until Will, Shelley and Jake are getting back into their car, and waving goodbye.

She even speaks the words out loud, very loud and very firmly, 'Last time.' And she closes the blue-butterflied mobile phone cover; puts it in her apron pocket where she will either feel it vibrate or hear it ring should he attempt to contact her.

'Last time.' She repeats the words, even more loudly, even more firmly. Opens and closes and puts away her phone.

'The *very* last time.'

She opens and closes and puts away her phone. She reminds herself of Ben as a little boy, asking for yet another, 'annuver yast' crisp. And then she starts to worry again. He'd sounded off his head last time they'd spoken on the phone.

Is she going mad? Talking to herself? She thinks perhaps she may be, and so instead of speaking to herself, she speaks to Tim,

'Last time, Tim,' and then she strokes him. Aware of her fussing even in his deep sleep, Tim purrs his gratitude. She ought to fuss Jack more, show him more affection; poor man. He says even less these days. They do still make beautiful love on a Saturday afternoon, but they rarely talk.

She hears them Willl and Shelley walking down the drive, and her heart lifts a little.

She forces her mouth into a smile, heads for the kitchen door.

Shelley immediately pulls off his Jake's duffel coat. They are very careful not to let Jake overheat after that awful scare at his birthday party, and thank goodness he has not suffered any further febrile convulsions.

Underneath he is dressed as a skeleton, a black tight-fitting all in one body stocking with luminous bones.

'Oh wow! A skeleton!' she says.

His new Spiderman velcro flashing trainers look huge on his feet, but his body looks so thin and vulnerable; not scary at all!

'Look what I won at Hunter's Halloween party, Nana.'

Hunter, what a name!

He studies her grandson's latest noisy plastic toy whilst he tells her how to make it talk, how to make it walk.

'So how are you mum?'

Will asks her, as she serves up hot drinks; biscuits. She knows they are both still angry with her, *and quite rightly so, and quite rightly so,* and so she bites her tongue, stops herself from saying 'Well, I'm a bit worried about Ben.' They didn't want, they didn't deserve to hear that.

'I'm fine,' she says; she can't bring herself to say 'I'm good' like they do nowadays,

I'm not good, I'm bad; I'm not good, I'm bad,

She's not good, she's far from good; she's bad; a bad person.

'Yes I'm fine, thanks,' and she smiles;

Don't mention Ben; don't mention Ben.

The bag of big bricks she's bought from the charity shop keep Jake amused for a long while; although Tim soon disappears upstairs. Jake loves it when they clatter down onto the wooden floor, although he pretends not to, screwing up his eyes, putting his hands over his ears, shouting, 'Oh no, not again!'

Once he and Will take turns and manage to build a really tall tower using up every single block. Jake raises his hand to smash it to the ground, but Will stops him in mid air,

'Wait a minute, Jake, what do you think will happen if you *very slowly* and *very carefully* remove just one block from the middle.'

'Will it stay up?' he asks, eyes and mouth open wide.

'Try it, and we'll find out,' he says.

He does and is shocked when the entire tower tumbles, rattling onto the wooden floor. 'I thought it would of stayed up!' he says, 'Did you, Nana?'

Later, Will and Shelley are looking at something on Shelley's phone. He has his arm around her and they look happy and relaxed sitting on the settee in front of the fire. Oh dear, she'll need to fetch some more logs soon. But, because as well as playing with the bricks and having sandwiches and chocolate, she and Jake have coloured in, stuck stickers, read two books and Jake is now he is getting a bit restless.

'Nana, are you actually sure your telly doesn't work until 6 o'clock in the evening?'

She's always assured him that this is the case, not wanting the television or videos to become a babysitter as they had for Ben.

'Daddy, check if it's mended now. It is dark. It might work now, if it's dark.'

He looks up, sighs and she senses he might be about to warn Jake that it's almost time to go. And she doesn't want them to go. She wants them to stay a while longer.

'Look, Jake, we're almost out of logs for the fire. Now that you're five and a bit, I think you're big enough to help Nana collect some more; do you, Daddy? Mummy? Even though it's getting dark now and it's Halloween night?'

'Do you think you're brave enough, Jake?' Shelley teases.

'Hunter's mum said there's no such things as ghosts anyway.'

'Oh well that's me told then!' laughs Shelley.

'But then we must get back. '

'Let mummy pop your coat and gloves back on then, and you can come and help Nana get another basketful.'

'Yay!' Jake says, delighted.

'Do you want to hold the log basket or ...' she has secreted a small torch into her apron pocket, which she pulls out '...or the torch!'

'The torch!' he says.

'You lead the way then,' she shakes her long dark hair from out of her collar, pulls on her black woolly hat with the annoying pointy bit that insists on sticking up at the top of her head.

Holding the wicker log basket, she walks slowly, so slowly, cherishing this short time left with him, as well as the peace and the crisp, cold air. Jake reminds her so much of Ben at his age. But, of course, in those days, she'd forever been rushing about, snatching things from him, impatient to get to work or to just get him to bed so that she could settle down in front of the TV and have a glass of wine or three, or, and probably even worse, letting him do as he wanted, watch TV or play on video games letting him eat yet annuvver yast one because she couldn't be bothered, yes, she might as well face it, because she simply couldn't be arsed; was too exhausted to stop him.

Goodness, she was so determined not to make the same mistakes with Jake.

He holds the torch steady with both hands as she's shown him to, shining its light towards the shed at the top of the long shared drive.

'That's it, nice and steady so that Nana can see the way and doesn't trip over with the basket.'

It's hard to see you Nana, you're all dressed in black.

'Well don't you worry, I'm behind you, all the way.'

After a few steps, he turns facing her with the torch,

'Are still you all right Nana?' he asks, and her heart and her eyes flood with love for her little grandson; her second chance.

She wipes a tear on the corner of her apron.

'Sorry did I shine the torch into your eyes?' he asks and her love and tears well up again.

'Just a bit of an itch,' she says with a sniff, and she has one of those premonition-type of feelings; she has a sore eye, is trying to sort it out in a mirror, and something awful, terrifying is happening behind her.

'You're guiding me wonderfully.'

How she wished she'd had someone to guide her back then. For he and his torch were guiding her like a star; like the star on Christmas Eve had guided the wise men and the shepherds to the baby Jesus.

'Here we are, behind the garden shed, and here we have the Winter log store.'

He touches all the rounds of wood, runs his gloved fingers over them.

'All these logs have come from trees; the trunks of trees and from their branches.'

He shines the torch closely at the patterns on the wood, the moss, the rings, oh! and a little spider hurries away! It must have come to look at your spiderman trainers flashing. They're almost as bright as the torch!' The spider scurried away.

'Look at all the neat piles. They're nearly as tall as me!' she says pointing to chest-height.

'They're way taller than me!' he says, pointing the torch up and beyond to the quink-ink and bruise-smudged sky.

She puts down the empty basket.

'All these great big heavy logs came in a truck just after your birthday and the man who drove the truck left them in a great big untidy heap on the drive and then Grandad had to pile them all up into neat rows. He had to move them one at a time. It took him absolutely ages. They're very heavy and because they're round, they can roll about, and could easily fall, just like those ...'

'Was he cross?' Jake interrupts her, head down, pointing the torch at his feet.

'...Was who cross?'

'Was Grandad cross...?' he looks ashamed on behalf of his Grandad, 'did Grandad actually be cross with the man who drove the truck and left the logs all untidy?'

She laughs. So rapid, her mood swings; from tears to laughter in a just a few minutes.

'No, Grandad wasn't cross. It was the man who drove the truck's job to bring us the logs; just to deliver them, not to stack them up. Grandad knew he'd have to stack them.'

'Did you help?'

She lifts a log from the top row, surprised as always by its weight; its density: almost as heavy as a stone of the same size, but sharper, slippier, harder to handle... Harder to handle, just like ...

Slippy, sharp, hard to handle. And she remembers how he'd slipped out of her all those years ago; silent and blue … Like a fish out of water.

'No not really. Grandad likes doing things like that… I took him a drink of beer out. '

But then she remembered she'd said, we should have asked Ben over to help, something for his CV, give him a tenner? Then he'd been cross. 'Why should we pay him? He should do such things out of the goodness of his heart.'

And, of course, he was right … in a way.

Jake was shining the torch on the logs, shuffling his feet in his spiderman trainers on the gravel and the dead leaves, making a scrunch-scrunch noise whilst Nana stared at the top row of the logs.

'It sounds like I'm eating a big lot of crisps!' he said, but fell silent for a moment, sensing his Nana was not really listening, and she wasn't, not properly she thought, just like when she used to ignore Ben when he was a little toddler wanting more and more crisps asking for a 'yast one,' and then 'annuver yast one.'

'Nana?'

Get in touch, please Ben, please get in touch.

'Nana?' she sensed that this was the second time her little grandson had spoken to her.

Anything just to know you are all right.

'Can I put the logs in the basket?'

'Yes…'

Anyway, she told herself, when they're back inside, she will nip up to the bathroom, give him another ring…

…but first put the torch on the gravel, pointing at them.'

'That's right.'

give him another ring.

'Ready?'

Jake nodded, his face distorted in the torch light.

'Here's log number one.'

Yes, she'd try him again…

'Use both hands. That's right.'

She'd try him again and if he did answer, then she'd be able to relax and enjoy her evening with Jack when he was back from work, and they'd gone back home; she might cook him something nice, have a few drinks…

'Mind, it's very heavy.'

… to get rid of this awful fidgety, lightweight- limbed feeling.

'Fuff! It *is* heavy!'

'Yes very heavy.'

'I never actually thought it would of been so heavy.'

And if he didn't answer, and if he didn't answer…

'That's it, bend down, and slowly into the basket.'

Don't put all your eggs into one basket.

'Right, Jake. Now I need to get each log from the very top row,' she said, her voice tightening as she stretched up again. She must remind him what would happen if she didn't get them from the top row; remind him what had happened with the plastic bricks…

Oh, of course! Her hand paused. Why hadn't she thought sooner? She could ask Will to call in Ben's flat on their way home, quickly check he was all right.

And if he wasn't and if he wasn't? …

Jake and Shelley could stay in the car, whilst he nipped in. She'd slip him some petrol money. She'd only got a twenty pound note but she didn't care.

Pleased with her idea, she raised her voice and her tone up a cheerful notch.

'And then one at a time, I'll hand them down to you.'

But if he wasn't all right, if he wasn't all right?…

'And your job is to count each one and put it carefully into the basket, and we'll see how many we can fit in.'

'Can I choose the next log?' he asks.

And if he wasn't all right?…

'Nana?' he asks.

'When the basket's completely full, I will lift you up and you can pick your very own special log from the top row and you can carry it in to show mummy and daddy.'

She reaches for the eighth log,

'All right? And then daddy can put it on the fire for you and you can watch it start to burn before you go.'

She reached up again to the top row of logs, making a big exaggerated stretching noise 'Oo… oof!'

Something vibrated in her apron pocket.

'Dring!'

And there, her hand stopped. Suspended in mid-air, fingers curled.

His ring tone.

Her left-hand dived into her pocket.

Thank God.

Whipped out her phone.

Thank you God.

Pressed the green button with her thumb.

'Ben?' her voice is that tight, scratchy one.

'Mum…?'

Rumble.

Thud-thud-thud-thud.

Rumble.

'Nana…?'

He's standing still.

He's not moving.

He's grasping his chosen log.

He's not protecting his head.

'Nana!'

He's not protecting his head. He's not protecting his head, his beautiful face, he's not protecting his brain.

Jake clutches his prized log and he screams.

She drops her phone, grabs him around his waist, tiny beneath his coat, and she drags him, his ruby red Spiderman heels raking through the tiny pebbles until they are inside the shed. He holds on tight to his chosen log even as the wood continues to rain down and roll. And then she lies him on his side, She shouts for help above his cries; yes, his cries.

Thank God he's crying…

She's thinking about the plastic blocks he'd knocked over in the house ; she should have warned him not to take a log from the middle of a stack, and she's thinking about the slot machines *shove ha'penny* they sometimes used to go to when they were little; the shove ha'penny game. Why is she thinking like this? She should be finding her phone.

Ringing an ambulance.

He was conscious.

'Don't let any more logs fall on me Nana!'

She holds him tight.

'I won't, my brave little boy. I won't.'

She gently strokes his hair, at the same time feeling for any wetness or stickiness on his scalp, then lifts his hood up and places a cushion from the old deckchair beneath his cheek. Then she gently touches his body all over to locate for any obvious injuries or pain, and tucks her coat beneath and around him.

Blood is slowly pooling upon his left temple. And his leg is bent behind him. His skeleton leggings are rucked up above his spiderman socks and the Velcro spiderman shoes.

His leg is bleeding. Blood. Blood red beneath the torchlight, black when the light moves from the wound. Blood is pooling; blood is dripping.

But he is crying.

'Shush my brave boy; shush my lovely; my brave little boy.'

He is crying. Crying so piteously, a wounded animal sound, a hurt, shocked sound. Now louder, purer, clearer in the shocked silence which has followed the ending of the logs' thunder roll; indignant, shocked. But, he is crying. Thank God. Thank you, God.

She soothes Jake as best she can,

'Brave Boy! My brave, brave little boy. Naughty, nasty old Nana,' presses tissues to his wounds to help stem the bleeding, which seems to have eased a little.

And she hears the kitchen door open, 'Mum? Jake?' And then Will was coming up the drive.

'The fire's just about dead now! What are you still doing out here?'

And she hears Will gasp as he sees all the logs higgledy-piggledy where they've rolled, and he sees his son lying down in the shed, and charges over to him, and she's reminded of the day at The Jungle.

'He's going to be fine!' she shouts.

He's alive; he's going to be fine; not fin, thank God, not fin, she thinks, suddenly recalling hers and Ben's private joke; she's bad, not good.

'…you need to call an ambulance…' she yells '… My phone's over there!'

Will grabs the phone from where she'd thrown it and she sees him clock the name on her screen, hears the raised voice at the other end and even now, and she knows it's so wrong, but even now she feels a swell of relief that it is not his off-his-head voice,

'Mum!! It's Ben. Are you OK? What's happening? I wanted to talk to you.'

And in the torchlight, Will's face contorts into that of a stranger.

Then she can hear Ben's voice at the other end, beneath the sound of Will who is trying to yell and scream down the phone at him, 'Fuck off you fucking Druggie Cunt!' but he can't scream because his voice is trembling so. And as he tries to yell, Will stares at her, he stares at her, he stares at his mother in utter disbelief, in utter disgust. As though she is an evil stranger. As though she is the worst of the worst witches on this awful Halloween Night. And she wants to die.

And then Shelley is there, and she is so frightened; so scared, trying to hold her little boy's head and crying.

'Shh,' she says, trying to soothe her daughter-in-law, as Will presses 999, her phone clenched to his ear.

'Shh! Shelley, Jake's going to be fine,' she says, touching her hair, but Shelley pushes her hand away, tosses her head, shakes her off.

'He is not fine,' she croaks, 'He is not fine, thanks to you.'

And Jake cries all the more.

As they wait for the emergency services to reply, Will says to Shelley,

'Go and get a duvet.'

Then he looks at her; he looks at her, his mother, our nameless narrator, his eyebrows raised in the half-darkness, then he looks at the wood, then back to her; in disbelief and disgust again, shakes his head slowly.

'That's what happens, you see…' he says to her, his voice weak and tight, his eyes flicking to her over his glowing phone which he clutches, waiting for a response, '…that's what happens when you take your eyes off a five-year-old, your five-year-old grandson; that's what happens when you answer the phone because it's that druggie bastard at your beck and call again. That's what happens when you always insist on putting that druggie bastard first all the time.'

'I don't,' she begins, 'I don't…' but no one is listening, and she whispers, 'I don't put him first.' And her tears fall upon Jake's coat. 'Honestly…' she whispers, 'I don't …' But she does. She knows she does.

As Will begins to speak to the person on the other end,

'Hello. Yes. Paramedics please.'

He gives their address.

Then, 'Sorry?' he turns to try and get a better reception, takes a few steps and rolls on a log, almost falling.

'Shitting hell!'

He kicks it and it flies towards her, hitting her sharply on the shin. He doesn't apologise, and she is glad. She wishes it had have hit her in the eye.

I should never have taken my eye off him.

When they'd finished questioning them, the paramedics said that because it was getting colder, they should carefully move him on a count of three, put him in the car and take him to A&E themselves; quicker than waiting for an ambulance.

As Shelley gently strapped him into his car seat, then sat next to him, holding him as close as she could, Jake examined the cut on his leg and asked,

'Will I have an actual proper bandage on it?'

She'd wanted to go with them to the hospital. She wouldn't be a nuisance to them; she wouldn't have a panic attack; she always felt safe in hospitals.

'Can I come with you?'

Will had turned to her, but had not looked at her, had stared beyond her, perhaps searching for the better mother she had been in times gone by, he'd shaken his head slowly; said nothing.

'Please may I come with you?' she asks again,

Shelley, in a shaking voice said,

'I don't think so.'

'I will ask Jack to bring me, then. He'll be back in an hour or so.'

'No. Please don't.'

'I want Nana to come and look at me in hospital,' said Jake, but his parents ignored him.

'Well, please let me know how he gets on.'

'You'll have to ring the hospital and enquire,' Shelley snapped, 'because we'll not be getting in touch with you.'

'She's right, Mum,' said Will, calmer now. 'It was bad enough what happened at the Jungle. Whilst ever you're still in touch with *him*, we want nothing to do with you. I refuse to let you put Jake in danger ever again.'

And then they were all gone. Leaving her alone with the most immense guilt she'd ever felt.

That night, hating herself because once she'd rung the hospital and had been reassured that Jake was indeed fine and was being kept in overnight just as a precaution, she had rung Ben. She didn't, however, mention to Ben, or Jack, that they'd said they would not be in touch with her whilst ever she remained in touch with Ben.

And then she'd felt even worse.

She lay in bed, literally beating herself up, thumping all of her bruises, especially the one on her shin, the one that Will had caused when he'd kicked that log. She was determined to make each of them hurt even more; was determined to make them look darker still.

And as she finally tumbled into sleep …

Perhaps I'll sleep like a log; but I doubt it…

…she saw the logs falling; falling again, this time slowly covering Jake. And in the dream she was aware that she had got plenty of time to lift the logs off him, but instead she stood and watched and waited until the logs obliterated him.

Then, in the dream, she removed each log and slowly, so slowly placed them in the basket one at a time, why was she taking so long? Why was she being so careful? And with just a few logs left, she uncovered him sitting naked in the middle of the pile; his skin blackened, charred. She pushed at him with the poker and he yielded, became soft; a rapidly pulsing heart of flaming orange.

Chapter Thirteen

The ground tilted and her head felt strange; her vision shimmered. She breathed deeply, trying hard; trying so hard to fight off the panic attack which sat in wait on the miserable bus-stop bench, alongside her and the little old lady and the large young girl.

Despite her efforts, Panic began to attack her from all angles, expertly playing all of its cruel tricks, mental and physical.

Panic had won again.

And, once more, she found herself lonely and terrified in her own private Hell.

She was still functioning; oh yes, she was still functioning, at least to a degree, determined as she was to visit him, to check he was OK in 'real life' as she thought of it. A text or even a telephone conversation was all well and good, but nothing could compare with a proper overnight visit.

Yes, she functioned; as she supposed he functioned some of the time; at least to the outside world. She functioned, gathering her bags together, checking her coins, standing aside so that the little old lady might embark first, but she was trembling and sweating, her heart thumping as though she'd had to seriously run to catch this bus, and she was clawing with her left-hand as she always did, clawing frantically, involuntarily, at a section of her hair, as though to pull Panic itself up by its root growing deep inside of her head. She couldn't stop herself.

The driver didn't bat an eyelid; took her money, printed out the ticket which she tore off with shaky fingers and the bus doors slid together, closing with a deep sigh.

She vaguely knew the two women already on the bus; they worked in the Spar shop, but she pretended not to see them, looking down, as she sat in front of them. She piled her bags upon her knees; a comfort to her, like a cushion, or a child, or Tim. The heavy carrier bags weighed down and stuck into her trembling legs, but nonetheless she held them close, with both hands, so that the clawing of her hair became more of an effort and so lessened.

After all, she deserved the discomfort. She wore her shoulder bag over her coat, and because she was sweating so, wished she felt strong enough; confident enough to remove it. Such a small thing to do, but impossible whilst she still had Panic to contend with.

'Her youngest's a druggie...' said one of the women behind her, then paused so that her next words might have the maximum effect on her friend, then continued, a little louder, '...been in prison and everything.'

'Why, what did he do?'

'Dealt drugs; hard drugs. To the year tens at All Saints.'

She stiffened. As if he'd do that. He was a good lad. Despite his addiction, he had morals. That. Was. So. Not. True. Plus, he'd always said he could never deal drugs, because he would never be able to resist taking them himself. So that was a total load of bollocks.

Did they not get that it was the fault of the person before him, the person who had dealt him drugs, introduced him to drugs, the drug pusher as they used to be called. The drug pusher and his drug pusher before that and his drug pusher before that for ever and a day?

'Oh 'eck,' replied the other woman.

She managed to shake back her hair in a way that she hoped might indicate she'd heard them but that she didn't give a toss, because she knew for a fact that that was not true.

'Her hair needs a good wash,' said one.

Her face became hot.

'A good brushing would help 'n all. Looks a right state.'

She knew this was true. She'd not had time to wash it this morning and she'd been clawing at it. Feeling her face become warm she resisted the urge to flatten it down.

Two fingers, one contained within a plain silver band, followed by a denim-jacketed arm appeared beside her right shoulder; long beautiful pale pink nails, poised ready to press the buzzer to stop the bus.

'Pass this on to your dirty druggie son. Yeah?'

The fingers turned, opened into a V sign which jerked upwards towards her, then slowly turned again to push the button.

Then Long Nails leaned over and spoke close to the side of her head; all chewing gum and garlic and hairspray,

'Tell him to fuck off and make sure he stays fucked off forever!'

Yes, people, especially other mothers, knew exactly which buttons to press to hurt her.

Her friend followed her off the bus, loudly clearing her throat, 'Ahh! Hmm!' snorting; gozzing phlegm up into her mouth from the back of her nose.

Cows.

Her eyes prickled, and to avoid their glares from the stop where they'd disembarked, she lowered her head and rummaged in her bags of stuff for him; tins of food, pot-noodles, biscuits, a jar of hot chocolate, a cleaning spray, a book, a newspaper, some apples, a bottle of wine for herself …

Flop!

A big green glob of mucus hit the window.

Dirty Bitches.

Nonetheless she could feel her panic subsiding because, after what had just happened to her, it was perfectly ok, perfectly normal and acceptable to be feeling like she was, anyone would like she was; heart racing, trembling, frightened.

It was only when she was feeling like that for no reason; when she felt terrified for absolutely no reason, that the panic overwhelmed her and she truly thought she would die on the spot; or else slide from the face of the earth. Thank goodness the attack had not grown into a full-blown one. She'd have had to have ring a taxi to take her straight back home and that would have cost a good twenty pounds or more.

And so, feeling slightly more normal, for the first time since she'd got on the bus, she felt able to glance around; there seemed to be only herself and the little old lady on the lower deck now. A CCTV camera pointed out her wrinkled, still-pretty face as she removed a handkerchief from her cardigan sleeve, dabbed daintily at her nose.

Then the CCTV panned to a woman she'd not noticed as she'd boarded. She was a mess, especially compared with the trim little lady. Hair bedraggled, sticking out at one side; a fat, miserable face. Oh my

God, it was her. Her cheeks blushed deep red until the camera left her.

Up to the top deck it roamed, picking out the silent youngsters, including the big girl who'd got on after her, all hunched over, bowed low, praying to their phones. Ah, on the back row in the middle seat was that lady again, that lady who'd been on the bus when she was coming home after going to Ben's the day he was arrested. Funny place to sit; she wouldn't have sat there, she'd have felt unsafe, like she might tumble into the aisle.

The lady had tried to comfort her; and she'd turned away, willing her to leave her alone, because she felt ashamed? Embarrassed? She'd been holding a massive bag of smelly dirty wet washing. Yes, it was definitely her; she was wearing that pink mac again. She saw that she had a pretty face, blonde hair, olive skin. The lady suddenly smiled into the camera, almost as though she had suddenly become aware she was looking at her. She felt a small fission of, of what; she didn't know, it felt like the tiniest weeniest electric shock, followed by a lightening of her limbs.

Ten minutes later, the bus stopped at the terminal where it always turned around and she knew to get off. She and the little old lady waited for all the kids, reluctantly pushing their phones into their back pockets, as they trudged down the stairs to college. Strange, the lady in the pink mac never came down. Perhaps she'd decided to stay on for the ride back; or perhaps she'd somehow just missed spotting her. She had been in a bit of a dream since she noticed her; relaxed; panic well and truly gone. Although as she left the bus, she felt anxiety returning because she such had an appalling sense of direction and always found it so hard to pinpoint which block of flats his was; everywhere looked the same.

Which way to turn?

Which way to turn? The story of her life…

Ah there it was. She spotted it more quickly than she normally did. He normally left his living room window open when he was expecting her, probably to let out the stale cigarette smoke. Today it was shut; the curtains closed; probably because it was quite chilly. Unless he was still asleep, of course.

Block 6. Flat 6.

Double six. Lucky double six. She remembered playing board games with them at

Christmas; why only ever at Christmas? That guilt again. You get two turns if you roll a double six, two chances, she'd told them. Move on six places and then rattle the dice in the little cup again; roll them out upon the table, once he'd got a double six again! 'Do many people get double six three times?' he'd asked her, his eyes wide, 'Have you ever got a double six three times?'

A second turn. That's what he needed now. A second chance. She pressed the number 6, then adjusted her shoulder bag, and checking the two folded tenners were pushed well out of sight down in the slots in her phone's case, out of temptation's way, then felt through the plastic of her bag the shape of the emergency credit card hidden in a tear at the bottom of the lining and pushed round further to sit upright at the bulky base of its handles. She picked up the two bulging Sports Direct bags again.

She looked up,

Smack bang, Smack Head, Smack head banger, Smack in the middle of the other windows, his with the black curtains drawn, presumably against the dark and early morning chill;, another with a skull and cross bones flag flapping through the window pane, its border trapped inside the occupant's living room; linings of blood red curtains ripped; a Saint George flag twisting and turning frantically upon its pole, tattered and weathered above carelessly closed red curtains, their white lining ragged and torn.

She heard the click as he picked up the handset in his hallway.

She spoke through wind-swept hair into the grille. It reminded her of the grille at the prison; the grille where the kind guard had sat, where the smell of food made her feel nauseous yet hungry because she couldn't face breakfast before a prison visit, where the smell of food mixed with cold frosty air.

'It's only mum.'

There was a pause, a sound, of static, perhaps. Maybe he'd not heard her. She blew the hair from the corner of her mouth,

'It's mum,' she repeated, a rush of anxiety already making her claw at her hair again.

She considered putting down the bags, decided against it, as she had them in a firm grasp and the goods could quite possibly roll down the slope and, more importantly, the bottle of wine could quite possibly smash.

'Are you up and about?'

She told herself that, of course, she'd probably woken him. The curtains were still closed. It was after all still early, not yet eight o'clock, although he was normally awake and anxious, craving the subutex which he picked up from the local pharmacy each morning at 9.30.

Maybe it a good sign, perhaps he had enjoyed a rare good night's sleep; she hoped so. Perhaps he was at this moment rubbing his eyes, fumbling for his first rollie of the day, or he already had his first rollie of the day in the corner of his mouth, and was fumbling for his Poundland lighter.

Still he didn't speak but there was another click, then quiet, followed by a series of loud beeps which seemed higher pitched than normal: beep-beep-beep. At least he'd let her in; he must be up. And she pushed open the heavy main entrance door, then held it open still beeping, turning awkwardly with her heavy carrier bags of tins and clothes and toiletries, her shoulder bag swinging around her waist, bumping into the side of the door, the hair back in her mouth.

She trudged up the dark grey concrete stairs, the bulging Sports Direct bags, too heavy to lift any higher, scuffed the edge of each step. Surely steps in gloomy places like this should be painted in a luminous yellow? But, there again, perhaps places like this didn't warrant safety features. She tried to move her hair with the inside of her forearm, smelling the fabric of her coat, damp with the drizzle, wiped her nose, as she reached the top. The door was closed. He was probably in the bathroom.

She knocked on the door, then when he did not answer, pushed down the loose metal handle, recalling for the first time in absolutely years, a dream she'd had, oh, twenty years back in which she'd been slowly opening an attic room door, and its handle had become cold, white, fingers beneath hers, and had taken her somewhere terrifying...

There was the usual smell of roll ups; a cool smoky fug; junk mail and final demands all over the paint spattered linoleum in the hallway. He didn't bother opening envelopes these days; he'd learned they never contained good news; he'd learned they were best ignored.

'Hello?'

She peeped into his living room.

'Are you all right?…'

The television wasn't muttering to itself; that was strange.

'… Only you normally say, "Come up"?'

He didn't reply.

In the early morning darkness and behind the closed curtains, she could barely see him in profile, seated on his black needle-cord sofa, bent forward as though at prayer, his elbows on his knees, head in his hands.

Had he gone back to sleep? Or perhaps he wasn't very well. He quite often felt really ill, 'rattling' he called it, before he'd picked up his Subutex from the pharmacy. She'd make them both a cup of tea in a minute and give him one of those biscuits she'd brought; that would make him feel better. Then they'd walk down to the pharmacy.

She put down the carrier bags, and tried the light switch; nothing. She wasn't surprised. He'd gone and let his electricity run out again. She'd give him a fiver to put on his meter, and after the pharmacy, she'd walk down to the Co-op with him to cash it in, and make sure he kept the receipt, and then she'd buy him some bits from Farmfood… She hated to think of him hungry in the dark and the cold.

It was too dark in here; she could hardly see him, she'd have to let some light in. She tiptoed across to open the curtains.

And then he was sobbing.

'I'm sorry, mum!'

And then he was shaking his head, speaking into his hands. She bent towards him, moving back her hair, struggling to focus.

'Whatever's wrong?'

'I'm just so sorry mum.'

She felt a faint pressure on her throat, the pressure that preceded her tight strained voice, the voice that was hers most of the time now: that familiar, that horrible, choked up, stressed lumpy, gulpy feeling.

But this time the feeling tightened, this time the feeling tightened, and became cold fingers.

Cold fingers followed by coffee and warm chewing-gum breath. She remembered the woman on the bus, cigarettes and gum. Most of the adult population were held to ransom by at least one addictive substance.

She swallowed painfully, making an almost comical squeak.

A growl; hot on the nape of her neck.

'I'm afraid your druggie son owes me.'

Her fingers reached inside her coat pocket for her mobile phone; familiar, warm, its butterfly-patterned cover slightly rough beneath her thumb.

'Not a good start, I hate chasing debts, and this my very first pitch round here.'

Her fingers curled around the phone cover's magnetic fastening, its tab fastener worn, creased then cracked from wear and tear.

'And what you going to do with that?' he hissed.

'Police?'

'Police?' he imitated her strained intonation perfectly.

'Yeah,' she said, her other hand resting upon the zip of her shoulder bag, strangely calm.

'I don't...' and with his left fist he pushed her hand beneath the pocket, 'I don't fucking think so!' he pushed her hand and her phone up and out of her pocket.

And her phone, become an open book, lay face down upon the stained flo-tex flooring. A scrunched up, shreddy, felty-looking tissue followed it.

Ben began to lean forward on the sofa, as though to reach for his mum's phone.

The hand remained around her neck.

'And you can fucking sit still...'

His voice was become louder, high pitched,

'...you greedy little drug-gie!'

on the word druggie his fingers pressed harder at her throat.

Ben's eye caught hers, his tears glinting in the darkness.

'I'm so …'

'I said shut it! Now then, what have you got for me?' he asked the back of her neck, his thumb twisting tight her long hair.

'Twenty quid?' she said, shuffling her feet.

'You can do better than that.'

His fingers clambered into her left-hand coat pocket.

'I can't.'

'For example what have we got in in *this* pocket?'

And she felt a pressure which she prayed to God, she prayed to God, Ben had not sensed, a pressure of two or three fingers up and through the lining of her empty coat pocket up and pushing against the centre seam, against the crotch of her leggings.

And then his knee was thrusting just behind the fingers. One… And she prayed to God that Ben did not notice. It would break his heart. Two… But God. IT HURT. God it hurt. Three… It hurt almost as much as her heart hurt; almost as much as her heart hurt, as it broke for them both.

'Get off me!' she hissed, hoping that Ben would think she referred only to the persistent pressure round her neck.

She shifted her legs.

And, face hot, hating the sudden involuntary indignant scalding tears, she stamped her feet; the feeling of his fingers and the hot tears making her recall weeing herself at infant school.

His fingers moved away with a twist and a pinch of her clitoris.

'"Temper temper" as me dear old nan used to say,' he chuckled.

'Druggie Waster, Unfasten yer dear old mum's bag.'

He reached for the zip.

'I'm so sorry, mum'

He was crying, big desperate croaky sobs.

'Clumsy twat! Undo the buckle on the shoulder strap, then give me the whole bag. Give me the old bag's bag. Greedy little druggie!'

And she remembered all those years ago when he was just a toddler, just a toddler, smiling at her over that family-sized bag of crisps. And she remembered him cajoling her into allowing him, 'one yast one' and then, having eaten that, 'annuvver yast one… please, mummy'.

Hand still around her neck, although with less force now, he clasped her shoulder bag awkwardly between his elbow and his bent right knee, emptying it of its contents.

And she hated that she was ashamed of its contents in front of that bastard, just as she had been in the Court in front of the security man; she hated the screwed up bits of toilet roll, the crumbs in the corners, the post it notes with scribble on and bits of fluff and hair upon their sticky strip. But she didn't deserve anything nice.

And on the carpet her mobile phone, like an open book, began to ring and to vibrate and to move slightly, a border of bright light seeping from its edges.

This could be the end of everything

So why don't we go

Somewhere only we know?

And God how she wished that they could go; that this could be the end of everything. Oh, to just go. Go. Disappear. Leave this world together. Leave this world and take their problems with them.

He began to hum along with Keane.

'Surprisingly good taste in music,' he sneered.

He had a nice voice.

Smash!

The ironing board beside Ben collapsed. She thought she saw the white of his ankle move back quick as a flash back to the settee. Had he done that deliberately?

Then she realised; of course, he was trying to make the man downstairs come up to complain. Please come up; please come up and see what's happening.

The familiar thump-thump-thump from below again, and maybe a raised voice?

She felt his fingers tighten briefly as maybe he thought he'd heard something too.

'No purse?' his voice had dropped to a whisper.

'No.'

'So where's the twenty quid you mentioned?'

She nodded towards her phone which was playing Keane again.

This could be the end of everything

So why don't we go

Somewhere only we know?

She hoped it was Jack checking she'd got there ok. Then just as quickly she hoped it wasn't him, because he'd say that he'd told her so. And he'd want to involve the police and …

'Druggie, Bring it here, and turn the fucker off while you're at it!' he hissed then opened the phone, pulled two folded tenners from its card slots. Put them into his pocket.

'And stop fuckin' cryin, will you?'

God how she hated him for saying that.

'Fuckin' cry baby.'

Bastard. God she wanted to kill him. She stared as hard as she possibly could at the cruel cunt. But he was studying her iphone.

'Half-decent phone, I'll take that, too, and the bag as well, while I'm doing.'

Oh no, she remembered her credit card was in the very back slot pushed up into the lining, just in case, just in case he might have been desperate, might have been as he quite probably would have been, able to persuade her to give him more than she could really afford to.

He looked inside it, put it on his shoulder, tossed back his hair, posed like a woman then made a camp gesture, and asked,

Is it a Designer bag? Don't know much about them. Not like my missus.'

God, she hurt inside. But at least his actual fingers hadn't touched her, it was all through her leggings, and she remembered Long Fingernails from on the bus.

'No it isn't. It's not worth anything. It's from Skeggy Market, but it was a present from my mother.'

'It 'twas a pres-sent from ma moth-ther!'

He sang 10CC under his breath, studying the bag, this way and that.

'Ah don't like cricket – oh no, I love it…'

'… And … I don't like druggies,' he sang, chuckling through a ball of phlegm, which he spat out onto the carpet.

'I said, I don't like druggies!'

He aimed a kick at his shin and her entire being felt that pain overtake the pain insid of her; one hundred-fold.

She wanted to scream at him, to scream at him that addicts were created by people like him, that addicts provided his income, his daily bread. It was he and other dealers that encouraged addicts, put temptation in their way every day. Texting; tempting; pestering when they were at their most vulnerable. She'd seen the texts on his phone, 'Come and join your mates. It's Happy Hour!'

Bang! Bang! There was a rapping at the door.

'That's an fucking copper's knock. You say nowt druggie, and I'll say nowt; but I'll be back.'

And she hated herself as she heard her voice through her bruised throat whisper to the man,

'If you promise not to hurt him, I promise you'll get your fucking money tomorrow.'

Their eyes met for the first time and she thought she saw at the back of them, she thought she saw a flicker of understanding, maybe even a flicker of sympathy.

He nodded once, silently and slowly, and handed her back her phone, then reached for his own from his back pocket. Without the need for further words, she texted him her number.

He flung her bag back at her, 'Heap of shit anyway,' he hissed.

Ben had gone to open the door.

She opened the curtains, put her scarf loosely around her neck to hide any bruising.

'I was just saying, someone's complained about the noise again,' the young policeman said as he walked into the living room, followed by Ben. Why ever didn't she shout out what had just happened? That she'd been damaged and humiliated and was now standing there hurting and stinging; bruised and broken. What was stopping her? Her heart absolutely raced.

'A friend of me brother's just dropped me mum off,' he looked around, smiled at her.

'Mornin,' the dealer said with a grin, as yet unknown to the local copper.

'Me mum's going to spend the day with me, help fill in some job application forms and stuff.'

God, he was good.

'Hello, yes, I remember your mum, Ben. We've met before, haven't we?'

She smiled wearily, 'Yeah, fraid so,' she said. He was one of the nicer coppers; and she'd met a heck of a lot of them during her time. This young man actually seemed to believe in the old adage, 'there but for the grace of God goes me.'

'So,' he continued, pen poised above his little notebook, 'what was all the noise all about?'

'I don't know. We've just been talking, that's all… Oh, me ironing board fell over,' he said as if he'd just remembered that. Perhaps he had. They all stared at the collapsed ironing board's gravestone-shaped, fag-burned cover; saw an ash tray and a mug weeping out their contents on the floor beside it.

'Yes, I must have put it up wrong. But that's all. I've not even got the tele on. I know it was him downstairs. I can't do anything without him moaning. I don't know how he'd have managed living below the girl upstairs when she was at her worst.

So he still believed that Her Upstairs had been out to get him?

The policeman walked over to the window.

'No, your downstair's neighbour's gone out. I saw him driving off whilst I was sat in my car doing some paperwork.'

The policemen gazed out at the neighbouring flats, and the blue sky and the green hills beyond.

'No,' he said quietly, 'it was a woman.'

He turned back to them, closed his notebook and slid his pen back into the little resting place at its side.

'I was just on my way to visit your mate at number 55 when she stopped me,' he continued, 'I'd not seen her before. I couldn't place her accent but she's definitely not local. She must have supersonic hearing or something…'

Or perhaps she was off her head, like half the people on this estate; hallucinating, suffering aural hallucinations just like he had used to do, she thought but didn't say.

'…Anyway, I don't know where she went, just seemed to vanish.'

He replaced his hat, then walked through the doorway. Catching his heel slightly upon the collapsed ironing board, he turned back to them, and said,

'She was wearing a bright pink mac.'

Chapter Fourteen

'Mum, you'll be glad to know, the police have caught up with that bastard who tried to take your bag. Apparently he was on the run; he's charged with manslaughter,' Ben told her.

Who'd have ever thought she'd have ended up living a life like this!

She'd still never told anyone what had really happened that day, but the news was good and had helped Ben to persuade her to stay overnight with him for the first time, especially as Jack and Antony have planned a footy videos evening in, doubtless with plenty of drinks and a takeaway. She plans to have a good heart-to-heart with Ben; again, to make him a 'do-able' action plan.

She packs an overnight bag, fills a carrier with tins of food, with old newspapers she's saved for him with the crosswords and the articles he's told her he likes reading because he knows, and she knows, that that's what she wants to hear. She adds a packet of biscuits she'd forgotten about, half a loaf of bread from the freezer, a family bag of salt and vinegar crisps, two bottles of wine, some shampoo that she's no longer keen on, a bathbomb she thinks he might like the smell of, some fruit she knows he will probably not eat, and she checks the bus times.

A couple of women whisper about her, and pointedly glare at her as they disembark. She hates it. She has always wanted people to like her, even if she doesn't particularly like them. Has never been able to understand those lucky people who are able to say things like, 'He or she can please themselves. I don't care what they think.'

And so she stares straight ahead through her own personal kaleidoscope of suspended tears. She doesn't turn or blink lest her eyes might begin to run, for if they do, she truly feels, she truly fears, she might just cry forever…

With heavy bags and a heavy heart, she steps off the bus and into her weekend.

She looks up at the flats with their ragged Saint George flags, as always, flapping; trapped in tight-shut windows, or dangling, tangling; hanging themselves on makeshift poles. She presses the buzzer, hears the click, the clearing of his throat, a 'Hello' as he flicks the switch upstairs to let her in.

And she slowly climbs the concrete staircase, laden bags scuffing against each step's new hi-vis edge, her wedding ring clinking lonesomely against the cold metal handrail.

'You go and put the kettle on,' she says, 'I won't be a moment.' For a moment she needs to compose herself, 'I'm a bit out of breath.' She needs to take a few deep breaths, to lean upon the window sill, palms pushed down flat upon the white gloss paint, a moment she needs to rest her furrowed brow against the glass, to look out at the neighbouring flats. She closes the curtains which don't quite reach in the middle,

And, of course, as she'd always known she would, she suddenly thinks, why has she come? What is she doing here? Why is she not at home simply pretending to be reading and pottering; pottering and reading? For she could do without this… She really could.

The smell today is more stale food than roll ups; a sour smell. Not old cooking; maybe something rotting? And she sees straight off that the four black refuse sacks that were there two weeks ago are still in the kitchen, leaning against the spattered wall, waiting to join the other rubbish in the communal skip.

Big, bulging black bags; one not tied at its top spews its styrofoam and its crushed cans emptied of strong, cheap lager. She is sorry to see the cans; he's never been a big drinker. Perhaps they are a mate's. She can't be bothered to ask. He will just say what she'd rather hear; he will just lie. Each sack jostles for a comfier resting place, pizza box corners protrude through their flesh as they elbow one another out of the way.

She tries the light switch; nothing. She had meant to bring a replacement bulb; his electric must have run out again. She touches the kitchen radiator; no, that's quite warm. She must ask him to take out the bulb; see what sort of replacement he needs.

She picks up the cans and the containers; wearily ties the top of the bag with a double knot. She doesn't need to speak. She's too tired to speak. He watches her with the whites of his eyes; sways forward onto his toes, sways backwards onto his heels.

'I'll take them out later, mum,' he slurs.

She unpacks the food she's brought with her; stacks, the tins of tuna, of beans, of soup, of custard, of macaroni cheese upon the unopened tins she'd brought with her the last time: puts a multipack of salt and vinegar crisps next to the kettle, tries not to notice the syringes glinting in their shrink wrap at the back of the dusty shelf beneath.

The television mutters quietly to itself as it sits upon the carpet in the corner, its remote controls long since lost or sold along with his self-control, its picture fuzzy, grainy, its matching chrome and glass stand and coffee table both now allegedly broken. She knows for sure that they, along with a second hand X-Box and games which she'd brought him and at least half a dozen other items, sit in wait in somebody else's living room, forgotten about until the next time his benefit money fails to match his craving.

The flowered melamine tea-tray which used to sit prettily beside her bread bin at home, now shares the stained carpet at the foot of the sofa. It is covered with curls of tobacco, filters and Rizlas, a disposable lighter, tiny squares of card, a bent teaspoon, a trainer lace, a cheap lighter, a ball of kitchen foil, a safety pin. A lidded metal push-down ash tray stands, an urn filled with ash, in the middle of a pile of empty self-seal polythene bags like those used for spare buttons; perhaps twenty or so of them, each with a caricature of a moustachioed man, and the word 'Happy' in upper case letters. Spice. Mamba. Surely he wasn't selling it? But why would he need so much? That's what he'd been introduced to in prison.

The erect ironing board now serves as a tall, gravestone-shaped coffee table. Its striped cover is tea and nicotine-stained a dark, dark brown, and is covered with unread print outs and hastily folded leaflets, given by the well-meaning, shoved in a pocket and forgotten about by them and by him; is heaped with letters, final reminders, medical appointments, eviction threats, all pushed back into their envelopes and ignored; is strewn with lists and bullet-pointed action ns in her handwriting that he knows, and that she knows, and that she knows that he knows, he will never act upon, but which make them both, more particularly her, feel better at the time.

She puts her stuff in the bedroom; her nightee, a few toiletries, spare clothes; she disguises her tablet with the quilt. She wears a little purse on a shoulder strap across her body. It contains her mobile phone, two twenty pound notes, her weekend return bus ticket.

It looks like he'd recently sold the dream catcher which used to hang over his bed.

It wasn't a girly dreamcatcher as most dreamcatchers are; rather, it was large, its nets and feathers bruise-coloured, purple and black; clusters of golden beads at the top of each bundle of feathers glowed; stars in the dark. She'd spent ages agonizing over which one to buy him on their holiday last year, which they'd spent in Lanzarote rather than Praia da Rocha. Praia da Rocha held too many memories. She couldn't contemplate going back there.

She'd attached the dreamcatcher high up onto the light pull above his bed, although she now knew he never slept in his bed, he preferred to lie on his squashy black sofa in the living room, and she'd said 'Now, each and every time you turn your light off to go to sleep, the dreamcatcher's net will capture and hold onto the good dreams, and its feathers will sweep away all the nightmares that have gone before. Because, you must believe that the good dreams are just around the corner; those stars are only just out of reach.'

And their eyes had met.

'Do you remember 'Reach for the Stars'?'

There had been the briefest hesitation, then, he'd nodded, slurred,

'S Club 7.'

He'd given a slight smile; and she saw that through the haze of drugs, he did remember; he did still remember those happy times in Praia da Rocha especially when he had won the Best Boy Dancer that time he'd taken little Kenny to his first ever disco, and tears had filled his eyes as he lifted his hand to stroke the feathers, and he silently touched each one of the stars in turn.

He remembered.

And she remembered.

Oh, how she remembered.

I've got you and you've got me, so

Reach

and he'd stretched and he'd reached

for the stars

so that even his gel-spiked hair seemed to stretch and to reach,

>*Climb every mountain higher*

and he'd stood on the tiptoes of the trainers he loved to keep so white and so clean,

>*Reach for the stars*

and he'd punched the air with his fist,

>*Follow your heart's desire*

and he'd sung along;

Reach for the stars

such a smile upon his face.

>*And when that rainbow's shining over you*
>*That's when your dreams will all come true*
>
>*There's a place waiting just for you (just for you)*
>*Is a special place where your dreams all come true*
>*Fly away (fly away) swim the ocean blue (swim the ocean blue)*
>*Drive that open road, leave the past behind you*
>*Don't stop gotta keep moving*
>*Your hopes,...*

She still believes that despite his start in life; his horrible conception, his harrowing birth, the lack of quality time with her, the broken marriage, the he surely did have everything to live for. Absolutely everything. Opportunities there for the taking. Wonderful things just within reach. But she'd obviously wrecked all that for him; for both of them.

He swayed on his tiptoes, then onto his heels, his head and his eyeballs tipping backwards, as he slurred,

'Have you got everything you need mum?'

'Yeah, I'll be fine.'

She has got everything she needs; far from everything she wants, she does have all she needs.

'When she goes back into the living room she can tell that he has either taken something more, or that whatever he had already taken is kicking further into his brain, his senses, his body, his eyes, his organs.

And he paces, and he rambles, and he repeats himself.

'It's a good book mum this is.'

He fans through the pages of Andrew Marr's The History of the World.

'What do you want to watch on tele?'

He crawls across the carpet on his knees, clutching the open volume like a prayer book, or Paddy's Bible in one hand, fumbles to open the little flap at the bottom of the screen, struggles to manually change the channel. He's obviously sold its remote control.

'Do you want to see a bit of the news?'

'Yeah ok, if you do. I'm just going to get another drink.' For she needs more than tea. Is glad she's brought plenty of wine.

He stands and fans through the pages again; channel flicking and magazine flipping just like she wishes she was doing.

'It's a good book mum this is. The news, do you want? It's a good book mum this is. I'm on page 63. Do you want to watch Coronation Street? I'm on page 63. It's a good book mum this is.'

And so they sit, or rather she sits, sipping wine from a black mug which she's rinsed, in the darkening kitchen, in surprisingly hot water, running her fingers around its inside to feel for any bits of cup-a-soup. She sits and he paces, and talks and goes outside to smoke. She thinks about saying 'Take the rubbish out' but she can't be bothered; says instead with no question mark, 'It is just normal fags you're smoking, isn't it?' And of course he says, 'Yes.'

'Good,' she whispers, shaking her head; tears almost spilling. She sips her wine, and tries to relax, tries to concentrate on the television soap opera which she used to think was far-fetched. Now she lives in her own soap opera.

It's hard; it's so hard to relax. And she wants to be at home with Tim on her knee with a proper glass of wine at her side, a jacket potato doing nicely, smelling nicely in the oven. And she has to remind herself that if she was at home she'd be forever checking her phone for missed calls, she knows she'd be stressed and distracted and miserable.

After a few minutes he comes back in.

'Can I borrow your phone, please, mum? Just for a sec?'

She doesn't reply, just sighs, knowing that if she asks why, he will only lie to her. And, as he reaches across to the arm of the lone armchair for her phone, she catches the smell of him; a smell of recent sweat; of animal fear gone stale. He texts rapidly for a few seconds and then immediately deletes the message.

'Why don't you have a nice bath whilst I'm here?' she asks him.

'I can't be bothered mum. It's too cold.' And he shudders at the very thought.

'I'll run it for you.'

And as she re-fills her mug with wine, she says, 'We could light that scented candle I got you for Christmas,' and nods her head in the direction of the imitation Yankee candle, still in its plastic box, sitting on the dusty mantlepiece next to a photograph of the naughty giant's boot rock at Praia da Rocha, a dish of faded pot pourri, a chewed pen.

'We could play that nice playlist I've got on my tablet.'

And she retrieved it from where she'd hidden it from temptation's way beneath the bed cover.

'OK. I'm just going out for a last smoke, then.'

'All right then. I'll just nip out and have a last fag,' he says, suddenly sounding a little more normal, and she calls to him, head down as she rummages. 'Take some of that rubbish out with you,' but he doesn't reply.

She replenishes her mug, finds a box of matches and collects together a couple of the less unpleasant towels, some hotel-feebie slippers brought back with the redundant dreamcatcher.

She lights the candle, balances her tablet on top of the toilet cistern, and finds the playlist which she'd devised that night about a year ago; when she'd truly thought her distorted, swollen face would never, ever recover from all the tears that she'd cried. That night when she'd thought she didn't care if it didn't. And she'd planned to sit in the bath with a bottle of red Radox bubblebath to disguise the blood, and a sharp pair of kitchen scissors.

She opens the window a tiny fraction. Catching the tender wound on the inside of her arm, she remembers his anger when she'd opened it fully last time she was here. She'd been cleaning up the mess; the splashes of blood, the vomit, even what looked like shit, whilst he'd slept fitfully on the sofa. The bathroom had all steamed up in a bleach-smelling fug and she'd opened the window to let out the the steam and let in some fresh air. Ben had woken up and he had been cross with her, had come storming in, taking her by surprise, talking with a rollie clamped in the corner of his mouth as he slammed the window tight shut with a horrid bang that made her wince, and then he'd held her arm and he'd said, 'Don't mum, please don't open the window, don't open the window because then people know that I'm in, and they'll come bothering me.' He'd held her arm tight, squeezing it tighter still on each hissing 'don't'. Then he'd gone outside for a smoke.

And she'd cried in that newly-cleaned bathroom, she'd cried briefly, hurriedly, quickly sobbing away the immediate, the urgent onslaught, the worst of he shocked, noisy tears, knowing there'd be many more to come later when she lay in bed that night.

She had hiccupped and tried to roughly wipe her eyes and nose on the nasty, smelly towel she'd used to try to buff up the taps, even the chain of the bath plug. And then when she was finished, she'd scrubbed at the centre of the mirror, round and round, she'd wiped the mirror with the corner of the rough towel, until, through a hole in the mist, her frightened and miserable and guilty face stared, accusing, back at her. Her sad eyes in the mirror had slowly softened, reminding her that he hadn't meant to hurt her, although she had seen that her arm was bright pink and swollen where he'd twisted her wrist.

But that was nothing compared to the constant pain in her heart.

And, above the opening bars of *'Somewhere Only We Know'*, and above the belching and hissing of the air-blocked hot water tap as it belched into some form of air-blocked life, she thought she heard him say 'All right mate?' as he went out of the front door of the flats.

And, as she sipped more wine, and as the hot, hot water began to trickle, slowly oh, so slowly, not more than a drip at a time, into the burgundy bath, she remembered the baths she'd run for herself when she was expecting Baby Ben.

She'd lie in the hot bubbles, stroking her neat pregnancy bump, loving the baby beneath, feeling and watching his elbows and knees beneath her tightening skin; stretched like the too-full bin bags. Had he been reaching for the stars even way back then? Or reaching for annuver yast one? How she'd loved those alternate Friday nights when Dan and Maria would have Fred and Will, and she could have a break. She'd lie down in a deep, hot bubble bath. She'd lie down. And she'd cry. She'd cry and sob and wail into the water.

And when he was new born, long and slim, all knees and elbows, she'd bath him and on her knees as if at prayer, she'd sob again 'We've been through so much together. I love you so much.'

And the truth was they were still going through so much together. And the truth was it wasn't getting any easier.

She bit at the shrink wrap on the bathbomb she'd brought with her, tore it away with her teeth, as Ben did with his syringe wraps. She crumbled it; pink ashes on the bottom of the bath, and it started to dissolve slightly in the hot dribbling water. It reminded her of Calpol. How she wished a couple of teaspoons of gloopy Calpol would help Ben, as it used to help with little Kenny's constant ear infections.

She put a bleach stained tea towel on the linoleum, to serve as a bath mat, the large beige towel on the lukewarm radiator.

'Oh, mum,' he came into her and she turned off the taps, not wanting to run the water cold.

She stood and turned to him, ready to chivvy him along. Swaying slightly, he bent his head and rested it upon her chest.

'Oh, mum,' he said again. 'I am getting there, aren't I mum?'

Her eyes suddenly filled with tears, and so that he wouldn't see them, she played for time, placed a hand upon his hair, felt she could almost feel the pulsing of his temple.

'Please tell me you think I'm getting there?' Heavy, lank hair; she touches his forehead with a soap and watery hand.

And, as she sometimes, well, more than sometimes, does, she wishes she'd bothered to have him christened, bothered to have him baptised. And with a contortion and a rolling together, a folding in of her lips, that prevented her from even telling her best friends everything, and a great guilty sob of a gulp, she knows that 'bothered' is the correct word: for she hadn't bothered, had she? She'd been exhausted, but determined to get back to full-time work six weeks after his birth, running to pick him up from the nursery if her bus was late, and literally picking him up when she saw him, his face all lit up and smiling, swirling him round as he clutched his book bag and his painting and his daily activity sheet. And when they saw them, the pissed off nursery nurses, no longer looked quite so pissed off that they'd had to wait after 6 o'clock, because Ben was liked, was always liked, even by the Screws in prison.

Surely, she should have bothered to have him baptised? But, she'd known that nobody else would bother to arrange the occasion. Dan, and her own parents were agnostic, she and her friends of no particular opinion. And yet if she had have suggested it, had have rung the local reverend to make a date, had have attended a couple of services which she would probably have quite enjoyed, how easy would that have been?

But then again, like the breast-feeding, or lack of it, Fred, Will and Kenny hadn't been baptised, and they had all turned out 'all right'; meaning by default that Ben had turned out 'all wrong'. 'Turning out all right' made them sound like baked apple pies, but they did all had girlfriends and wives, and jobs; why, Kenny was a junior school teacher, no less! And of course Will and Shelley had little Jake, *the apple of her eye*; her second chance.

But, when she was feeling lazy she would convince herself that having Ben christened would, have been hypocritical, an end justifying the means, it would have been hypocritical because she knew she wouldn't have continued to regularly attend church, and, well, let's face it, she had never been baptised herself. Then, again. Perhaps that was the reason why things were as they were? Would things be different as regards Ben, had her parents have had *her* christened?

She recalled that weird occasion with Susan and Asher, which they both talked about from time to time. She considered mentioning it now; decided against it.

He lit the candle on the edge of the bath with his lighter and then with a shaky hand from that same flame, the nub end of a rollie, then laid his head against her chest again as they both stood. She found herself swaying slightly as though rocking him; trying to comfort him by gently rocking him.

'I think so,' she said. 'I think you're getting there,' she lied, 'don't you, Ben?'

Then she sniffed, and she felt his brow lift and furrow beneath her hand,

'Are you all right?' he asked her chest; her breast.

The breast she'd never tried to feed him from; the breast she'd never offered; the breast she'd never ever even proffered. Another reason to feel guilty, perhaps, although she'd not been able to breast-feed the twins, and had chosen not to breast-feed Kenny, and, here she goes again, they'd all turned out 'all right'…

'Yeah, I'm fine, she sniffed again, trying to sound more upbeat, 'A steamy atmosphere always loosens up my sinuses… Probably does me good… Anyway. You get undressed and have a good long soak. I'll go and sort you out some clean nightwear.'

But he still didn't move. Spoke to her chest, her breast again. Slurry, as though on the cusp of sleep.

'Will you undress me, mum?'

She opened her mouth to say something. She wasn't sure what; and she wiped her eyes, fiercely with both hands.

'Sit on the edge of the bath, then. I can't reach you way up there!'

She tried to laugh at his height, although no means tall by today's standards, he was a good five inches taller than her, and when she thought about him as that toddler, asking, and being handed, 'annuver yast' crisp, he seemed impossibly tall.

He sat slowly, awkwardly. Still swaying slightly. Gnawed, grubby fingers dangling between his legs, head bent low.

'Arms up!' she said, trying to sound cheery.

And he raised his arms, 'Reach for the Stars!' he sang, trying, but failing to punch with a fist.

As he raised his arms, slowly, limply, revealing large dark patches of sweat beneath arms so thin that the sleeves of his grey hoodie dropped to pool about his elbows as he did so.

'Yes,' she says, her voice cracking, 'let's reach for the stars!'

A grown man, Ben raises his arms not to enthusiastically answer a question at school, not to reach for the stars, but for his mother to remove his top; hands up, submitting, admitting defeat in fighting his addiction.

She pulls him free of the stained dark blue hoodie, flinching at the marks on his arms, one was recent; raised, a heroin blister, like a deflated strawberry- coloured party balloon; a blood and semen filled used condom.

Hands up
High
Punching the sky
Eyes bright
Trainers pristine-white
Hair gel-spiked
He'd sang and
He'd danced to
'Reach for the Stars'
All to live for …
Now his stained, scorched
fingers are
Clasped by his mum
and
Defeated by his habit
she lifts his
stick-thin arms
Needlessly needle-marked
and helps him to
Undress
for a bath
which they both know
will not get him
Clean…

Chapter Fifteen

Our nameless narrator often feels as though she has no mouth, no words to say, or rather, no words that will be listened to; no words that will be heeded, acted upon. That why she's nameless; that why she's breathing out useless, empty speech bubbles. That's why, when she's anxious, her mind works overtime, because she's always had to bottle things up.

Bottle things up. Bottles of wine. Never bottled up. Always well and truly emptied.

She gulps down some wine; an attempt to fill those voids.

She looks again through that personal kaleidoscope of shimmery tears; wonders if this is how the world looks to him when he's on a high; wonders if he's ever really on a high. She doesn't think so. He's merely trying to equal, or rather, to 'better' that first high. He rarely seems genuinely happy.

Everything is steamy, yet shiny and glimmering, even the music seems distorted as the candle flickers. The steamed up mirror on the wall reveals an impressionist portrait of herself, left behind after a hurried wiping of the steam a couple of weeks ago.

The squiggles where she'd wiped the mirror showed up once again in today's steam, revealing an accurate caricature of the face she now has. No longer pretty. No longer looking younger than her years, her mouth so often these past years down-turned, its lips rolled in, has sprouted long deep lines on either side, as though etched into her skin, remaining even when she forces, or is forced to, smile. There is the beginning of a vertical line across the bridge of her nose, her eyelids are becoming floppy, hooded, her worried eyes, haunted. On a bad day she doesn't look very much younger than her mother. Considering all the stress she's under, she wonders, will she last *that* long?

Then, she realises, she *has* to. She has to last that long for Ben's sake. What would happen to Ben if he no longer had her support? Or, or, and a huge breath catches at the back of her throat, would he be better off without her? Would he have been better off without her from the word go?

Would he have, and her heart starts to break, would he have been better off, the thought hurt her so deeply that she could barely bear to think it, for again she'd been hypocritical because when he sometimes said so matter of factly, or sometimes cried that he'd never asked to be born, that he wished he'd never been born, she'd always, automatically, said things like, 'Don't be silly, please don't say that … 'And he'd normally, normally but not always, say 'oh mum. Don't worry mum. I'd never … you know, I'd never… I'd never hurt you like that.'

And she wanted to believe him, God, she wanted so much to believe him, but was that wanting, that willing herself to believe him, was that a cruelty to him? Would he be better off… she forced herself to form the word in her mind as she looked over his sweet head at the miserable, ugly caricature in the steamed up mirror, would he be better off Dead?

Dead.

There, she'd formed the word. She went a stage further, raised her own head as though reaching for the very stars herself, clicked her tongue at the back of her top teeth ready to give the word a voice. Would he be better off Dead? For then he would be at peace, wouldn't he? For then he would not have to keep up the pretence, because a guilty pretence it was, wasn't it, or otherwise, of resisting that last one, of resisting another last one, and then, inevitably, yet another last one, another last one.

And she considered, hating herself for daring to think like this, that if he *was* Dead, and therefore at peace, she would surely, eventually be by default, at peace herself?

'Get a grip.' Dan's words from all those years ago echoed in her ears.

'Skin a rabbit!' she trills as his G Star Raw counterfeit T- shirt left his body.

'Skin a *what*?!' Ben asked, raising his head, a flicker of amusement in his far- off voice, a sudden startling twinkle lighting just like his Granddad Frederick's lit up his dull, drugged eyes, a slight phlegmy laugh. She is grateful for his reaction.

'A rabbit. Skin a rabbit. It's what my grandma used to say.'

He was skinny as a wild rabbit, his eyes though not as they were sometimes, wide and anxious; a rabbit transfixed in a car's headlights, but glazed, almost goat like, distorted; their pupils tiny, seemingly unseeing, as though looking beyond and through objects rather than at them.

Although the fair hairs on his arms were raised in goose-bumps, a smell of fresh warm, wet, sweat rose from his body, far nicer than that earlier animal smell of fear.

And then there was the scar tissue that looked like her own post-four children's stretch marks, where she knew he'd pared away layers of skin with her vegetable peeler.

'Where's the peeler?' she remembered saying, 'I was going to peel some of those cooking apples from Grandma's garden; make a nice crumble.'

She'd struggled instead with a knife, and had found the peeler weeks later in his bedside cabinet.

Ben's ribs protruded so much they seemed like a separate entity, something that could be removed, replaced with a different part; like those figurines he used play with, 'Transformers' were they called?

And there was, had he got another tattoo? She'd caught a glimpse of something blue on the inside of his elbow but no, she didn't think it was a tattoo at second glance, it must be dye from the dark blue hoodie; dye mixed and diluted by sweat. That would irritate the eczema he was prone to there. But it should come off in the bath. She must remember to tell him to put some of that hydrocortisone cream on.

She began to say, 'You've lost a lot of weight...' but he was still chuckling.

'Skin a rabbit. 'Skin'. See, mum, you've made me want another smoke now.' And, although she knew he was partly joking, her heart plummeted; she'd said the wrong thing.

Again.

'Just a normal rollie then,' she said, pulling off the lace-free pumps, their soles now just plastic grids; their rubber eaten up by anxious pavement- pacing.

Sometimes, in between benefit payments he told her, he picked up other people's nub ends from the ground, put them in his pocket, opened them up onto to the melamine flowered tea tray and gently re housed the second-hand tobacco, and, should he get lucky, any other stuff, into his own rizla papers.

The socks she recognised as a pair of Jack's old-man socks, Jack had more than enough socks. She never thought that Ben might actually wear them; the thick grey cable knit socks with the burgundy emblem. There was a hole in one heel and beneath that a pair of trainer liners. He'd worn them to compensate for his shoes' missing soles. And, swallowing her wine, she begins a loop of painful thoughts once again;

his soles were missing; was his soul missing?

Should she have had had him baptised?

His toenails were long, grubby, yellowed. He stuck out one leg, off came one trackie-bottom; stuck out the other leg, off came the other trackie-bottom. Her heart broke when she saw 'Lucky Pants' emblazoned on the elasticated waistband of his cheap boxers.

'Stand up,' she said and he stood, balancing on her arm, which was still a little pink from when he'd twisted her wrist the other week. Sometimes at night it helped her sleep to pinch and pull at the wound; to make it hurt all over again.

He removed his pants, and she tried not to look at the stains. He stood scratching at his pubic hair and the skin beneath looked sore. Itchy, like that the skin would be underneath that patch of dark blue dye on the inside of his arm.

His penis hung flaccid. She didn't think he had sex these days, certainly, not with a girl, or at least he'd never mentioned a girl. There had been a full packet of Durex in his kitchen drawer a few weeks ago and they remained there still, amongst the forgotten washcloth and Jay cloths, the useless tin opener, a nearly empty box of Swan Vestas, the wrong type of batteries and of kitchen light bulbs, the warrantees and guarantees and offers of increased cover that there is no way on this earth he would ever need, all for goods he'd long since sold or swapped for drugs.

'Right.' she said, 'In you get.'

The bath was nicely deep; the water very warm.

As he turned to climb in, she saw a few spots on his bottom; a bruise, quite a big one, and wondered how he'd done that.

'It'd better be good and hot, mum'

And he climbed in tentatively,

And then he sank into the strawberry-smelling deep, hot, bubbly water, with a loud 'Ahh!'

And his white body turned slowly pink, almost red, and his novice tattoos turned a darker blue as the water touched his naked flesh.

'Oh, that's so nice,' he said, voice deeper than usual.

'It looks nice.'

The foamy water clung to him, wrapped itself around his shoulders, like a shawl. Like some kind person standing behind him; his rock, supporting him; his or her arms around him. She had used to feel like that when she was relaxing in the bath, or when she'd taken a mug of tea back up to bed at weekends. And then she would have sighed out a grateful 'Ahh!' of breath, because sometimes, sometimes things didn't seem quite so bad. 'That's so nice,' she'd tell Tim, or Jack if he was there, and not at work, and then she'd wriggle her bottom back further and lean her shoulders well and truly back into the propped-up pillows.

Of course, that was when she was still able to relax, she pondered, swooshing the hot water around with her fingertips, swooshing the wine around her mouth with her tongue; she'd only brought two bottles with her; she had to make it last. She couldn't be bothered to walk down to the Co-op for more.

'I might have a bath after you.'

And she pictured him as a new born baby, covered in pink and white vernix, his skin a shocking blue.

And she pictured him as a toddler, always eager to please, always smiley, squirmy and lively.

Then as a little boy sitting in his Matey bubble bath, playing with the container of the little sailor boy who reminded her of him, froth all over his head, blowing bubbles from his fingers.

> *There was a little boy called Ben-Ben-Ben-agen*
> *He grew whiskers on his chin-agen'*

And then suddenly; shockingly, as an adult, dead and blue in a burgundy silk lined coffin. A coffin like Dan's empty guitar case all those years ago.

'Will you wash my hair for me, mum? Make me all nice and clean.'

God, how she wished, how she wished more than anything that she could make him clean; permanently clean. Clean. Cleaned and freed from drugs,

'Make me all nice and clean, again.'

And he looked up at her, and as she looked down at him, 'Please, Mum,' and she reached across to the edge of the bath, knelt to pick up the chipped Pyrex jug, remembering how, years ago, she had filled it with Jack's flowers.

And he still bought her flowers. Jack was a good, kind man, and she was neglecting him.

She took a deliberate deep breath, as though it was herself anticipating an imminent pouring of water upon her head.

'Right. Are you ready?'

'Are you ready for the waterfall?' she tried to tease him with little drips and drops as she had when he was little; but these drips and drops were mixed with her tears.

How, oh how very much she wished he was young again, eating his salt and vinegar crisps; she would no way allow him to have annuver yast one if she had her time again. She'd been too lenient, surely she had, too wrapped up in her own world; her marital problems, her other children.

'I'm ready.'

He dunked the half- fag end into the water where it hissed its protest before its life was cut short, then bled dark brown on the side of the bath.

Ben lowered his head.

'Here it comes. Here comes the waterfall.'

She poured the water several times, darkening and flattening the hair which he never touched; never shook his head as he had always done when swimming. He stayed still as still, as though deep in thought; or deep in prayer. Perhaps this would serve as the ultimate of baptisms? A true cleansing of body and soul.

Then she said,

'This will be the yast waterfall. We've got to shampoo yet, and rinse all that off, remember. And I'd like you to save some hot water for me.'

The water pouring from his hair still looked slightly grubby.

And so she asked,

'And annuver? Anuvver last one?' she asked him.

'Another,' he nods, choosing to either ignore the irony, or perhaps he hadn't heard properly through the water; he was leaning forward now, holding his feet.

'Are you ready for the very yast waterfall?' she teased again, louder this time, pouring little drops, her arm now aching to release the entire jug.

'Ahh that feels so good, mum.' He sighed, remaining still, head lowered, then clutched his feet.

'Can I have just annuver yast one, mum, just onve more annuver yast one before we've done? Before we've Fin.'

Then she squeezed plenty of shampoo into her hand, rubbed it between her palms and then firmly massaged it into his thick hair, a fresh lemon fragrance overtaking the vanilla of the candle, the strawberry of the bathbomb, the sherbet of his subutex breath, the sweat from his clothes, the stench of the half-rollie closeby.

Her fingertips reached right down through his thick hair to his scalp. She felt him relax. A little. Smile. She screws up her mouth, her eyes, her brow, wished she could reach deep down into his brain, wished she could pull out whatever it was that had made him like he was. She imagines strands of disgusting, putrid, burning slime. She'd pull and she'd pull and she'd pull as though her life depended upon it, for *his* life surely did; wished she could perform trepanning; creating holes to release the demons within him.

Tears came again to her eyes, and her nose began to run, an itchy tickle she longed to stop. She lent down to her hands which were immersed in his wet lathered hair, tried to wipe her nose, then her eyes with the back of her wrist.

Ouch! A sudden sting from a stray fleck of the shampoo she'd not been keen on. At least shampoo, she thinks fumbling for the towel beneath her knees, turning to face the cruel caricature in the mirror, as the pain increases, at least shampoo, unlike the burning tears permanently on call, permanently at the ready and waiting for the vaguest invitation, at least the tears from shampoo could be quickly rubbed and rinsed away.

'Ow! Shampoo in my eye!' she mutters and stands, fumbling for the towel beneath her.

'Ahh, mum,' Ben slurs, sympathetic, 'Rinse out. Plenty water.'

She turns to wipe free the new steam on the mirror, then rubs at her hot stinging eye with a wet frayed corner of the towel, aware of a contented exhale, 'Ahh!' as she hears him slowly lower himself into the bubbles.

The sting is gone in a couple of seconds, and she grimaces at her reflection as she often does when she visits the loo here, remembering that feeling she'd had a while ago when she was cleaning a mirror and something bad was happening behind her. What had that all been about? Sometimes she was convinced she was going mad.

She grimaces at the reflection superimposed upon the caricature. Her right eye swollen, bloodshot. The pupil of her left eye sits rather too close to its inner corner, and she knows that she has drunk nearly one bottle of wine on an empty stomach, is slowly becoming drunk.

But, she promises herself, after a nice hot bath. she will warm through a tin of macaroni cheese in his latest microwave, eat it straight from his melted plastic bowl, dip in a couple of slices of the bread she's brought with her, dipped in, no toast, his toaster has gone leaving a pile of stale crumbs which she will wipe up in the morning and no butter for his little fridge is also missing.

Yes, she will definitely have a nice hot bath.

She turns from the mirror to tell him this, then realises she'd not heard him come up for air.

'Ben?'

Apart from his feet and his knees, his entire skinny body was submerged beneath the bubbles; his face was submerged beneath the bubbles.

'Ben?'

He will raise his head in a second.

She knows he will.

She remembers all the times when, exhausted, she'd made herself take him on the bus for swimming lessons on Saturday mornings and during free time he'd jump into the pool, and his thin body would plummet and her heart would plummet along with him as he sank into the depths of the turquoise, chlorinated water, leaving just a froth of tiny bubbles.

Oh, how her heart would plummet, and the echoing laughter, the shrieks, and the splashes, the discordant shrills of the grumpy lifeguard's whistle would fade to nothing as her heart descended and drowned ready to join him in the depths. And then on the cusp of his mother's scream, maybe sensing her distress, although of this she never told, why had she never? Why had she never told him that she worried desperately when he did not come up straight away for air? That she was desperately worried that he might have drowned. That she loved him that much.

And, just as her lungs might have surely burst from holding her own breath, his head would shatter the blue surface, his hair darkened, flattened, he'd shake free his hair which he'd worn long and straightened with her straighteners then, and, like a wet dog, he would scatter drops of liquid diamond as he'd stared about him through eyelashes clumped into dark points like holly leaves; momentarily disoriented. Then he'd catch her eye, just like had had that horrible day in Court, and, oh, the relief as he would wave and smile at her, then turn and swim his easy front crawl to join his mates.

Chapter Sixteen

'Ben?'

A second on, and his face remains hidden beneath the creamy-pink bubbles; the ends of his long feet are there to be seen, resting, pointing slightly outwards, as Jack's always do in bed, like a mermaid's tail, either side of the chain of the bath plug. His blue-white knees are bent, raised, safe above the water.

Blue-white. Blue. Little boy blue. Baby blue.

'Ben!'

'Ben!'

She grabbed the point of his chin; tried to lift it.

A gurgle; a guttural gurgle and then his chin dipped back down. Why the fuck had she run the water so deep? She grabs his chin again. So slippery.

Chin up! Chin up! That's what people told her. Keep your chin up!

Her mind is too full; her mind is bursting, her chest is bursting, her heart is bursting. She holding up his chin. And she's feeling; scrabbling with her free hand for the towel which had sat in a heap beside her, beside herself.

Beside myself! I'm beside myself! Beside myself with fear!

Oh no! the towel was out of reach, on the floor under the mirror. 'Ben! Ben,' she whisper-shouts all the time; stretches with all her might for the towel, which she manages to shove beneath his chin.

Then she catches hold of the chain of the bath plug, determined to release the bathwater. She tugs until the chain pulls free, but it hangs; a useless rosary between her fingers. She scrabbles between his feet to pull out the plug. But the plug remains stuck tight. And she knows she is wasting time.

Scream-whispering his name over and over, she grabs the Pyrex jug, scoops it into the bathwater, pours it into the sink, bailing out.

Bailing out… bailing out… how many times had she bailed him out?

But again, she was wasting precious time, having to stretch up to the sink.

Always wasting time. She'd always wasted time, like when she listened to that stupid man from SPODA. Time waster. Waste of space.

So she began to pour each jug of bailed-out water onto the discarded clothes on the floor. She must be careful not to slip on the water.

She must be careful not to slip up. Then there'd be two of them in a mess. But she had slipped up. She had slipped up, already hadn't she? She had slipped up a long long time ago.

Her mind was incredibly alert. And yet... why the fuck hadn't she brought her mobile phone in with her? Terrified, shouting loudly now to rouse him, she struggled again for a few endless, useless seconds, she fumbled with desperate hands, between his heels for the fast-tight plug. But all she managed to do was to dislodge the towel beneath his chin.

He gurgled. He gurgled. Not a nice little blue baby gurgle. An old man gurgle. A dying man's gurgle.

She squashed his clothes together, shoved what she could beneath his chin, used the trackie bottoms to try and grip beneath his arms, to lift him up. But although he was thin, he weighed heavy; a dead weight.

He weighed heavy on her mind. Had always weighed heavy on her mind. A dead weight.

Dead. Dead.

And he slid back down, his head now flopping to one side.

'Stay awake!' she screamed.

'I'm going for my phone.'

A gurgle. A gurgle that was more alert?

'I'm going for my phone!' and she pictured herself grabbing it off the arm of the only chair in the flat, she could already feel its worn butterfly cover in her hand, yes, she would grab the phone, she would open it, she would swipe it, she would press the keyboard, for 999 was not on her contact list. Thank goodness she'd charged it fully this morning, a lifetime ago. She pictured herself, she heard herself, surprisingly clearly, requesting an ambulance, clearly providing her son's date of birth, his address, even his postcode.

But the arm of the chair was empty. Both arms of the lone chair were empty. Empty with nobody to hug. She lifted her coat off the back of the chair, shook it; pushed her hands into its pockets. One of those matted bits of scrappy tissue that were everywhere. Nothing. She threw it and her scarf onto the sofa. She pushed her fingers beneath the chair's hard worn cushions, felt dust and grit and dirt with rubbery fingers and Ouch! a tiny prick of pain at the side of her thumb nail reminded her of the splash of shampoo in her eye, something sharp, a half open upholstery staple.

She dropped to her knees, peering and swooshing her hands about beneath the chair as she had done when running the bathwater. Bastard bathwater. Why had she even mentioned a bath? Why had she not been content for him to stay smelly and dirty? Because, if not clean, at least smelly and dirty he was alive!

Why had she stared at her disgusting drunken face for so long, fretting about a tiny shampoo sting whilst her son ...

Desperate to feel her phone, which must have fallen from the chair, peering dizzily into dusk for her precious butterfly phone... Nothing. Just a glistening piece of cellophane in the distance, the torn off top of one of the individually wrapped herbal tea bags she always brought with her.

She grabbed the smaller of the chair's cushions, ran back to the bath, lifted his chin, shoved the cushion beneath,

Chin Up. Chin Up. Keep your fucking chin up. Chin Up...

A gurgle of greeting, Even a slight smile,

thank fuck thank fuck thank fuck.

'Where the fuck's my phone...?'

'Soo-reee, Mum.' he whispered.

'What do you mean. Sorry?' she yelled. 'What the fuck does Sorry mean?' she yelled. 'I need my phone! I need to ring a fucking ambulance for you.'

And suddenly, as she felt another little prickle of soreness at the edge of her thumb nail, she knew. She knew. She fucking knew why he was saying 'Sorry'. And she fucking knew that the glimmering cellophane beneath the chair was far from the top of an individually-wrapped herbal teabag. And she fucking knew why her phone was missing. And she knew, she knew for the very first time, she knew why some mothers chose to wash their hands of their druggie offspring.

She ran back to the living room to find Ben's phone because surely even if a phone was out of credit, even, perhaps its battery dead.

Dead; dead; dead

Please God, the emergency services could still be contacted. Please God. Please. She grabbed his phone from the ironing board. It was an old push button one with a blank cracked, crazed screen. She couldn't see, she couldn't see properly, her eyes sore from tears and shampoo, from tears and shampoo, and suddenly she remembered when he was little in the bath, she'd run out of baby shampoo and she'd used a little of her own and it had got in his eye and she'd caught him rubbing it and shaking his head, and it was only later, only later when he was tucked up in bed that she noticed one of his beautiful eyes was bloodshot.

She was evil. She fumbled in her little shoulder bag for her reading glasses, why on earth hadn't she kept her phone in there with them and the many times folded ten pound note, at the ready, safe close by her side? She pushed the handset's buttons but its screen refused to give away its secrets. She shoved her reading glasses onto the top of her head.

She thrust the phone to his face. Began to yell, 'How…?' She reached out for his hands to dry them. But his lips now had a vaguely blue tinge and despite the damp atmosphere they were dry, and his breathing was noisy.

And at the back of her mind, and within her buzzing ears, she heard some people; some people she'd thought of a few years ago as friends, say that he was Waste of Space, Leave him Be, to Let him Die, tell her He'd caused her Nowt but Grief. She'd be Better Off Without Him.

She propped his chin up further to maintain his airway. Then she struggled, as she had the last time, standing on tip toe to open his bathroom window. Cool dusk air floated into the room; the steamy fug floated out to join the cool dusk air, and she did not care if people knew he was in.

He needed help and fast and she would die to save his life. She would do anything. Two lads wearing trackies and hoodies stood on the steps to the small neighbouring flats opposite. Both were hunched over their phones stroking, scrolling them one was about to light a cigarette, the other had his free hand in his pocket.

Their phones? Through her swollen eyes she could see that the youth with the rollie was holding her phone, her phone, its diamante lilac and blue butterflies glistened next to the faglighter's flame, shimmering and fluttering in the dusk, trying to escape their worn, cracked case.

'Oy!'

'Oy!' she yelled. One of the youths raised his head, then looked back down at her phone.

'Oy!' she yelled again.

The rollie lad took a deep drag, raised his head, looked her straight into her swollen eyes.

'I need you to dial 999 for me. Please. It's Ben!'

'Right on it, love" he yelled back, dialling even as he spoke, and tears filled her eyes as she ran back into the bathroom.

'So soo-ree mum,' he slurred, pupils rolling up, almost disappearing beneath his eyelids. His lips were darkening, his face a baby-blue, a thin stream of vomit like spent semen, or like formula milk,

Why had she fed him SMA formula milk instead of her own breast milk?

and a sticky froth like the Matey bubble bath he'd loved as a child clung to the corners of his lips. He shifted slightly, turning his face as though to kiss her, and then there was a loud and fierce sucking sound, a slurping sound as his feet freed the bath plug, permitting its water a sudden, rapid release.

'I love you, mum.'

And then, a horrendous, deep, hoarse, a wailing, a rattling from his very core.

A solid turd topped with mucussy blood floated in the escaping water then dark diarrhoea; urine.

She moved her hair behind her ear and she leaned very close to her son's face, and, holding her own breath, she listened for a full ten seconds. She listened for sounds of breathing. She prayed that she'd feel his warm breath on her cheek. She listened and she prayed, strangely calm, she listened and she prayed for signs of life.

There were none.

'Please come back, Ben.' she whispered, 'Please come back.'

And so she knelt upon the floor and she leaned forward as if at payer, and she placed one hand on top of the other and she interlocked her fingers, seeing the swelling at the base of her little finger where his syringe had stabbed her in the dusty darkness, seeing the bruise on her wrist which she'd blamed on a heavy shopping bag, when Jack had questioned her about it.

And she discovered the place in the centre of his chest where there was a shiny scar from self-harming with her vegetable peeler, beneath which she knew his heart was floundering dangerously.

And there she pushed down hard; she pushed down hard and fast; she pushed down hard and fast thirty times.

And after thirty times, she tossed back her hair and she took the point of his chin between her thumb and her index finger, and she tilted it gently back to open his airway, and she pinched shut his nose with the thumb and index finger of her other hand, and as she did so, she tossed back her hair, aware of the ponytail band upon her wrist but not wanting to waste the single two seconds it would take to tie it back out of her way.

And she lowered her lips, which if she had have looked in that steamed-up mirror, would have been colourless with shock, she lowered her colourless lips to his blue lips, and she stretched her mouth to form a seal around his mouth, and she blew into his lungs, for a full ten seconds; a long slow breath. And, as she did so, she saw from the corner of her eye, that, as she filled his lungs for him, his chest was rising from his still, pale blue body. His chest rose as she breathed for him.

A desperate Mother breathing for her dying Son.

She lifted her head, tilted his chin, pinched his nose, and slowly and firmly breathed for him again. She tasted the taste of the inside of him. She smelled the smell of the inside of him.

And then one hand on top of the other, she again interlocked her fingers and she pushed hard and quickly upon his chest. And she felt a crack as one of his ribs snapped, like a stick of celery. But she carried on, she carried on; the edge of the bath pushing against her arms, the swelling of her little finger spreading dark pink across the base of her hand. She carried on, thirty long hard times and then she tossed back her hair and she tilted back his chin and she pinched his nose and, becoming light headed, she breathed for him, she breathed slowly and deeply for her son, tasting him; sour vomit, tobacco, something sweet, salty crisps.

Salty crisps.

'And annuver'

She breathes on her inhalation, then lowers her head to breathe for him again.

'Annuver.'

And again, she sees his chest rise as she breathes her love, and as she breathes her life into him. She is exhausted. She hopes to God that those lads have got through to the emergency services.

She is exhausted but after a moment, when her arms become so heavy; so pained; so shaky and weak, something kicks in and she seems to get her second wind, a second breath. Annuver yast one. And everything seems heightened. She seems to be watching herself from above. Perhaps she has died. Perhaps they are both dead.

And on the final two of her latest series of thirty chest compressions, she tosses back her hair and she shouts, 'Annuver yast one! Please God. Please God grant him Annuver yast life Please!' and as she bends her head, there is a surprised gasp, and she sees that Ben's chest has risen on its own. His chest has risen without her breath, and she sees the warm pink glow of life itself travel rapidly from his blue feet up and over his entire body; totally replacing the blue.

A scum has formed around him now the water has dispersed, a grubby, creamy scum of shampoo and bath bomb, of faeces, of vomit and urine, of blood and of sweat and of tears.

'You're going to be fine, Ben, the ambulance is on its way.'

She gasps and hiccups through sobs as supporting his head, she turns him onto his side, into the recovery position, so that his airway remains open, so that if he is sick the vomit will not choke him.

Then she runs into the bedroom to grab the two pillows and the duvet; the one pillow, she flings onto the floor to kneel upon, the other to lean upon; her shaking, rubbery limbs are bruised and aching; the duvet she pushes down the side of the bath to keep his poor, poor body upon its side; to keep his poor, poor body from turning over. He breathes shallowly, quickly in and out, in and out.

Thank you, God, Thank you God. Thank you from the bottom of our hearts; thank you for granting us Annuver yast one.

She needs to keep him warm; she needs to keep him warm until help comes. Where is help? She runs into his living room to get the throw from the sofa. Unusually, he has folded it neatly and it sits in the centre of the two cushions.

Beneath the throw is a piece of lined, folded A4 paper, 'MUM x 'on the front.

She opens it, feeling so sick, her breath too big, too heavy for her lungs, escapes slowly, painfully in tiny whimpers as she reads, Ben's heavy handwriting,

'Dear Mum

Please believe me when I say that I'm so sorry you're having to read this. But also please believe me that I'm of sound mind when I'm writing this (whatever that might mean!!!!) In fact, I have taken nothing as you describe it 'dodgy' for days now! But, being totally serious now, that's the thing, mum, I just know I can't keep it up. I want to get clean so, so very much, for your sake more than anything. I want to make you proud of me, mum. But know, I know beyond an inkling of doubt that that's never going to happen. No matter how hard I try, no matter how long I manage to go without, I will never be free of that craving. I. always want more. I'm so sorry, but I do. I will always want a last one, and then I'll always want another last one. Just like with the crisps when I was a little boy. And I know I can't cope much longer, and I know you can't cope much longer, and honestly, totally and completely and utterly honestly, all I want to do is sleep. Sleep. All I want is for this nightmare to end. All I want is to be at peace. And all I want is to know that you too, are at peace with me.

If you've read this far, I think you've probably guessed by now that I've taken an overdose. I have deliberately, very deliberately, totally deliberately taken a long-planned overdose. and, sorry mum, but I've sold your phone to do so and to prevent you from quickly getting help (because I am a bad, bad person mum. Yes, don't deny it, I am!!!) I am so very sorry mum that you've had to go through all this. Truly I am. You mean the absolute world to me. I wouldn't have lasted half as long as I have without your undying love and support. But please believe me when I say I no longer want that support. I want to die. I am ready and happy (yes, honestly, happy!!!) to die. And I do not want anybody to resuscitate me. You might have even seen 'DNR' on my arm?! …'

Oh My God. Don't do this. Don't do this. Don't do this me! Please don't do this to me.

'…Please. I really don't. I know you'll cry and you'll grieve and I know the guilt will seem unbearable for a while, but believe me, mum, it will only be for a while and it will be the best for all of us, and most of all it will be the best for me. '

She went back to the bathroom, clutching the letter to her breast. She went back into the bathroom where her naked son lay in his makeshift coffin, its side lined with damp blue polyester.

She laid the blanket over him. Stroked his head. His eyes opened.

'You read the letter, mum?' he asked, sounding more normal than he had for a long long time.

'Yes.'

She stroked his head, and then the relief made her face twist, become ugly, and she couldn't stop it, and as she reached for the candle she said,

'and I'm going to fucking burn it. I'm going to fucking burn it because I'VE NEVER FUCKING SEEN IT.'

'Please don't, mum.'

He grabbed her hand, but he was too late; the letter was quickly consumed by flames.

And she saw that the mark on the insides of his elbows that he'd mentioned in his letter was not, after all, dye diluted with sweat from his shirt but dark blue marker. And she saw that, although slightly faded, the solid, tattoo style letters he'd always formed so beautifully clearly read 'D.N.R.'

'Do. Not. Resuscitate.'

And she felt herself slipping off the edge of the world, as she put down the letter and she slid to the pillow on her knees beside him and she wrung her hands, begging and praying.

Begging and Praying. Praying and Begging. What was the difference? What was the difference if you were desperate? And desperate she was…

She wrung her hands and she winced at the pain on her wrist and at the pain spreading from her nail. And she felt hopeless, and she felt helpless and she let her nose and her eyes run and she let her bladder empty onto the wet, wet floor, because no one and nothing could help her. Because nothing mattered. Nothing mattered any more.

'What's up mum?' he slurred.

'What's up?' She looked at her son, then shaking her head, lowered it again.

Whats up? Nothing's up. Everything's down. Down. Down. Down. DOWN.

'Mum. I'll only do it all again.'

The candle and black ashes from the letter toppled into the water with a hiss.

'I'll only do it all again, mum.'

And she knelt in the puddles of bailed-out bathwater, and of tears and urine on the linoleum. She knelt down, head low and hands clasped, she knelt down upon the lino and she shook her head, and the tears flowed and burned, and her urine flowed again, and she choked and all she could say was, 'No,' all she could say was, 'No…'

And then in such a quiet whisper she didn't know for sure that her dry lips were even moving, she didn't know for sure that she was uttering any sound at all, she began her mantra.

'I beg you I beg you I beg you'

And he began his,

'I beg you I beg you I beg you'

A banging at the door;

and still 'I beg you I beg you'

A loud voice.

Thank God, thank God, the ambulance.

***

The door opened.

Thank God, thank God, thank God.

Reassuring sounds of pagers and of rustling, stiff, crisp uniforms smelling of fresh air and hospitals and something else; fried meat? A bacon and ketchup sandwich first thing that Friday morning?

Kindly, urgent and yet hushed voices; men's and women's.

'They're here, everything's going to be fine,' she whispered.

'Aw, mu-um...'

He slurred through swollen blue lips, sticky with a drying, dying? froth of spittle. She leaned forward, as though at prayer, which of course she surely was. She leaned forward in the inch-deep water, wanting to wet his lips, to kiss his temple; to baptise him twenty years too late; wanting to hold him.

But,

'Let's have you out of the way, now, love.'

And so she moved, barely able to stand on ridiculously rubbery, pins-and-needled legs, and she pressed herself against the wall, the back of her head against the mirror which fell to the ground, its blank, steamy glass front landing face-down, surely cracking into thousands of shards, surely pre-empting another seven years' bad luck.

The two paramedics lifted Ben from his coffin bath and onto a stretcher. They attached an oxygen mask, a blood pressure cuff; needles, monitors, clips; they shone lights into his eyes and they covered his naked body, not his face, thank God, with a silver sheet.

They asked her if she was ok; she replied, 'yes,' with a question mark at the end. And then, they asked her questions; his name, date of birth, what had he taken? And through body-wracking shudders, she answered as best she could, wrapping her arms tightly around herself for she felt stone cold, and there was no-one there to hug her.

'On three. 1. 2. 3.' and they raised the stretcher; as pall bearers might lift a coffin at a funeral.

'I'm coming with him,' she told them.

She followed from the bathroom, crunching on the broken mirror, and into the passageway.

But a female police officer stepped in front of her, blocking her way. She placed a firm hand upon her forearm. She wore a hi-vis jacket and a no-nonsense face.

'Not just now,' she said.

'But I want to go with my son!' she cried.

'No,' she said, 'Sorry. Not now. Right now, you need to change out of your wet clothes and come down to the station with me and my colleague.'

Oh my God, oh my God, oh my God.

'But …'

You know your son's in the best possible place.'

And the police officer handed her her overnight bag, had found a dry, grubby towel from somewhere, motioned for her to sit upon the bed where she had laid her coat and shoes.

'But …'

Her shocked thoughts were so muddled, so frantic they sapped her equally shocked limbs' energy and co-ordination and so clumsily and so infuriatingly slowly she removed her skirt and the tights and knickers which were soaked with bathwater and urine. She wanted so much to hurry, for surely if she got this over with then she'd be allowed to see him. But she could not hurry, her fingers felt numb, as though they were lined with the grubby towel; her brain, too.

She dabbed herself with the bleach-and- toothpaste-spottled towel. The towel smelled of Ben, and she wanted to carry it with her, to smell that towel until it smelled of him no more.

'Please… I was saving his life. Please believe me, I was saving his life,' she said as she struggled into leggings.

'I tried to save his life.'

The woman's colleague joined them in the bedroom. She wore latex gloves, and held a sealed, tagged plastic bag containing her son's crappy old mobile phone.

'Why are you doing this?' she asked of nothing and of nobody, as her wet clothes were placed into a similar bag, a plastic tag fastened, labelled and cut to fit.

'You need to bring your immediate belongings with you to the station. Handbag, phone, money, any medication, that sort of thing.'

'I can't bring my phone because my phone's,' her voice began to break but she took a deep breath, finding a flash of irritation from somewhere, 'my phone is fucking lost…' she told them with an edge of irritation.

Yes, our nameless narrator's phone was fucking lost; lost just like her and her son, lost in the system, lost in the fucking stupid system which had let them both down from day one; was to this most awful of awful of fucking days, still letting them down.

'Really? Well, we can talk about that at the station,' said police officer one.

She continued, in a whisper, calmer now, for what would be the point in getting angry, it could only delay things. '…but, everything else is in here,'

She removed the damp strand of hair which had stuck to her dry lips; was it one of his hairs? If so, she'd like to keep it; she made a mental note that she'd deposited it on the top of the rucksack.

Everything I've got is in here.' Then she pointed to, she touched each of her dampened, tiny rucksack's straps, which she still carried like a baby on her body like a mother koala bear. Why had she not allowed him to cling to her like the maternal mammal she had been put on this earth to be? She again touched her lips, then the rucksack's straps; a desperate genuflection; murmured a desperate prayer.

Silence, apart from 7 Club Seven still singing in the bathroom and a vehicle purring outside. Surely not the ambulance? Surely the ambulance should be well on its way to the hospital by now? Surely it should be arriving there round about now, because The Royal wasn't far away. Surely they would let her ring there from the police station. God, she hoped so. But with a start, she realised she couldn't remember hearing its siren.

She shuffled into her shoes and stood; was handed her coat.

The first officer was pulling something from the side pocket of her dark cargo style trousers. A sudden flash of silver, a cold clink of metal. Car keys perhaps?

'I am arresting you on suspicion of attempted manslaughter.' she said.

'What?'

Oh, my God. Oh, my God. Oh, my God.

Her arms were pulled behind her, the insides of her wrists pushed together, and she heard and she felt something tightly turning, squeezing, almost as tightly as her head and her heart and her lungs were being turned and squeezed.

And once again she was slipping off the edge of the world…

'I now need to caution you …

… hyperventilating, tremors wracking her body.

'You do not have to say anything but it may harm your defence if you do not mention when questioned something which you may later rely on in court…'

And the three of them began an awkward, bumping walk down the concrete steps, passing other police officers who were cordoning off the area with red and white cones and ticker tape.

'Anything you do say may be given in evidence…'

And she saw though her dry, desperate eyes, the lad who'd had her phone; the lad she'd implored to ring for help.

'He knows what happened!' she tried to yell, lurching forward and stumbling in an automatic attempt to point, to gesture with fingers were shackled behind her back, inside the handcuffs.

'Be assured, we will be speaking with all of Ben's neighbours later today.'

As she sat shaking in the police car she suddenly thought with such a fission of relief that it almost scalded her, she thought of the suicide note. And she gulped, cleared her throat, opened her mouth …

And then she thought, of course, how stupid stupid stupid. She had burned Ben's suicide note with the candle.

Stupid Stupid Stupid…

***

Although Ben didn't write particularly largely, he did press down hard when he wrote, and the police were able to read what he had written by making a rubbing of his writing. The skeletons of Ben's wishes remained upon the next page of the notebook she had bought him, so that when he pleaded with them that he had, wanted to die and when he pleaded and she pleaded that she had saved his life, they believed them. Even the letters on the underside of his elbow were visible under magnification.

Thank God he'd never heeded her when she'd said, 'Don't press on so hard.' And thank God she'd not been scared to press on hard and deep with her CPR, even though she had snapped one of his ribs.

And so she was free to go. And Ben was hospitalised in a special unit for three months, supposedly a rehabilitation unit, but people told her there were 'drugs everywhere'.

She visited him in that unit just the once, then he was permitted no visitors.

It was a strange, sad time.

Chapter Seventeen

After his spell in rehab, Ben returned to live in a different flat although on the same estate. She still rang him three or four times a week and went to see him every six weeks or so, staying overnight and usually combining it with a trip to see Will, Shelly and Jake.

A community Hub had opened just around the corner from Ben's new flat and Ben had been asked to help run it. It suited him down to the ground; he loved talking to people, and got on well with everybody, particularly the older people. They were running some courses there and he had completed one on Alexander the Great. He'd loved every minute of it and had filled two big notebooks with his heavy handwriting.

By all accounts he was doing much better, although she knew he was still crushing up his daily Subutex and injecting it; and she also knew he was still smoking a lot of weed.

But even though he'd sounded fine and had been quite chatty the last time she'd spoken to him, in fact the last several times; she was determined to do everything she could to keep it that way. She would never let down her guard.

She knew from experience that he would never be free from the temptation of drugs, or from the depression and the anxiety which stalked both of them. She knew that a bender was quite possibly due, and she'd wanted very much the comfort and reassurance of knowing that Ben was all right; not off his head or miserable.

She sought that reassurance all the more so that particular cold Saturday afternoon because she was having two friends round for drinks and a light supper later, whilst Jack went out with Antony She'd love be able to tell them that Ben was fine, to talk about things other than Ben for a change; she wanted to be able to relax and enjoy her evening.

And so, mid-way through making her quiche-with-a-kick she texted him,

'How are you? X'

She was quite pleased with that; short, and to the point, not nagging, not mumsy, and as always with a kiss at the end to let him know that no matter what, she loved him.

She took off her wedding ring, and began to rub the butter into the flour to make pastry.

A couple of moments later, her phone shrilled and vibrated from the familiar confines of her apron pocket, where it always nestled amongst used tissues and reading glasses; a cossetted marsupial in its mother's pouch.

She pulled it out; opened its cover, that modern day prayer book. *Whoops!* She should have wiped her hands; she should have learned from the logs incident; always over-eager to answer her blessed phone lest it was him.

She bent down to the tiled floor, scooped it up, unharmed. Oh good. As she'd hoped, the message was a reply from him. She squinted.

It looked like just the one word. What was it? It looked like 'Fine.'

She felt positively giddy, both with having leaned over suddenly to reach down for the phone, and with the rush, oh, the rush of relief; the rush of pleasure, that had coursed through her veins, giving her a split-second high surely as exhilarating as any drug he'd ever taken.

As the feeling settled warmly in the very centre of her being; only then did she realise just how very anxious she had been; just how anxious she *always* was.

These days she had become used to hiding her emotions; even from herself.

She wiped her hands and put on her reading glasses to see his reply properly, but the lenses steamed up in the chilli-fug of the kitchen and, still clutching her phone by its open case, she opened the window to let the steam out to play with the frosty air, wiped the spectacles with the corner of her apron, and then dabbed at her eyes as they misted.

Yes, she was right, he'd just put 'Fine'; well, 'Fin' to be precise.

Obviously, he'd meant 'Fine'; he'd just missed off the 'e'; it was easily done.

'Fin'

Fin

People missed off letters and digits all the time; he'd have been walking round town with his ear-thing shoved in, that modern-day umbilical cord; he'd not have been concentrating. Why she'd even seen young girls texting as they steered pushchairs! How on earth they managed to do that she could not imagine; if she ever needed to text when she was walking, she had to stop in her tracks, and stand perfectly still, preferably leaning against something.

Blinking fiercely through chilli fumes and emotions, she rinsed and wiped her floury hands and rang him back, thinking that before she'd got through to him, he'd probably have re-sent her the message, complete with the missing 'e' and a kiss.

Even if he sounded irritated with her and was blatantly trying to hurry her off the phone, she had decided that she was determined to talk to him at least for a couple of minutes. In fact, she didn't care if he was irritated. So much the better if he *was* impatient with her, so much better that than those days when he'd been sobbing his heart out or screaming in terror, or didn't even know who she was.

And so she went into the back yard where the reception was usually better, her hair blowing into her mouth and eyes, hunched against the weather, her screen and her fingers slippery with rain. She pressed and scrolled.

But the wind was blowing cold rain straight at her, and she could hear nothing. She went back into the kitchen, cardigan wrapped tightly around her and leant against the worktop. She could still hear nothing. No voice mail message. No ring tone. No engaged tone.

Strange. Of course, her signal might be iffy at the moment, especially with the weather as it was. Or, and more likely, he was changing his battery, or perhaps his phone had died again. He changed his phones all the time. Her Contacts list had at least ten Bens listed. She'd given up asking him why he used so many different phones. She had a good idea why, and didn't want to know. So long as she was able to make contact with him she didn't really care which phone he was speaking from.

Anyway, she must forget about Ben for the time-being, and get on. Her friends would be here soon. She'd not seen them for ages and was looking forward to it. She'd make do with texting him. After all, he'd told her he was fine. What more did she want? She really must try to get a grip, to leave him alone a bit more; after all as people, especially Jack, kept telling her, he was now 'a grown man.' And so she texted,

'Just tried to ring you couldn't get thro. But as always relieved to hear you're fine…'

And then, in a flourish of renewed determination to cut him a bit more slack, a flourish of renewed determination for which she could well and truly have kicked herself for later, she continued the text,

'…Just ring me when you can please. Love always mum xxx'

That message; that stupid message had given him carte-blanche to ignore her; that message had given him an excuse not to ring or text; the perfect excuse not to ring, or to reply to her texts.

Why the fuck had she put, 'Just ring me when you can please'? Why had she then turned back to her blessed pastry-making, humming along to her favourite radio station? Even pouring herself the first of the evening's many glasses of wine? What was wrong with her?

'Just ring me when you can please'

How pathetic was that? For fuck's sake.

Why on earth hadn't she kept her phone on call-back?

Why hadn't she caught the next bus, or rung a taxi, gone to find him? Because she'd have had one of her blessed panic attacks; that's why. Because she was a useless, anxious, nervous wreck.

Well then, why hadn't she paid someone to track him?

Why hadn't she demanded he ring her immediately he got her message?

Why hadn't she bribed him, blackmailed him; anything?

Twenty-four hours later, after a short, exhausted, slightly drunken night's sleep filled with confused dreams about him and all his brothers as children, she reached for her phone.

No message.

No missed call.

Fingers sweaty, greasy with nerves she tried again to call him, and texted all the other contacts on she had for him on her phone. Non-one knew anything.

Then she typed,

'OMG Because I've heard nothing I'm now thinking the worst and you can't blame me, After all, we both know it nearly happened before ... I stupidly, as always, took it that you were fine and had just missed the 'e' off? Surely you didn't mean 'fin', did you? Fin as in 'finished'? 'Fin' as in 'the end.'?

And she immediately scrolled back to his message, opening up its properties, agonising over its implications ...

And later that day she typed on the phone which she clutched tight as tight in her hand.

'OMG ... I still can't reach you and I know it's only been a day but 'Fin'? You were telling me you've reached the end weren't you? Again. And this time... Please put my mind at rest. First and foremost, let me know you are alive. Secondly, where you are. Please. I won't come looking for you if you don't want me to, I promise. I just want to know you're alive. I love you so much.'

'You may even have another new phone by now. I hope you have. But if so, I'm begging whoever is reading this on my son's old phone to please reply to me. I just want to talk to my son. Please just tell me how and where you got this phone. I promise on my son's life that I won't grass on you, won't dob you in no matter what you've done or are doing. I just need to contact my son. It will only take you a minute, please. I am frantic with worry.'

Despite trying every single contact or organisation, including social media, hospitals and the police she heard nothing; received no messages. It was as though he had slid off the end of the world. It was as though he'd finished with her; finished with his life.

It was as if he had never existed in the first place.

✳✳✳

Twelve months later

It was still on her mobile phone, there on the screen, that one word. Should it disappear, any last vestige of hope would disappear too; would vanish into thin air, just as he had done.

Each and every morning, the second after shutting off her alarm clock, ignoring the sleep belatedly beckoning her, she'd prop herself upon her elbow, renewed with a cruel fresh hope, and look to see if there'd been any new message from him.

And then, because there never, ever had been, she'd lie back down, her head slumping into her pillow in the darkness, and with a heavy sigh, she'd blindly scroll back in time to his last text, the thumb of her right-hand knowing just when to cease its rapid swipes, knowing precisely where his final message lay in wait for her to study yet again.

And she'd gaze at the date and the time he'd sent it, wondering if there was any significance. But, there was none. Even so, back in time she'd return again and again, each and every morning…

Sometimes, even now, almost twelve months later, her heart would begin to quicken; to pound in fresh hope; because if the last, she could never bring herself to refer to it as the 'final' text; if the last text was meant to read 'I'm fin', why had there been no kiss at the end? No kiss. He'd always put at least one kiss at the end of his texts, even when he was totally pissed off with her. Surely he'd have sent her one final kiss?

'Why no kiss… surely I deserve a final kiss from you? I know you didn't want me to give you the kiss of life but surely you know that any mother would do the same in my position. So why no kiss? Sometimes I feel so angry with you. So hurt. And then again, no, I shouldn't say such things. I'm pissed off cos I'm pissed. Nothing different there, I know. I'm drinking a lot again. We are more alike than we realise you and me. Yep, pissed as usual. Anyway you know how to contact me; you know where I am. I wish to God I knew where you were! Your loving mum xxx

Nothing.

Why was there no full stop? After all, she pondered, he had bothered to include the apostrophe in 'I'm', and he must have added that apostrophe manually because, all of his phones had been the most basic of basic models, £2 with a £10 top-up; no predictive text facility.

She continued to agonize over the meaning of that message; analysing it this way and that. She thought some more; after all, he knew she liked playing with words, he knew she was sometimes given to writing mainly melancholy little poems. He would surely know she'd be analysing his text.

Or, and a wave of guilt would again wash over her, more likely, he probably didn't care; had probably given up on her, like she deserved.

'I hope to God you've done nothing stupid. You know and I know that you're capable but I'd hoped you'd got through that now. Please. Please, please get in touch. I'm begging you. I will do absolutely anything on this earth to help you. Love you for

all time Mum xxx'

Nothing.

Why no final 'e'? Perhaps it had been missed off because he had been interrupted by something or somebody? Maybe something or someone unimaginably awful?

Perhaps someone had grabbed his phone off him, before he could add the 'e' and the kiss; or the 'x' as a kiss was portrayed, she'd think, the guilt gnawing at her heart, and then she'd be off on a different spiral, because, of course, e and x spelled 'ex'; 'ex' as in previous; 'ex' as in had been-and-gone; as in 'over'; and therefore, in meaning, surely similar, to 'fin'?

For fuck's sake get a grip! She'd tell herself, and then,

'... For fuck sake's Ben get in touch. I'm beside myself with worry. And, I know you'll despise me for my weakness, I know you'll despise me for all of this but, because of all this shit, I'm drunk again. Please just let me know you're ok. I won't contact you if you don't want me to. Just text me. One word. Just one letter so that I know you're alive, an 'e' or a X would be good. Please. Love from mum xxx

Nothing.

'... I've now tried every number I can possibly think of and it's like you've fallen off the edge of the earth. I'm just praying now. I truly don't know what do to. Please, just one text. I promise I won't try and find you if you don't want me to, and I'm sure you don't cos I'm evil. I've realized that now. I should have realized it many years ago. I don't blame you if you never want to set eyes on me again. And you don't have to. You truly don't ever have to set eyes upon me again, ever, ever, ever again. Amen. I know I've been a useless, greedy drunken mother who isn't fit to live. But please just a text to let me know you're alive.'

Nothing.

Nothing. Well of course, of course, Whatever did she expect? And at this point in her circle of torturous thoughts, she would sometimes start to cry. For, of course; it was obvious, the word could not have been 'fine'; not in a million years. Not in a million years could it have been 'fine'. He was not stupid. He'd put 'fin' and that's precisely what he meant.

'Fin'.

Why should she presume he'd occidentally spelt the word wrong? How dare she presume? He was a clever young man. How could she ever have even had the gall, she, the totally useless mother, how could she have ever in a million years have had the gall to for a split second consider, nay even believe, he might actually be 'fine'.

Great God, she did not deserve to exist. She should be made to wear horse-hair sacking and walk upon mile after mile of beds of nails for the rest of her miserable life. God she surely deserved such misery, and more.

'I get it… I get you meant 'Fin' and I appreciate that you were sober and clean enough to share our long ago secret word with me. It means such a lot, but if you are not yet Fin, if you are still alive, whatever state you're in and if you're in too much of a state to even text please ask somebody to do so on your behalf. Please. I really am begging you. I will read and pick up any message I get. I don't care who it's from. xxx

Nothing.

Things will change for the better. I promise. I will pack up work. I will help you. God, I will even get you heroin if that's what it takes to have you in my life for just a while longer. I will even sell my own body for it. That's as low as I've sunk. And I know, God how I know, I should never say such a thing. I have sunk as low as I possibly can. X'

Nothing.

And then the guilt and the heartache would rise again, and she'd think, of course, the reason he'd not sent her a last kiss, had merely typed 'I'm fin' was because he'd have finally realised that, actually, he really, really hated her. Detested her. She didn't deserve a kiss. He'd had time to think and to realise that yes, he should have always hated her; hated her from giving birth to him, that unplanned, skinny blue baby with an AGPAR score lower than both his elder twin brothers; through to nurturing him into the addict he'd become.

And he must now know that this had happened because when just an innocent toddler his dreadful mother had confused him by yet again and again allowing him another last one, annuver yast one, another last fatty salty crisp.

But it never was the last. It never was the last, was it? Because she was too tired, or simply could not be bothered; was too lazy, too self-centred to argue or to reason with him. She'd never defined boundaries; she'd not been consistent; she'd constantly given out mixed messages. She'd palmed him off at nursery, and upon others all the time, My God, she'd even had another baby! It was obvious. Of course, it was no wonder he'd added no kiss. God knows, she didn't deserve a kiss.

'Fin' was his way of telling her, his rubbish mother, that he was finished, that he was about to end his miserable life, that death was an imminent and welcome alternative, and that, by disappearing off the face of the earth, he would ensure she could no longer interfere; that she could not and would not stop him this time. She could and would not give him that kiss of life again. She'd raised him from the dead to face yet more misery. Christ, whatever was wrong with her?

***

Jack had been talking about going on a short holiday abroad, but not too far afield: what about going back to Praia da Rocha on the same week as they always had done before the kids got too grown up and the two of them started to holiday as a couple rather than a family, travelling to the Canaries rather than to Portugal.

A 'holiday'? for fuck's sake?! She didn't deserve a holiday. She was too anxious to enjoy a holiday. Everyone was telling her a holiday would do her 'good'. But, as she tried to explain to everybody, she honestly didn't *want* to feel good; she didn't *want* to feel any better, she didn't *want* to even come close to getting over him, to forgetting him; she didn't *want* to stop thinking about him. She didn't *deserve* to feel even the tiniest bit better.

If anything, she deserved to feel even worse than she did. She needed to suffer like he had done, and if he wasn't dead, she needed to suffer far more than he was suffering now. And, ideally, she needed to suffer alongside him.

'All the more reason to go. Take your mind off him,' they said.

'I'm fine,' she said, then straight away thinking,

Fin, Fin, Fin.

And on the surface she appeared to be fine. She was getting up and going to work. She had even stopped taking the sleeping tablets and anti-depressants which she'd been prescribed, keeping them, instead, in her bedroom cabinet drawer.

Yes, although she was obviously stressed and worried, she appeared to be doing well, her but her friends and work colleagues agreed with Jack, a break away from it all would do her the world good.

Apart from her sad face and her quietness, she had them all convinced she was fine.

'Fin'

She stared yet again at that message, at the time and the date that it was posted; she stared at it for the several thousandth time… A year ago today, and she was no further forward.

'Fin'

So often she had pictured herself in the bath on a Saturday afternoon whilst Jack relaxed, after a hard morning's work, watching a football match downstairs.

So often she had planned what she would do. She'd make Jack his favourite snack Saturday lunch, then tell him she might be in the bathroom for a couple of hours. She was going to colour her hair, her grey roots looked awful, then she was going to treat herself to a facepack lying in water fragranced and oiled by a lavender bath bomb; lavender was supposed to help you sleep.

And as Jack watched his football, he would be pleased, relieved that she appeared to be starting to think about herself, and what she wanted, instead of just about Ben. Perhaps she was finally coming to terms with things…

She'd have candles and music playing, the same playlist that they'd had on that day when she'd prevented Ben from taking his life. The bath would be deep and hot, and she would be drinking plenty of wine as she sat on the loo and texted Jack, Fred, Will, Kenny and her parents. She would then save those messages in draft form.

Then, just before the bath was deep enough she'd go into the bedroom and grab the old makeup bag from the back of the top drawer of her bedside cabinet. The old makeup bag in which she'd been stashing the anti-depressants and sleeping pills she'd been prescribed eleven months ago. She'd remove every one of them from their blister packs in case she, as she surely would, became too slow and clumsy to remove them. as their effect took hold on her.

She would take half the tablets and then send the texts, then immediately take the rest with what remained of the wine.

What on earth would Jack think if he knew what she was planning on doing? Despite everything, she knew he thought the world of her. He must do to put up with her and her constant misery.

She glanced at him. She rarely looked at him now; sometimes wondering if she resented his continued quiet presence whilst Ben was missing. And that was a terrible way to think; that was so unfair.

Jack had just put jacket potatoes in the oven, he'd fed Tim, he'd washed up, he'd set up the wood burner, fetched in logs for later. He was a good, kind man. And she was wrecking *his* life, too.

And now he was leaning on the window sill, broad shoulders hunched, slender hard-working fingers splayed, staring grimly out of the kitchen window where the pots and the troughs that had once been filled with such beautiful pansies and violas this day two year ago year were now full of weeds and dead flowers. The few pansies which had risen again were thin and tangled, their long pale stems and limp leaves flailing and falling and failing to thrive, leaning over the tubs' edges like arms reaching; beseeching for help.

She was neglecting everyone; everything.

She looks again at him. She was most certainly neglecting Jack!

She was being so selfish. They were both approaching retirement age and yet he'd been working today for nine hours on top of a ladder in high winds and rain. How could she keep on forgetting about him? For goodness' sake he was suffering too.

He was suffering alongside her. His lips were turned down; there were new lines between his eyes and around his mouth. Quiet, as usual, he looked tired and drawn. And she realized with a nauseous lilt to her stomach that the reason he was quiet, that the reason he said very little these days was for fear of being snapped at by this woman; by her, his wife of twenty years whom he now barely even knew.

And yet despite all of this, aside from the occasional frustrated outburst,

'It's not right. Whilst I'm at work in all weathers; he sits and waits for his subby and his benefits and for the Jeremy Kyle show to start. It's all wrong. It's all wrong!'

And she totally got where he was coming from, she really did, but…

Jack didn't know the half of it. That she had regularly posted him cash; that she posted him cash in between two folded sheets of typing paper; that she posted him cash, his address typed neatly on a label, and stuck on an envelope with the Council's logo in the top left-hand corner. No one would ever suspect such an official looking envelope contained two ten pound notes.

Sometimes she'd also enclose a long letter or one of her bullet-pointed action plans to go with the money, maybe a motivational or 'Thinking of You' type of card, but more recently, she had just written 'For Food only' or 'towards trainers' or 'for electric' or whatever excuse he'd provided her with during that particular telephone conversation followed by 'Nowt Dodgy!' and a kiss, always a kiss to salve her conscience.

She'd then stamp the letter with a red 'First Class' and slide it into the middle of the pile of office post waiting to be to be franked. Yes, many times she'd even risked losing her job to help him. To help him? What rubbish! More like, to feed his habit.

Yes, Jack did have a little rant from time to time.

And although she totally understood where he was coming from, she still found herself incapable of taking Ben's side over Jack's. Why did she always feel the need to protect Ben. Why could she never agree with him, or even just keep quiet? It would have hurt her. It wouldn't have hurt Ben.

She felt a sudden jolt of surprise that Jack had actually stayed and, against all the odds, was still there for her and, therefore, for his stepson.

***

That night, that night twelve months after the text, he stirred when she'd made a slight noise replacing her water glass upon her bedside cabinet. The bedside cabinet that held her stash of tablets.

'Sorry,' she'd said, then turned over, back facing him, reaching for the tepid comfort of her hot water bottle.

'I didn't mean to wake you. I really ought to start sleeping in the spare room.'

'No,' he said, 'don't worry, if you want me to, I'll go sleep in there,' he said, 'because it really and truthfully doesn't bother me you waking me because – yes, I know I sleep a lot better than you, of course I do, but nowadays although it might appear than I'm fast on, I'm never, ever properly asleep; I'm never deeply asleep. The slightest thing wakes me up.'

She hadn't realized this, and asked him warily almost as though to test him.

'What do you mean the slightest thing?'

He closed his eyes and looked pained.

There followed a couple of seconds of silence and then she croaked, 'You mean, when I start to cry, don't you?'

'Yes,' and his voice cracked, '…I mean when you …cry but…'

And she began. She began to cry.

And he put his arms around her for the first time in months.

'…of course I mean when you cry…'

His voice had become hoarse,

'Of course, I mean every night when I hear you cry and then sometimes…' he hesitated, sounded surprised, 'when … you pray? '

She looked into his eyes.

Whispered,

'Yes, I do pray. 'Please come back. Please God bring him back to me. Every night I pray.'

She'd never been religious. But she had been thinking more and more lately that surely there was an after-life; surely there ought to be something better to come after all their suffering?

Otherwise what was the point in even existing?

And he murmured, his lips touching that place on the side of her neck where she had a little mole, which she used to love him to kiss,

'Every single night when you cry just after you think I've fallen asleep, and I know that, even though I've tried so hard not to disturb you you've woken and everything's come flooding back. And I wish to God

I could stop it all flooding back.'

She shook her head, put on her bedside light, looked down at her hands; neglected, ugly.

'...And then you creep out and stand at the spare room window beside the bed where he used to sleep, where his bed is still made up for him. Where one of those blessed dream-catchers that you took an absolute age to choose from that little shop in Praia da Rocha; where one of those blessed dream-catcher still hangs uselessly, from his light pull. And I know that you sit on his bed and I know that you stifle your sobs. And I know that you do the same all over again every single night at 3am...'

She shrugged, and the movement caused the tears to spill.

'I know you're taking sleeping pills and anti-depressants, love, but they're not working properly, are they? Don't you think you should go back to the Doctors? Perhaps they could prescribe something different or stronger?'

God, what would he think if he knew she'd barely taken any of the anti-depressants; that they were lying in an old makeup bag waiting to kill her?

Time stood still and in the first time for months, she put Ben briefly to the back of her mind, and she realized just how much Jack had done for them, and she realized just how much she still loved him.

God, how she loves him.

'I so want to help you, I so wish I could comfort you, but I'm scared of saying the wrong I really, really do, but ...

God, how she has neglected him.

She reaches for his hand. It is shaking ever so slightly.

'I so want to help you. But ... I'm frightened of doing or saying to wrong thing.'

Still not looking her in the eye, he tried and failed to lift his lips into a smile, his head bent low, his thumb and his forefinger pinching the bridge of his nose as his eyes filled with tears.

'I feel so useless; so helpless.'

She wiped away her tears with her fingers, then said, 'I will come on holiday with you.'

'What?' he asked, looking directly at her for the first time in months.

'I will come to Praia da Rocha with you, just so long as I can get the time off work.'

'Really?' he said, his lips lifting into a smile. And his face lost ten years in just a few seconds.

And they held each other tight.

When she told people her plan, they were pleased for her, told her they knew she was doing the right thing.

Best thing for you, and everyone else. He'll come back to you when he's well and truly ready; you'll see. They tried to convince her that he would have made a fresh start. Best thing for him. holiday is certainly the best thing for you; exactly what you need; just what the doctor ordered, and it was; the lovely Dr Bridgewater had herself advised her, cool hand on her hot wrist as she'd tried to contain her tears, 'Any chance of taking a holiday this Summer?' And, yes, she'd sobbed with a question mark, 'Yes, I think, I suppose so?'

Everyone was telling her, with an uncomfortable smile, 'On holiday, there'll be no more stress.' She'd half nod and half smile and think, *No more stress?!* 'No more stress. No more worrying.' *No more worrying?!* No more ringing him every day, not knowing what he's going to sound like. No more visiting him. No more watching him inject himself. No more finding needles down the side of his settee. No more putting yourself at risk. No more putting your whole family at risk.'

'*But... But ...*' she'd say.

'But, what? It's *your* turn to chill now. You've done *your* bit.'

Bit, bit? They were right there. If she'd done anything useful at all (and she hadn't) it was a miniscule 'bit'.

'It's time for you to forget,' they'd say.

She knew they meant well, but ... Forget?! She would never forget. She could never forget. She didn't want to forget. She didn't deserve to forget; she didn't, would never deserve or earn, the bliss of ignorance, of ignorance is bliss.'

'It's time to move on. To take a well-earned holiday. Get some sun and sangria down you. Write some poetry. Draw a line beneath what's happened. Move on. Concentrate on yourself and Jack. But, make sure you go somewhere different, somewhere totally different. Perhaps a cruise? You always used to say you quite fancied a cruise…?'

It's true, she had in years gone by said she'd fancied a cruise. But a cruise? A cruise, now? All those other people. All unavoidable; all curious. All that organising; all those unknown rules and regulations, all that money spent on an unfamiliar holiday which she very much doubted she would enjoy, certainly at this moment in time. And more importantly, as she kept thinking she didn't for one moment *deserve* to enjoy.

No, she didn't *deserve* a holiday. And because she didn't deserve a holiday, she decided that if, in order to quieten other people, she *had* to take a holiday, she would go back to Portugal, back to Praia da Rocha where she knew the memories of the family's previous holidays lay in wait and raw; ready to torture her.

She deserved to be tortured.

She didn't tell Jack that was her reason, of course she didn't, once she'd decided, she barely even admitted it to herself; she didn't tell anybody; she said and she told herself that she believed she'd find some comfort in the memories she had left in Praia da Rocha.

And to Ben she texted,

I'm sorry Ben You probably don't care anyway, and I don't blame you, but I really can't take much more of this. After all, all I want is the opportunity to say 'Sorry' to you, then once I know you're fine, or even God forbid, if you're not fine, I promise I will leave you be. If I can't find you I have to presume you have got your wish and have ended things. Anyway just to let you know, if you are alive and reading this, for Jack's long-suffering self, he has offered to take us back to Praia da Rocha for a couple of weeks. I have promised him and I have promised myself and my friends and your brothers etc. etc. that I will try my hardest not mention you whilst I am away; that I will – as if I ever could – try to forget about you.

But I have added my own proviso that I am sharing with you and with you alone, that if I have not heard from you by the time we arrive home on … I will take my own life. By now I have a good stash of pain killers, anti-depressants, high blood pressure tablets, beta-blockers, and God knows what else. I know this sounds like blackmail but it really isn't. At least then we might be together again then. I have been beginning to think more and more lately that there may be an after- life; that there has to be something better than this… x'

And so, believing herself both brave and stupid, they have returned to their beloved Praia da Rocha.

Chapter Eighteen

Praia da Rocha

At six o'clock in the morning she sits on their balcony in Praia da Rocha.

A seagull startles her as he silently swoops by; wings stretched wide, embracing the star-filled sky; its underbelly golden. It leaves in its wake an upturned soft feather which floats upon the breeze; a teeny, weeny empty cup, as soft as new born baby Ben's hair had been.

She sips her tea, and watches a straggle of people talking in the loud, slow slurs of the drunk as they wind their way back to their hotels.

The sound of the toilet flushing startles her and she conceals the make-up bag in her dressing gown pocket; turns abruptly to the left so that she can disguise her weeping. The sudden movement causes more tears to spill, and she is reminded of that day on the bus, however many years ago now – it's all a blur, that day when the lady in the pink mac had tried to comfort her and she'd turned sharply away from her; had willed her to go away; to leave her alone. Why ever had she done that? That dear lady had *wanted* to help her; might have been *able* to help her. Things could have been so different. Things could be so much better for both herself and for Ben.

She hears the kettle being re-filled, cups and saucers rattling, and, calmer now, she gazes across the sea at the gold and silver lights of nearby the quaint fishing village, Alvor. In the approaching dawn, they are pulsing, breathing; a living entity awakening to face the day. Glimmering and glistening, a sea of jewels; or a sea of fallen stars…

And she begins to whisper-sing to the stars, now distorted, and stretched by her falling tears. She begins to sing his favourite song.

'Reach for the stars

Climb every mountain …'

She stops every few seconds to wipe her eyes on the belt of the dressing gown as her voice cracks.

He had loved that song so much.

And then Jack appears, puts down the cups and saucers, places his arm around her shoulders, and hoarse, joins in with the words,

'…BUT I've got you and you've got me so…'

and she knows what he is meaning, she knows what he is implying, and she is grateful, so grateful to him in so many ways; but …

She places her hand on top of his, gives it an apologetic pat of thanks.

'I know, I've got you and you've got me so …'

And yes, she had Jack and Jack had her, but she no longer had Ben and Ben had not got her; had he ever really had her? Had her total love and support?… It was all her fault.

And the chances are that he has relapsed or died, and the chances are that she will never, ever see him again.

She should have left him to die in peace as he had wanted.

***

Although it is early, the noisy seagulls have already visited the pale, honey-coloured sands, hopping and jumping and cackling, leaving a trail of arrow-shaped prints behind them; a treasure map for them to follow. And now, having breakfasted on the sea's tasty pickings, they fly high above; an ever-changing, ever-moving dot-to-dot puzzle.

She and Jack carry their provisions for the day; flip flops, books, water. Ten euros for a sunbed. Whatever next? But they agree that they, and more particularly she, would struggle to sit upon a towel all day as they'd used to do when they'd brought Ben and Kenny.

'You'd never get back up again. I'd have to leave you here!' he laughs.

But she doesn't smile; doesn't even bother to protest with a playful slap;

In fact, that might not be such a bad idea, she thinks; grim-faced. To sit upon the sands like the naughty giant's boot rock, in a place filled with mainly good memories, until the skies darken and the tide approaches to drown her in a comforting salt-water blanket.

She looks down at their shadows upon the sand, the two of them carrying their stuff form a black and sepia tableau; strangely incomplete. Why incomplete? Yes of course, it is the children who are missing. Ben and Kenny, who they had brought here every October half term holiday for nearly ten years; always sitting in the same place, opposite the naughty giant's boot- rock.

with their shared inflatable Ninja turtle; the arguments they'd had about whose turn it was to wear the ring around their tiny tummies; their buckets and their spades, and those blessed fishing nets.

Far younger then, the two brothers neat and cool and trendy in their bandanas, their T shirts smelling of fabric conditioner, their October half-term holiday-length hair smelling of the banana shampoo they used to like, comfy and at ease, bare legged in their loose cotton shorts. They'd be carrying their buckets and spades, and those blessed fishing-nets, bickering good-naturedly, about whose turn it was to wear the shared inflatable Ninja turtle rubber-ring; racing ahead up the slope laughing, sliding back down, loose sand flying.

'Mind the sand doesn't get in your eyes!' she was forever shouting, and she is reminded of that shampoo-sting in her eye when she was helping Ben to take a bath. Why couldn't she have put up with that tiny little sting; instead of turning away? …

Had she always buried her head in the sand? …

On the crowded beach, they are lucky to find a sunbed in the exact spot where they used to lay down their four towels, looking out at the 'naughty giant's boot-rock'; that massive boot-shaped rock just a couple of hundred yards away from the brodiere-anglais foaming hem of the turquoise sea.

✳✳✳

On their earliest trips, she had used to tell Ben, and Kenny, if he was still awake, a bedtimre story she'd made up about how the rock boot came to be. The story used to particularly placate Ben when he was over-tired, or had a holiday tummy ache, or if the fish he'd finally managed to catch in his blessed fishing-net had somehow slipped back though the holes before she could take a photograph of it, or if, all those years ago, he'd fallen, or dropped his icecream.

If only it had been so simple to make things better for him once he hit his teens.

They settle themselves in between two empty sunbeds. She is glad they've come early. She anoints herself with suncream and puts all she will need for the day close to hand, all she will need, but not all she needs not by any means, because as always there is a massive void within her. And the memories of happy holidays are fast flooding back, to further crush her heart.

She closes her eyes beneath her sun glasses, sees blood red orange; permits a lone tear to trickle. There will be more tears later she knows, but she has bought with her tissues, and a suitably sad novel; a reason; a justification to wipe away tears.

'…Once upon a time there was a giant who lost his boot. We saw it today, didn't we? Over there in the sea. We saw where the lace holes were, didn't we? We saw where the sole of the 'boot' was a lighter colour than the rest of the boot? Point to the sole of your foot…'

Kenny would normally be sleeping by this point.

'Well,' she'd continue, 'the giant with the big stone giant's boots, lived at the top of a giant beanstalk, a beanstalk like Grandad has in his garden, only a million times bigger. And every night when he should have been asleep the giant with the big stone giant's boots would climb down the beanstalk, and paddle in the sea.

'With his boots on?'

Ben had asked wide-eyed, the first time she'd told the tale, and Jack's eyes had met hers over Ben and the now-sleeping Kenny, and they had smiled at each another, and she had had to press her hand over her mouth to stop herself from laughing out loud.

'Er, Yes giants always paddle with their boots on.'

'Giants don't like the feel of the cold water…' Jack had added. '…or the little fishes between their toes.'

How she had loved them all so much…

'Anyway,' she'd continued, 'Giles, because that was his name, Giles the Giant, Giles's mummy and daddy kept on telling Giles not to get up in the middle of the night to paddle in the sea, but he kept on doing it.

They started to get crosser and more and more fed up with him because of course he'd wake them up, especially when he came back in and he was all wet. Then his boots would leave wet puddles all over the place. And of course because he was getting up every night to go paddling he was tired, and he couldn't concentrate at school. He was getting all his sums and spellings wrong.

He kept promising to stay in bed all night, but then he'd get up and every single night Mummy kept saying 'Do you promise not to get up tonight?' and Giles would always say, 'Yes,' but then he'd break his promise. Even his teacher was worried about him. One day his mummy said, 'Right Giles, be warned this is your last chance. If you go for a paddle tonight you will be punished!' Do you know what punished means?

'Yes, it means when you're like 'grounded?' Ben had said, with a serious face.

'Yes, exactly. It means like when you're grounded and you can't go out and you can no longer do what you really want to do anymore.'

Well, I'm afraid that Giles did go out paddling again that night. And do you know what his mummy and daddy did? No, they didn't ground him. They punished him even more harshly than that. They cast a magic spell that turned Giles into stone! Every little bit of him. So that he couldn't move – at all'

Ben had looked horrified, for a split second as though turned to stone himself.

Just for a short moment they turned him into stone.

One. Two. Three!

Just long enough to frighten Giles a bit. '

But … perhaps because they had been so tired and so worried, Giles's mummy and daddy got the spell just a little bit wrong and they permanently …

'Do you know what 'permanently' means?'

'Forever?' Ben had whispered.

'That's right… They permanently turned one of Giles's boots into stone. So when Giles the Giant tried to climb back up that beanstalk, he discovered that his left foot,

'Which is your left foot?' Ben pointed to his, his eyes never leaving her face.

'That's … correct.'

'Giles discovered that his left foot would not move and he had to wrench…

'What does 'wrench' mean?'

Ben pulled at his foot under the duvet.

'That's right. Well done… Giles had to wrench his foot from his stone boot because he was in such a rush to shimmy …'

'What does shimmy mean?' she'd asked and Ben had stood up, straight-faced, in his pyjama bottoms and had waggled his slim hips.

'Yes, that's right,' and she'd smiled at his lack of self-consciousness.

So Giles the Giant left his great big stone boot behind in the sea forever more. And there it still stands till this day with its lighter-coloured sole and its lace holes. There it still stands till this very day, the naughty giant's boot-rock, stands for the birds to sit upon and for the brave but silly show-off big boys to dive off.'

Then she had said with a flourish,

'… and that's tonight's story 'FIN!'

And Ben had laughed as she kissed him and then the sleeping Kenny 'Goodnight'.

***

And so today her heart broke as she watched those silly big boys diving off the naughty giant's bootrock, missing the surrounding smaller rocks by inches. And she remembered telling Ben, and truly believing at the time that he never would, she remembered telling him that she hoped he'd never show off and do anything so silly, because even though he was a strong swimmer, if he misjudged his dive, he could kill himself on the sharp stones. As far as she knew he had never dived off the giant boot's rock but, of course, what he *had* done - *she hated that she now thought in the past tense about Ben* - what he *had* done was far more dangerous. Wasn't it?

And now they'd come back to the giant's boot on Praia da Rocha beach and they lay on their sunbeds and they watched the people, mainly carefree but every now and again she'd see the signs of unhappiness that others didn't. She'd heard one lady at the airport, talking into her mobile phone, eyes frightened, brow furrowed, listening to her son or her daughter loudly slurring at the other end of the line, nonetheless still trying to act normally for the sake of the friend she was going on a well-deserved holiday with.

As the lady had put away her mobile phone, she saw her gesture to her friend; that shake of the head that said 'Please, don't ask'. Then, as most women do, she'd apologetically fanned away the approaching tears with her fingers. And her friend had smiled a sympathetic smile, and had patted her on the arm, 'Come on, love'; had manoeuvred her towards their boarding gate.

Mothers of addicts often are nice, kind people. Perhaps that's where she and others like her had gone wrong. Perhaps she'd been *too* nice? Perhaps she'd been *too* kind? She should have been cruel.

Sometimes it was necessary 'to be cruel to be kind'; wasn't that the saying?

***

'I think I'll go in the sea,' she said to Jack after she'd read for a while, rising from her sunbed and walking onto the firm, pale sand.

'Mmm'hhh!' Jack said, his voice slurry; slack with approaching sleep.

A fairly confident swimmer, she would float upon her belly. She loved to do that; to let the cool Atlantic Sea carry her safe within its womb, weightless, strangely complete; a gently rocking cradle. How she wished she was still carrying Ben in her womb; safe and sound. Knowing what she did now, she would do so many things very differently.

The sand suddenly sloped, and so she stepped slowly, carefully down the shifting slippery sand, and then ignoring the shock of the cold, waded in until the sparkling waves softly slapped against her breasts, making her nipples hard. Then, as she'd so often done, laughing at her children's cries of,

'Mum! Don't, because then you'll look like you're dead!'

She would turn her back upon the baby blue horizon, hold her arms out in front of her, beseech the healing water to support her; kick up her legs beneath her.

She'd not floated in the sea for years and was newly amazed by its coldness, by its strength and its noise. The water felt so very different to that of the hotel pools in the Canaries in which she'd occasionally manage a token dip; or to the warm, fragrant shawl of bathwater which, even during the very worst of times, had never ceased to give her at least some fleeting comfort.

As she kicked and stretched and tried to relax so that the waves might support her, she found herself remembering when she was pregnant with Ben, lying in warm bubbles, watching, fascinated as the limbs she'd yet to see, yet to hold, wriggled beneath the blue-veined skin of her neat pink bump.

She remembered bathing him as a few-days-old baby. He was longer, more slippery than all three brothers had been; thinner. He was no trouble then; he woke for his feed then settled back to sleep. He was a smiley baby; if he ever cried she could always find a reason. She remembered lifting him from one of his very first baths; sobbing and telling him how much she loved him; that she'd always love him; that she'd always love him simply because they'd already been through so much together. And as she'd sobbed, her hot tears had mingled with the water upon his skin; a makeshift baptism.

She continued to attempt to float on top of the water, limbs outstretched like a star-fish. But something in the sea felt different from previous holidays. Something was not right. Something felt wrong…

This time, years later, it seemed the very waves were become angry and impatient with her; determined to punish her for how badly she'd let her third son down. They rose, silent and sly behind her back, and they started to roar and to swell, and they swallowed her whole.

She struggled. She struggled desperately. And as she struggled, she recalled teaching Ben to swim; his face, set with concentration, tiny between those two gigantic orange-coloured water wings, his neck lifted up and out of the water like a pretty little tortoise, his soft mouth open, his eyes squeezed tightly shut against his own splashes. His skinny white limbs flailing and frantic; so determined to swim those few strokes to Mummy. She could still see his pearly baby-toothed smile as he reached out to her, ready for her to hug him, and laughing, to lift him up high, free from the pool; as though re-born.

'Well done! My clever boy!!'

He'd trusted her totally, unconditionally; trusted her with his life. And yet, she'd cut his life short. What a terrible way to re-pay him…

She managed to stand, but the deep water, like a whirlpool, twisted and turned her so that she was facing another way.

The wrong way? The right way? The incorrect way? The left way?

As always her mind started racing. *Which way?* Then she caught a brief glimpse of the horizon before she was flung beneath the water, down another slope of sharp pebbles and slippery masses of green weed. She fought, frantic to stand firm, to raise, and to keep, her head above the water; to breathe.

But the ground kept shifting beneath her feet, and then she was on her knees; sharp shells and stones. She was on her knees where she surely should be…

She was upon her knees. She should pray for forgiveness. She should pray to be saved.

And the water roared, angry all around her. She needed to pray. This might be the end. She might be Fin. She needed to breathe. And she knew she couldn't breathe. And she thought about him. She thought about him in the bathwater. And she thought about both of their lives…

And she remembered one night, lying in her bath, considering drawing or even of having a bracelet of perforations tattooed around her wrist, perforations for her to score, to join up like a dot-to-dot puzzle, ready then to rip or tear with a small sharp knife…

Then, she recalled, she'd begun thinking how strange that 'rip' in upper case letters made RIP, *Rest in Peace*, which is what she desired more than anything; which was what she desired for both herself and for Ben, more than anything in the whole wide world.

Then, she recalled, she'd begun thinking how strange it was that to 'tear' pronounced in a different way became *tear*, as in to weep; and she knew that if she allowed her tears to flow freeley, she believed she'd carry on weeping for both of them; forever.

The salt water would surely be almost as deep as this sea water was now…

She jumped and managed to pull some air into her mouth before she was tossed beneath the surface again …

She'd been thrown in at the deep end; and she was in far too deep; she was way out of her depth now.

And she tried to pray, then she found herself wondering, truly wondering whether to give up; whether to just give up her fight; allow the elements to take her.

Then she thought of Jack, of Kenny, of Fred and Will, of Shelly and dear little Jake. Because Ben had now been missing for so long, Will and Shelley now allowed her to see her grandson again. And for that she was truly grateful.

She must be brave; she must be strong for all of them.

She must not give up. She must not give up because there was a chance, just a chance that Ben was still alive; that she might just possibly see him again one day.

She recalled Ben growing braver in the local swimming pool water which had prepared him for his holidays here. She'd go and watch him on Saturday mornings, her heart sinking as he jumped into the deep end; her heart plunging into the dark depths along with his body.

She'd hear nothing; see nothing; her entire life put on hold until he broke through the surface, disorientated, shaking his long hair, scattering jewels of chlorinated water everywhere as he scoured for her amongst the people waiting behind the screen, just as he'd scoured the people in the court room all those years ago. Then, just as he had in the court room, he'd caught her eye and smiled.

And then, and only then, for who knows what might have happened to him in those few seconds that seemed like silent hours, who knew if he'd bumped his head or forgotten to hold his breath; then and only then, would her senses return, and she'd smell again the chlorine, see the other people, hear the comforting noise of the grumpy lifeguard's shrill whistle; the echoing squeals and splashes…

She felt so very tired, so very weak…

She thought again, of how easy it would be to allow the salt waves to take her; to become her pall bearer, to carry her off to her watery grave; over there where the sea was navy blue, beneath a baby blue sky.

And then she was thinking about their final family holiday together, the day after Ben's thirteenth birthday, the day she found the bong in his hoodie, the evening he'd won the boys' best dancer prize, and had gone out with some older lads, been sick all over Kenny's bed.

Thirteen; unlucky for some. Certainly unlucky for herself and for Ben…

It was strange how she was recalling past events. Didn't they, whoever 'they' were, didn't they say that if you were drowning, your whole life would flash before you?

Perhaps she was drowning? …

Halfway through their final family holiday together; halfway, that favourite point in the holiday, when they'd all relaxed into their stay, she remembered they had been for a couple of drinks and a bite to eat, and were feeling pleasantly friendly and a little giddy with each other.

Just as they'd been were about to settle down onto their towels where they always sat, opposite the Naughty Giant's Boot Rock so that they all knew where to meet up, whatever they decided to do, Kenny had suddenly yelled,

'Race you to the sea!'

Kenny had brought the blessed football with him; and, as one, they'd raced towards the sea laughing and kicking up sand; and then, as one, they'd run into the sea, ignoring the shock of the cold, laughing and kicking up water.

And, she remembered, she'd felt a rare fission of pride as she noticed other women looking at them, some smiling; some she'd thought at the time, with a touch of envy. They wouldn't envy her now; she knew that for a fact.

Then they'd played Catch with the football, each standing within their own depth; a football that splashed horribly, causing her to squeal each time it bounced upon the water,

'I don't know why you have to use a hard football! Why can't you get a blow-up beach ball?'

And they'd all tease and laugh at her whinings, and she'd laugh too.

Those were the days; when they'd all been happy.

And then, of course, on that same, final holiday, Ben had won the Best

Boy Disco Dancer at the kids' club, when he'd danced and sung to Reach for the Stars and had got the whole audience joining in.

But then … Well, she considered, the rest, as they say was history …

… And the waves continued to yell at her and to roar, daring her to ever darken their depths again. But at some point, she now realised, the waves had somehow turned her back around, to face the sands.

Or was it she who had turned herself around?

A star fish floated towards her from above. She'd occasionally seen a star fish dead, stranded on the sands, or deceased, cleaned and dried in souvenir shops. This one was very much alive and kicking.

She reached up and touched the star fish, surprised that it did not sting her; rather it felt like a tongue, a rough kiss perhaps.

Surely, some sort of message for her?

And so she clawed at the sand and shells and at the stones and weed with her fingers, and she fought and she fought to stand and to break through the surface of that deep, bubbling, broiling, living water. And then her body become suddenly stable; she regained her balance; and she stood, legs wide apart. And then she jumped, raising her arms and stretching them right to her very finger tips, until she could stretch no more.

Like a star fish, herself; reaching for the stars.

And she felt a warm force from way up high lifting her from the sea's depths, and back into the brightness of blue sky.

She had reached for the stars; and her body was become freed.

For a several moments, she whooped painful, terrified, terrible gasps. And as the air trickled into her starved lungs, water streamed from her; her eyes and nose, her hair, her body; from every single orifice as though her waters were broken once more.

Still the waves slapped her upon her back and shoulders; still the waves whipped her legs, as they shoved and pushed her. Weeping, gasping, punished and banished, she staggered back up that slippery, sliding slope before the beach's edge.

Chapter Nineteen

After the noise of the sea, there was utter silence.

Her breathing and heart rate returned to normal surprisingly quickly, and she felt the warm breeze already attempting to dry her wet hair and body.

And so, strangely calm, and with good strong steps, our nameless narrator walked back onto the beach.

Into a very different world.

Dripping water, she adjusted her bikini bottoms, realising there and then, although she was not sure why, realising there and then, that she was always going to keep whatever had just happened out there to herself.

Jack was still fast asleep. She tied on her sarong, drank some water, returned to her book.

When Jack began to stir, he fished in the bag between them for his bottle of water and for a big bag of crisps.

'I think I'll have annuver yast one,' he said.

'More-ish as ever,' he said reaching for another one, passing them to her with a smile.

It was a huge family bag, the sort they'd always bought when they'd come with Kenny and Ben, the green-coloured packet, their preferred flavour, salt and vinegar-ish but they were never quite sure. That's funny, she couldn't remember packing them this morning, or even buying them at the little shop last night; Jack must have slipped them into the basket.

***

The salt from the crisps mixed with her sweat, her tears, with the salt from the sea water that clung to and frosted the tiny fair hairs all over body, and when she'd had enough, had eaten her last and then another last crisp, she drank some more water, adjusted her back rest and lay down flat, her towel around her shoulders, a little, although not unpleasantly, dizzy; feeling inside her head a gentle rocking motion, not dissimilar to the slight turbulence they'd experienced on the plane when they'd arrived.

Somebody bent to spread their towel upon the end sun-lounger next to Jack, and a sudden cooling shadow fell across her face. Bit late in the day to pay the ten euros for a sunbed, she thought. Mind you, whoever they were, they were doubtless hoping that the chirpy chap with the cap and the bag round his waist would be more intent on stacking the sunbeds up ready for the next morning and clocking off, rather than noticing any latecomers arriving.

The person lowered themselves to sit, and the early evening sun peeped back round from behind the shadow and shone once more; a warm breath upon her face. She closed her heavy eyes against it for a moment or two, or maybe for longer? And she saw blood-red orange behind her sunglasses.

As she breathed in and out, on the cusp of the lightest of sleeps, she became aware of a vague ringing, and beneath that, the seagulls, the waves, now calmer, and the palm trees in the breeze, beckoning her hither with their spiky fingers.

There was some faint music too. Of course, it would be leaking from the person's headphones. Headphones, that modern-day umbilical cord; she smiled to herself.

Drifted off deliciously…

What *was* that music?

She came to with a start, and lifting her head and then her hand to her forehead, she was surprised, through silhouettes of shadows and flickers of a dusky fading sun, she was surprised to see Jack offering the bag of crisps to the young man who'd sat upon the sunbed beside him. She smiled again; he was getting more talkative, more sociable in his old age.

She heard the slight rustle of the bag, and, as the young man reached across for a crisp,

he said,

'Thank you,'

and, as the earphones fell upon his shoulders, the leaking music played louder.

    'Reach for the Stars, Climb every mountain…'

And then the trees and the breeze and the waves were become silent; and the seagulls, too. And she leaned forward too soon; too quickly and everything swam. But she said nothing. Apart from a gulp, she remained quiet.

She closed her eyes again until the feeling lessened, attempting to think rationally until the pumping of her heart and of her blood slowed.

A few moments later, she heard Jack ask,

'Would you like another?'

And her body stiffened and chilled in the fading sunshine.

Surely not? Surely not?

And she heard the rustle of the packet; and that music again.

    'Reach for the Stars, Climb every mountain …'

S-Club Seven

'Another crisp?' Jack asked again, and then a few seconds later, a rattle of the bag, and 'Anuvver yast one?'

And she screwed up her eyes. Was she dreaming? She pinched herself, using her fingernails on the inside of her wrist.

'No. No, thank you. I'm fin.'

That phlegmy little smoker's laugh, and then,

'No way would I have annuver yast one. I'm well and truly fin. Fin with drugs. I've even cut down on the fags. I know now that I'd be safer diving off that naughty giant's boot rock than choosing to have another last fix; another last one.'

He tossed his phone onto the sunbed where it bounced slightly and continued to sing 'Reach for the Stars' through its earphones.

'I might take a walk out to the rock. For old times' sake.'

And he turned to her with a laugh and it was his face; it was his face but softer.

And he pulled off his long-sleeved T shirt; revealing the familiar mess of amateur graffiti and the shiny scars of self-harm all over his body;

but the tattoos on his arms were no longer inter-twined with the pinks and reds of needle scratches from syringes; the tattoos were no longer competing with the love-bite like bruises and big blister bubbles; there were no pink tourniquet bracelets.

And then he was striding towards the turquoise sea with its broderiere-anglais lace hem. The giant's boot rock stood straight ahead; a motionless seagull acting as sentry from the rock's highest point.

She sat up, this time rising very slowly; as if from a coffin; as though from the dead.

She stood cautiously, and she began to follow him, surprised that she did not have to step around bodies, surprised that she did not have to move aside for beach balls and children and sandcastles. Surely there had been more people on the beach than this when they'd arrived? But of course, time was getting on. She'd slept a while.

Perhaps she was still asleep. Was she dreaming?

She hoped not; pinched herself; hard. Felt herself start to panic. What if he …

Was it really he?

… what if he walked out to sea then swam and never stopped?

Or what if he jumped off the giant's boot rock and banged his head; drowned?

'Ben!' she called, 'Please come back!'

And he turned, and he stood, and he smiled, and the smile reached his eyes and his eyes were moist and white; bright. No longer anxious.

Then he faced the sea again and began to walk towards it.

'Please come back!'

His eyes were certainly not blood shot needle-pricks; certainly not dead black holes.

'Please come back!'

And she recalled shouting and begging 'Please come back!' as she performed CPR on him in his bath all those months ago.

'Please come back!'

And she carried on walking up the cool sand, calling, now a little breathless; dizzy,

'Please come back!'

Walking, not running, because her legs were shaking and the blood in her head was roaring louder than the waves.

'Please come back!'

The words seemed distant, they seemed to echo and to slow a little up above her, and her chest felt as though it was being crushed.

And then he stopped his teasing, because teasing it surely was; and he turned and opened up his arms and his heart to her and she hugged him so tightly.

As she spoke, her dry lips opened and shut to form silent desperate words, kissing against his flesh.

'Please come back.'

He gently kissed her lips and the warm breeze seemed to reach inside the very core of her.

He hugged her close and she could feel no jutting ribs. And she smelled him; and she could smell no fear; no anxious sweat.

And she loved him. And he rocked her gently from side to side.

'Please come back.'

Was it her or was it him who was speaking?

And her breath fought for release in her chest. But suddenly she could speak no longer; she could barely breathe for the feelings ballooning inside of her, deep inside of her. The emotions inside of her were desperate to escape, as they'd been desperate to help little Jake, unconscious, trapped behind that netting in the Jungle playcentre that time.

Her emotions were desperate to burst through the netting covering her mind and her body, the netting which had just about served to contain her emotions inside of her; which had just about enabled our nameless narrator to hold it all together for so very long.

And she allowed Ben to support *her*; she allowed her son to support *her* for the first time since he was a child, and she heard herself emitting dreadful, howling, noises as he held her tight.

'Don't you worry, Mum. I have come back. I've come back to stay. I've filled Jack in with the important bits and I've got a very long tale to tell you, Mum. But all you need to know for now is that I have come back; I have come back a different person. I'm so very sorry and so ashamed for all that I've put you through. I know I can never make it up to you, but I will do absolutely everything I can to make you happy again; I promise. I'm going nowhere. I'm here to stay.'

And beneath the darkening sky, the healing, cleansing, cool salt water lapped around their feet.

And then Jack joined them, towels hanging over his arm, clutching Ben's phone and headphones from which S-Club Seven, obviously on repeat, still sang.

And the atmosphere of the moment changed.

Once more she could hear the seagulls and other people and the waves of the sea. Just like when she'd been having a panic attack, she always knew the attack was dying when she, once more, became aware of the sounds around her.

'What a surprise, eh, love?' Jack said, as he handed her her towel and passed over the phone to Ben.

'I'll let you tell your mum everything you've been telling me.'

Jack said as he wrapped the towel around Ben's shoulders, whispering,

'It's dropping chilly now'

And Jack gave him a loving squeeze as his voice broke,

'… when you're ready…'

And Ben released a small sob.

'… when you're well and truly ready.'

And she nodded her head in silent agreement, unable to speak for the tears which blocked her chest and her throat.

And the three of them stood, their arms around one another in the cleansing water; beneath the stars.

'You came back to me,' she breathed.

'Yes,' Ben said, 'I had a feeling you'd be in Praia da Rocha this week, October half term, and if you *were* here, I just knew you'd be sitting opposite the naughty giant's boot rock. And now I'm going nowhere, Mum.'

Surely she must be dreaming. Was she still drowning? Had she banged her head. Was she unconscious dead having some kind of hallucination? Was she dead?

'Mum.'

His voice broke.

'I'm going nowhere without you. When I think of everything I've put you through, I feel so ashamed.'

'I thought I was dreaming.'

She was sobbing, snuffling, hiccupping, but the tears that flowed cool down her face, felt so very different from the hot painful tears of the past years.

'And then you kept on walking away and I thought you were going to leave me again. I couldn't bear that. Where have you been? I texted you to ask how you were a year ago, about a year ago to the day, and all you put was 'Fin'.

'I thought you were telling me you were going to try,' and her voice shook, 'I thought you were telling me you'd finished, you were finished with life and were going to try to take your life again.'

She was filled with a sudden surge of indignation; able finally now to vent her anger, she spat,

'I thought you were … *dead.*'

'Mum…I'm so sorry. But please believe me I'm far from Fin or dead. I've got a second chance at life. I've been given 'annuver yast' chance at life, and I'm going to grab it and never let it go. I'm going nowhere. I'm well and truly clean… Thanks to …'

And he waved and beckoned to somebody.

She'd not been there a moment ago, she was sure that she hadn't; that blonde wavy-haired lady who wore sunglasses on top of her head, who carried a pink towel folded over one slim arm, flip flops in her hand, a beach bag over her shoulder; she'd not been there a moment ago.

And yet she looked as though she'd been there forever; completely settled, relaxed. She leaned upon a small outcrop of seaweed covered rocks; her legs in a silvery-blue narrow pleated maxi skirt were outstretched; her bare feet were crossed at the ankles, and rested in a shallow pool: a fish's fin, or, better, a mermaid's tail. She looked entirely at home, a permanent part of the scene, like the moon and the stars, or the Naughty Giant's Boot rock.

Ben continued speaking,

'… I'm well and truly clean, thanks to my…'

She caught her breath.

'… Thanks to my…'

She knew that woman, but where from?

'… guardian angel …'

Of course, she realised, as the lady began to walk over to them, a big smile upon her face, the fingers of her free hand, palm up, fingers splayed like a star fish. It was her. The same lady she'd seen several times before… although she couldn't remember where now.

'… Thanks to my new, very best friend…'

Even before she clasped the lady's proffered hand, she felt a weird sensation as if she'd suddenly become almost carefree; floating. What was it? Where had she felt that magnetic pull before? …

'Pleased to meet you,' she said in a confident, smiley voice, as though on the cusp of a laugh.

And she realised as she came closer, that the pink towel wasn't a towel at all, but a mac.

'For the past twelve months, Fin has supported and guided me every step of the way.'

Fin? Fin?

'Fin? That's all your last text said. That's all you replied when I asked you how you were. That one word. Then I heard nothing. The text you sent me a year ago.'

'Yes, I remember your last text. Just asking how I was, wasn't it? That was the last text I was to read for almost a year. It came through about an hour before I went to Fin's recovery cottage.'

He was rapidly scrolling through his phone.

'Yes. Here it is. I've still got it, and my reply, too… Well, what you *should* have received from me. I must admit I was having a final blowout before my rehab; perhaps I never sent it properly, but this is what I'd intended you to receive:

'Fin is a very kind lady. She is going to help me. Please don't worry if you don't hear from me for a while x"

'But, Ben, I never received that text, not the full text. Just that one word 'Fin' and I've been frantic with worry. I didn't know if you were dead or alive. In fact, in all honesty I thought you were…' she felt a sudden need to take a deep breath, and the word came out in a squeak, '…dead.'

'Oh mum … I'm so sorry. But even though I was off my head, I really don't know why you wouldn't have got the complete message…'

And she thought back to that cold and frosty afternoon. She'd been in the kitchen… Hadn't she been cooking her quiche with the kick for her and her friends to eat later. Hadn't she got raw pastry all over her hands? Hadn't she dropped her phone? Hadn't she tried to open the window? Hadn't her eyes been blurring and burning with fumes from the hot chilli, and then with tears of relief? Hadn't she fumbled about pressing buttons and scrolling her phone in the wind and the rain? She must have somehow deleted the rest of that text.

'I'm sorry too,' said Fin, taking her hand; it felt rough, like the starfish had.

'I know about everything. I know how hard you've always tried to help your son. You have exercised the patience of a Saint, you really have. I so admire you, and you must be very proud of yourself. Many people would have completely washed their hands of Ben. You must have felt absolutely frantic…'

'I was, God, how I was…' she sobbed, trying to smile her thanks to this person, this person who had actually acknowledged how hard our nameless narrator had worked to try to help her son.

'…But I know you'll understand that Ben was not permitted to have access to a mobile phone whilst he was recovering. Obviously, there has to be no contact whatsoever with the outside world.'

Ben then spoke,

'Mum, It was so hard, incredibly hard but I refused to give into temptation, to break free and I grew stronger by the day. I refused to allow myself another last drug because I knew it wouldn't be a last one, it would be just like the crisps, it would lead to another last one, "annuvver yast one". Instead of that little lad reaching into the crisp packet, and instead of that young man reaching for drugs and syringes, and fake highs, I reached for the stars.'

He pointed up to the Quink-ink blue sky.

'I reached for the stars, just like the song.'

'See. There they are, Mum. Look…'

And she breathed deeply and she raised her head to the myriads of tiny stars which were beginning to bloom like spring-time daisies, peeping through the veil of gossamer clouds.

And she was reminded of how she'd so often stood behind her voile curtains, sometimes the very thought of going into the garden causing her heart to pound, she'd stand gazing at the weather, at the quiet road, at neighbours walking dogs, but all the time really just searching for a solution; searching for him.

Through all the different seasons, through all the different times of day. And she knew now that the stars had been there in waiting for her, for him; for both of them all along.

All they'd had to do was to reach for them.

Ben grinned across at Jack who nodded and smiled back at him,

'And…' Ben continued,

'Kenny is on his way as we speak; even Fred is going to come from Skye; and Will and Shelly and little Jake!…'

She staggered and Jack supported her; Jack who had always supported her.

'…And we are all going to have a fantastic holiday in our favourite place on earth.'

And, amongst the stars, she sees the flashing light of a plane unzipping the sky, making its way to Faro airport and she just knows it is Will, Shelly, Jake and Kenny's plane. Jake has never been on an aeroplane.

How excited will *he* be?! How excited was *she*?!

She released herself from Jack's arms to give Fin a hug; to thank her again. But our nameless narrator was not surprised to find that Fin along with her pink mac had vanished; no doubt she was already on her way to help some other broken soul.

And our nameless narrator breathed deeply, finally feeling an inkling of something she'd not felt for many, many years; an inkling; just an inkling, that at long last everything might be all right.

Reach
for the stars
Climb every mountain higher
Reach for the stars
Follow your heart's desire
Reach for the stars

And when that rainbow's shining over you
That's when your dreams will all come true

There's a place waiting just for you (just for you)
Is a special place where your dreams all come true
Fly away (fly away) swim the ocean blue (swim the ocean blue)
Drive that open road, leave the past behind you
Don't stop gotta keep moving
Your hopes,…

FIN

Endpiece

How wonderful! Ben free of his addiction, a further week's holiday in her favourite place in the whole world, and Kenny, Fred, Will, Shelley and little Jake (his first time on a plane – he would be so excited!) on their way to join them.

She'd only ever dreamed of such things. Now, at long last, they seemed to be happening for her.

Or were they?

***

Of course, that was the happy ending she had wanted for her novel. That was, of course, the ending she had wanted with all her heart. That was the ending she *still* wants with all her heart.

That, dear reader, and thank you for reading this far, that is the ending *I* still want with all my heart. And if you are happy with that ending, please hold onto that feeling, and read no further…

For the others of you, I want to say…

I am the person who has written this story, I am the person you have known up to now only as 'she', or 'mum' or 'duck' or 'love' or 'my dear' by the other characters. Yes, my real name, or rather the initials I prefer the writer-me to be known as, may be on the spine or the cover of this book but, within its pages, I am the *nameless narrator*.

I am the nameless narrator.

Mine and Ben's story needs to be read; to get out there amongst the 'system' that has consistently and constantly let us down and let so many other people, so many desperate mothers and fathers, other family members, and carers; so many kind people involved in helping, or in trying to help, drug-users like my Ben.

My story could have been told by any of them.

But I'm afraid that happy ending is far from the true ending. And as I write these words, I can feel my face grow hot and contort, creasing in sorrow, my breathing quickens and gives way to short, shallow gasps and sobbing. Hot tears spill from my eyes, my reading glasses forming a brief sort of dam and then they trickle scalding and unchecked down my cheeks.

I'm so sorry to say that Ben rarely reaches for the stars now; he reaches for his tourniquet and his syringes.

But … who knows?

I'm tired, in fact, I'm exhausted, but I've not given up hope yet. I still have faith in Ben because some days he is fine; an absolute joy to be with, and he's definitely doing better than he was at one point in his life…

My worst nightmare…
My slowly recovering
Addict son
Slips back to where he once begun
because although I love you dearly, Ben

I can't live through that Hell again.

Yes, I still have faith, and if you are in a similar position to me, so should you.

Thank you for reading my book.

- CJK -